NAMEDROPPING

NAMEDROPPING

MOSTLY LITERARY MEMOIRS

RICHARD ELMAN

STATE UNIVERSITY OF NEW YORK PRESS

Published by
State University of New York Press, Albany

For information, address State University of New York Press,
State University Plaza, Albany, N.Y. 12246

Production by M. R. Mulholland
Marketing by Dana E. Yanulavich

Library of Congress Cataloging-in-Publication Data

Elman, Richard M.
    Namedropping : mostly literary memoirs / Richard Elman.
       p.   cm.
    ISBN 0-7914-3879-1 (HC : acid-free paper). — ISBN 0-7914-3880-5
(PB : acid-free paper)
       1. Elman, Richard M.—Friends and associates. 2. United States-
-Intellectual life—20th century. 3. Novelists, American—20th
century—Biography. 4. Journalists—United States—Biography.
5. Elman, Richard M.—Biography. I. Title.
PS3555.L628Z47 1998
813'.54—dc21
    [B]   97-45812
                                                                          CIP

10 9 8 7 6 5 4 3 2 1

CONTENTS

Part III. Relaxing at the Touro

ACKNOWLEDGMENTS

In one way or another, nearly everybody mentioned in *Name-dropping* was one of my teachers, and I have had many more dear mentors I have not mentioned.

This book is dedicated to Alice and Margaret and Lila, and with special gratitude to Fred Haines, Nick Delbanco, Herbert Krohn, and Prudence Crowther.

Visse, scrisse, amo . . .

—Stendhal

Much of this book was written over long periods of broken time while I was also otherwise engaged as a teacher, a journalist, a novelist, and free-lance ghost writer in New York, Vermont, Glens Falls, on Long Island, in Central America. As an aid to readers I've provided a resume of my career below. *Voila:*

Born, Brooklyn, New York, 1934.
Attended Syracuse University, 1951–55.
Gangway guard, Greenpoint, Brooklyn, 1954–55.
Attended Stanford University, 1955–57.
U.S. Army, 1958.
Free-lance writer and radio journalist,1959.
Director of Public Affairs, and later Drama and Literature, WBAI-Pacifica, 1960–63.
Free-lance writer, New York, 1964–67.
Lecturer in Literature, Bennington College,1967–68.
Professor of Creative Writing, Columbia, 1968–75.
Faculty, Bennington College Summer Workshops,1977–89.
Frequent trips to Nicaragua and elsewhere in Central America, 1978–87.
Visiting Professor of Creative Writing at State University of New York, Stony Brook, and other universities such as Michigan, Arizona, University of Pennsylvania, Wichita State, Notre Dame, and Tennessee,1985 to date.

As this book-length memoir was being put together over the years, some pieces were first published in magazines and quarterlies: "Post Time," in *Agni Review*; "Alexander Kerensky," in *Evergreen Review*; "Bernard Malamud" and "Bashevis," in *Tikkun*; "Sy Krim" and "Robert Lowell," in the *American Book Review*; "David Lamson," in the *Georgia Review*; "Susan Meiselas," in the *San Francisco Review of Books*; "Falta Nada," in *Raritan*; and a somewhat different version of the C. P. Snow piece in the *Boston Review of Books*. The author thanks these publications for permission to reprint in this volume.

Additionally, the vignettes on "Little Richard" Penniman, W. H. Auden, and Grace Paley appeared first in *Witness*, as did the pieces on Matthew Josephson, Jules Olitski, and Lucinda Childs in the *Notre Dame Review*. In a slightly altered version, the William Bronk memoir was read at the dedication honoring Bronk's gift of his papers to Columbia University and later was printed in the Butler Library publication *Columns*. The memoir of Alfred Kreymborg appeared in *Exquisite Corpse*, and *The Minnesota Review* published "Roberto Sosa." "Tears" appeared in the short-lived *Flatiron News*. The memoir of Richard Price appeared in the *Boston Review of Books*. "Homage to Isaac Babel"was broadcast on NPR and appeared in the *Boston Review of Books*. "Newton's Laws" was published in the *Bulletin* of the Society for Psychoanalytic Psychotherapy of Seattle, Washington.

PREFACE: POST TIME

There's the silence
of the clock,
of chance
incandescent
on the tote:
Horses
calm and separate
in their stalls
prepare for sound.

In the course of the same old race I find myself writing about knowing some people—how fame seems to set some people apart from us, once known: I was astonished by Ernest Hemingway's small, weak handshake when we were introduced at Scribners by John Hall Wheelock and by the jolt of force with which Elie Wiesel squeezed my hand.

How long ago seems knowing, too: when I first meet Isaac Singer he asks me, "Who is Mr. Saul Bellow?"

We're on the Upper West Side in his apartment next to the funeral parlor. A yellow parakeet hops around on Singer's bald forehead. Singer's great comic story of faith, "Gimpel the Fool," has only recently been published from Yiddish into English in a translation by Saul Bellow. They're both still a long way from Stockholm.

"Do you know him? Can you tell me who this Mr. Bellow is?" he asks. It was not always possible to guess Singer's motives in acting as though he was not impressed with worldly reputations. His features of a medieval Polish saint, even to a faint white-haired tonsure effect around the crown of his skull, were backlit by the glowing monitor from his mischievous incubus.

Not who I know, but how I knew the person once: My oldest daughter goes to school for a while in Lake Placid. Another parent with children at the school is J. D. Salinger. Divorce and single part-time fatherhood has made us comrades at a distance. Once we take Thanksgiving dinner together at the same long table at the school. He's quite a charming and sartorially elegant man in those days, more than fifteen years ago, and he doesn't seem to mind talking about his writing.

I asked "Jerry" once, as we were driving from our inn to the school in his Jaguar, if the world could expect another Salinger book someday.

Salinger said he wrote all the time and he had been working on something a very long time. I asked when could the world expect to see another Salinger book.

"My book?" His voice was low, confident, and confidential, from the driver's seat of his Jaguar sedan where he sat behind the wheel. "Richard," he said, "it's really nice not to have to publish anything until the work is completed . . . and that's real nice, Richard."

The last time I saw Salinger he was hitting ground strokes on the school courts with his son, who later became a movie actor. Did he ever seem troubled by his seeming lack of productivity? Not in my company. Nowadays I am forced to conclude other people's estimations of his well-being were of much less consequence to him than getting proper topspin, showing that to a son. In long tennis whites he looked a bit like one of the old timers, though slightly overweight, another grayer version perhaps of the Central Park camp counselor who appears in his early stories.

Who I have sometimes been with is also important. "Kiddo," Henry Miller tells me when we speak about my writing his life story, which I have been contracted to do, "don't you think you have a lot of nerve thinking you could write that?"

"Why not make up my life story, kiddo?" Henry Miller told me when he was an old man. He had a chronically sore hip. Said: "I made up my version of it. Why don't you? Or you pay me some of the advance you're getting, and I'll swear every word is the truth."

Ralph Ellison told me he once resented James Agee when he was a young writer because "Agee wrote about the poverty of poor white trash . . . and they were the people who kept my people down, I thought."

When John Paul Sartre won the Nobel Prize, Isaac Singer tells me, with the innocence of a centerfold spread in *Playboy*, "This man Sartre, he's not such a good writer, is he?"

I say I think he is, though different, of course.

When I recounted this story a few days later to Elie Wiesel, he said, "That's just Isaac's chutzpah. He's too arrogant to read Sartre, and this way he makes his insistence on not knowing seem like a reasonable position."

In those days Wiesel and Singer were both still writing for the Yiddish newspaper *The Jewish Daily Forward*. The collegiality of these two future Nobel laureates was largely a matter of incessant backbite.

The poet John Ashbery and I once met in front of his apartment building in Chelsea on a hot summer day. I was getting off my bike to run an errand. He invited me up to his place for a cool drink. Some weeks later we exchanged books: I gave him my autobiography, *Fredi & Shirl & the Kids*. He gave me *A Nest of Ninnies*, which he wrote with the poet James Schuyler.

We sat together on couches in his comfortable, though somewhat frumpy, living room, as though divided on opposite sides of a white picket fence. I tell him I admire his poetry of time as a sort of white noise. He tells me that, as an almost unknown in Paris, he also had to do a lot of hack work: crime stories, some porn, I believe, under assumed names. Under assumed names, both poets have chosen at times to be fugitives.

I've met Ashbery many times in many situations since that first quick pick-me-up drink on a hot summer day. I know his story; he knows mine. We usually try to be kind to each other. As poetry editor of *Partisan Review*, he published one of my poems.

This is about some famous and accomplished people I have known a long time, and some less well, in the course of my career as a working writer. After all, I'm a little tired of being confused for the biographer of James Joyce.

Confrontations rarely trouble me. At a dinner party once, about a decade ago in Albany, Toni Morrison scolded me about having a new daughter with a younger wife at my age. She said she was envious of me, but also thought it unfair that she was now too old to bear children.

I pointed out I'd never had a Guggenheim Fellowship, like she, or an endowed chair at a university, or a best seller. Wasn't that just as unfair?

Toni Morrison departed early that evening.

I was in Nick Delbanco's living room the night Donald Barthelme challenged John Gardner to a fist fight for what he wrote about him, in *On Moral Fiction*. I was also slandered by Gardner in that book as anti-Semitic because I didn't like my parents, so I found myself rooting for Barthelme, but Gardner wouldn't step outside, and Barthelme finally relented in his constant daring of Gardner and left the party. Bern Malamud said of Gardner another time when John appeared boisterously clobbered at a Delbanco party: "You should understand John, Richard. He's having his Bennington experience. You remember what that was like don't you?"

Once Cynthia Ozick called me up to make a statement in support of some Israeli incursion into Lebanon. I was then dating a Lebanese woman I liked a lot who still had relatives there, and I did not feel comfortable, I told Cynthia, supporting acts of Israeli aggression, despite the fact that I supported the principle of a Jewish nation in Palestine.

"I hope you and your Arab whore will be very happy together," she shouted into the phone and hung up.

I was in Malcolm Cowley's creative writing workshop with Tillie Olsen at Stanford in 1957. Cowley was a great admirer of Tillie's writings, as were most of us, and he was a great help to her in those days.

He was very hard of hearing and wore a device over one ear which was the size of an early Japanese transistor radio. When Tillie presented in class he turned up the sound level, but it was well known that when the rest of us presented he turned the sound down to a pleasing drone and napped.

At Stanford I also had some time with the Irish writer Frank O'Connor. He gave *me* some advice I still follow: Try to tell the story you're working on to yourself, or write it down, in a few sentences. If you can't, you probably don't have a story.

Henry Miller told me the following story. He married his first wife in Brooklyn when he was seventeen. She was his piano teacher, "an older woman." They had an affair on his mother's rug in Bushwick. "But afterwards," Henry said, "she was so frigid with me, kiddo, I had to fuck her through her nightgown."

The journalist Ned Calmer told me once he was a character in Henry Miller's *Tropic of Cancer*. He lived in the same hotel with Henry and June (Maud in the novels) in Paris. He said that when Henry and June went on tandem bike trips they wore his and her lederhosen with leather flaps that sprang open around the genitals for easy access.

June Corbett, as she now called herself when I interviewed her in her Elmont Queens flat, had switched her primary allegiances from Henry Miller to Amiri Baraka. She was old and beautiful and bleak, and she raised funds for Baraka's short-lived political party in a tiny apartment filled with Henry Miller memorabilia. She told me, "Henry saved my life when I was an alky living in a flea bag in New York. So I'll always be grateful to Henry for thinking of me out in Big Sur when he really didn't have to, but I'm a Marxist and a Black Nationalist, and politically he and I are worlds apart and always will be."

At Yaddo John Cheever told me that the first time he was in residence at that famed art colony in Saratoga in the 1920s, Katrina Trask Peabody, the widow of the newsprint magnate who donated the place after the death of her husband and child, was still in residence, with her swami and her Ethiopian holy man.

"The high point of every evening," Cheever told me wryly, "was after dinner when all the 'colored' servants were invited into the dining room to sing 'spirituals' to the assembled artists."

When I wrote a number of American writers in the seventies to inquire if they had ever been in the employment of the Central Intelligence Agency novelist Robert Coover sent back a postcard that said, "Alas yes." Novelist Peter Matthiesen, who worked for the Agency in Paris right after college, declined to answer any of my questions.

I enter this tiny New York hotel room. I've been standing in a dark hallway quite some time after knocking more than once at the door. The door opens, and I see a room plastered over with shiny aluminum foil—walls, ceiling, even the windows.

Lenny Bruce is standing, overweight and naked, inside a big white bath towel next to the bed. It's a bitter New York winter, and the room is close, with knocking steam pipes, a smell like camphor. Bruce's teeth chatter a little; he's got goosebumps.

"I was tanning myself," he explains. "Sometimes you need a little internal sun as well as what you can get outside. I was just trying to get a little brown."

The towel slips partly off his hip, and he grabs for it to pull it back in place. The overhead light against such shiny aluminum is a blinding waxy yellow, making the rubbery flab circling his waist all the more sallow.

"Don' misunderstand me, kid. The *emmes*," he says. "The truth is I was just trying to get a little sun inside me."

I

IN ADDITION TO GEORGE SPELVIN

MOTKE KAPLAN

I met Motke on the waterfront in Greenpoint when I was working as a guard on the ocean-going freighters. While I was watching the boats, he watched me for certain business interests in Newark and Miami, but it wasn't always clear what he was protecting—me or the contraband arriving from abroad.

Motke, or "Mutt" as we called him, a specialist in extortion and mayhem, was a short, round man with a bald pate circled by a fringe of light brown hair. His nose was wide with flaring nostrils, and his smile womanish. He worked only by referral, he told me, and called himself a contractor. "I have an uncle who does electrical contracting," I said.

"Kiddo," he said, "you don't care to know the kind of contracting I do."

He had very thick forearms and fists the size of pig's knuckles. He wore an old, yellow Cubavera jacket with the sleeves cut off at the elbows and carried a piece but never made a show of it. When he and I became friends he nicknamed me, "Junior."

Motke was a member of the Bergen Street Boys Club of Newark on detached duty in Greenpoint. His CEO was Longy Zwillman whom he called "Abner," but he also was connected in some capacity to Meyer Lansky whom he called "Booky."

"He keeps the books don't he?" Motke explained. He'd been arrested a score of times for theft, fraud, and violations of the Volstead Act during Prohibition. I never saw Motke being violent. He kept a handbook for the merchant seamen coming off the ships and gave good odds. Had a punchcard route in Port Newark. And he had a couple of Jewish women for whom he procured—Muriel and Lorna. Motke said the "nafkehs" were both hard-working girls with families who would "do anything for a guy within reason."

He told me he'd gone to grade school in Brooklyn with Barbara Stanwyck and knew Rita Hayworth when she was "in the life at Hector's Cafeteria."

"Are you sure?" I said. "She was a dancer."

"Dance my ass," he said.

I think Motke was probably celibate. He had a son in Greenwich Village named Roman. He said Roman had an Italian mother he hadn't seen in fifteen years. Seems she was also in the life, and Roman, who looked mulatto, played piano at the high yellow Village bar called the "Club Savannah." Motke called his son a "flic" and a "dickhead," and they hadn't spoken in a decade. "He uses his rear end irresponsibly" was all Motkey would say.

He'd fought welterweight when he was younger and raced bikes, and had a summer place in Lake Hopatcong. He said he'd been "muscle" when Gertrude Stein spoke in Chicago and couldn't "make dick out of what she was saying."

"Adolf Hitler," he said, "was my undoing as a bad guy. When I read about the camps I took care of business but started observing the Sabbath."

One hot summer day I went to work, and there was Motke chatting it up with a bulky looking man in a Panama hat and a double-breasted suit the color of vanilla ice cream. The man wore lightly tinted shades. When Motke waved me over, he said, "Mr. Genovesee appreciates the way you look after things around here" and handed me a fifty dollar bill.

I tried to return the money but Motke's companion said, "Think nothing of it. Just do your job."

"Yes sir," I said.

Afterward, Motke confided in me that his friend Vito had really liked my "Yes sir."

"It's good you showed him that respect," he said. "A man like that requires respect."

The local police knew all about Motke, but they never seemed to hassle him. He was just another member of the community and wasn't always looking over his shoulder.

He told me that in Havana, Cuba, the police were allowed to accept "gratuities, a good cigar, a cocktail on a hot day, a shirt, a tie. The little things."

"New York," Motke added, "is a two-faced whore. Everybody is on the take and pretends otherwise."

One day Motke told me he was leaving town for a while, a trip to the coast. Business. I never saw him again. For a long time that didn't bother me until I read about him in a book about Florida.

It seems Longy had made a deal with some West Coast people for Motke to be in on the skim in Las Vegas. Motke had allergies and didn't like Vegas. He was sent to Florida to manage a place I think called "Papa Bouchard's" in Key Biscayne which had back room gambling. Motke quarreled with a Cuban high roller named Perry Finger and was fed to some alligators off the Tamiami Trail; and then Longy had Finger reduced to blue fish chum and spread all over the beaches of the Florida Keys.

The author of this account says Motke was a favorite in the rabbinical courts of Longy and Lansky. At a memorial service at the Shelburn Hotel in Atlantic City, an honorary Boy's Club member named Guzik said, "You could always count on Motke. He was the cockstand of stand up guys from our era."

Motke had one gold tooth and a lot of inlays and used to sing a little Ira Gershwin song to himself whenever he got real agitated:

> La la so this is Venice
> la la you can tell by the smell
> and by the way they play no tennis . . .

Whenever Motke started singing that song you knew you should watch out.

ALEXANDER KERENSKY

I met my old grad school housemate Alexander Kerensky once, more than twenty years ago, in front of the Columbia University School of Social Work at Fifth Avenue and Ninety-first Street. I was hopping out of a cab, it so happens, with a copy of the Menshevik *New Leader* in my hand. Kerensky was, I imagine, on his usual early morning constitutional. The former first provisional president of the Russian government had aged since the last time we met, nearly ten years before at Stanford University, but he still knew how to dandle his walking cane as if practicing with the epee; and he still had a way of staring at you with his head cocked slightly askew, as if wearing a monocle, which he was not. I said, "Dr. Kerensky, hello. Do you remember me?"

Kerensky stopped, glared at me, glared again, his closecropped gray hair bristling. He ran the cane between his fingers like a pool cue. Finally he declared: "Certainly not!"

No wonder his government was so easily overthrown by the Bolsheviks. Can you imagine the King of Consensus, Lyndon Baines Johnson, under such circumstances? Probably L. B. J. would have shaken the hoof of a cow if it suddenly said, "Lyndon baby, don't you remember me?" If a democratic politician doesn't have that much opportunism, what else can one expect of him? Not only the small *d* democrats! I can recall photographs of Comrade Ulbricht being embraced by Comrade Brezhnev, which must have been like putting your arms around Grant's Tomb. I can also remember seeing former Senator Barry Goldwater in Fresno, California, on a hand-shaking tour shortly before he received the GOP nomination in 1964. People were complaining that Goldwater was a racist, so his campaign managers had propped one of the local colored folk within shooting distance of the caravan of press photographers. As he passed by, Goldwater's chief aide gave the candidate a furious poke in the ribs. Barry doubled over but he recognized what he must do, went "Hi there," broke his stride, and ran to shake the *prop* hand. "Don't you remember me?" the candidate declared, pumping furiously. "You shined my shoes here at the hotel ten years ago."

Which simply means that Alexander Kerensky was a man of uncompromising anticommunism. How would you feel if you had been chased out of the Winter Palace buttoning your trousers? But "the conscience of the democracy," as Lev Davidovich Trotsky called him sarcastically, was also a right social revolutionary—whatever that meant. When I was a leftist student, I thought it meant that Kerensky had bobbled the ball in the first quarter with first down and goal to go.

Imagine the scene: two young Russians growing up in the same hometown; it's twenty years later, a Simbirsk field day in the capital— Lenin goes to the left; Kerensky is at center. It's squat formation with John Reed calling the signals. Oops! Fumble! The Bolsheviks take over the ball on the Cadets' forty yard line. I would be bitter, too. But whether or not I would want to spend the rest of my life waiting for punt formation is another matter. The men who were now ruling Russia were, in effect, the same gang of conspirators who had tackled him on the playing fields before the Winter Palace. It was only in character for such a Kerensky to greet Khrushchev's later overthrow with a statement to the effect that Russia's new *emminence gris* had not yet revealed himself. For such a Kerensky to give up believing in Bolshevik conspiracies would, I suspect, be like the pope renouncing the mystery of the Holy Trinity. Somebody, after all, has to continue to uphold revelation.

But I am not trying to infer that the Alexander Kerensky who shared a bathroom with me in the home of Herbert Hoover's niece in Palo Alto, California, was a sore loser. Although he used to boast about how his two sons had refused to serve as Bulganin's and Khrushchev's interpreters during their visit to England in 1955, he was not unpleasant about it. Kerensky, as I remember him, was a charmer, a hand kisser, a well-oiled mechanical doll with a set of fine steel Swiss watch springs in his elbows and knees. Nothing other-worldly about this man; he would do his morning constitutional heel and toe fashion, as if taking part in the Coney Island marathon. Not once but twice I caught him peering down a sun-freckled bosom as he bent from hand to hand in my landlady's back garden at the wedding reception barbecue which she gave for my first wife and myself, shortly after we returned from our honeymoon. Having known the splendors of Petersburg society, Nicolai's court, the great world of the moneyed exiles, it was absolutely splendid of Kerensky to be trying so hard not to condescend at my wedding reception. He flitted from barbecue pit to beer case as if at an Imperial levee. Dazed by the heavy sweet scent of the lemon blossoms, rubbed bright red by the warm summer sun, perhaps a little bit tipsy from all the sherry, he was passing up his third hamburger in favor of a third frankfurter while Mrs. Maryk, my landlady—ever the well-brought-up widow of an India medical missionary—cooed: "Have another sausage Doctor. . . . *un autre saucisson* . . . they're *glat kosher* in honor of the bride and groom."

If this was a petty triumph for the Jews, it was a somewhat larger triumph for Kerensky. For Mrs. Maryk's Uncle Herbert had, after all, backed the Whites against the Bolsheviks, and the old Left-Right social revolutionary was forced to travel all the way out to Palo Alto to study his official papers, which Hoover had pirated for his Stanford library. But it must have seemed particularly bizarre (as well as hopelessly American) that he should have ended up lodging with Hoover's niece.

I remember the day Mrs. Maryk got the phone call from the university asking her if she could rent a room to Alexander Kerensky. I happened to be writing a poem in my room overlooking the lemon garden, when I heard a general commotion down below. Presently, Mrs. Maryk appeared in my doorway, handsomely decked out as usual in a silk print dress, but with her lorgnette swinging freely, her lovely gray hair-do all awry, her face flushed, her lips slightly parted, her great bosoms heaving, quite out of breath. Since I knew she suffered from a weak heart, I invited her to sit in the only comfortable chair. "Shall I get you a glass of water?" I asked.

"No, please, I couldn't . . ." Mrs. Maryk struggled with her breathing, measuring me shrewdly all the while.

"It's just too terrible," she declared then. "It isn't bad enough that I've had weight lifters and Arabs . . . and . . . homosexuals. . . . Now they want me to take in this Bolshevik. Mr. Elman, what shall I do?"

I asked: "How do you know he is a Communist?"

"Because," she gasped, "he was the president of Russia. They told me so."

"But, Mrs. Maryk," I said, "there hasn't been a Russian president that I know of since Alexander Kerensky."

"Yes. That's the man, Kerensky," she said . . . "O what shall I do?"

After I explained to Mrs. Maryk that if, indeed, the gentleman was Kerensky he was anything but a Bolshevik, she grew calm again. I said: "He must be a very old man, for that matter."

"An old Russian . . . what shall I do?" Mrs. Maryk lamented. She prided herself on being a tolerant person, and she presently was agreeing with me that she would probably come to no harm. "I just hope he doesn't like to stare through keyholes like that Turkish agronomist they sent two years ago," she concluded. Moments later, Mrs. Maryk was calling the university: it would be all right now if the Russian gentleman cared to see his rooms, she announced, with considerable pluck.

It was not until another week had gone by that I actually became aware that the man who left his teeth in a glass in my bathroom every morning was Kerensky. He seemed never to make any noises in his adjoining rooms. Perhaps he was poring over great sealed dossiers. I was too busy to care, still in the act of creating my poem which, as I recall, was quite long and rather symbolic, all about a peacock with glaucoma. I can remember only one phrase: "Sprung rhythm of your stuck gore—O my big blind bird."

Pacing back and forth in my room, I used to recite this to myself. There were peacocks near the Stanford campus. Late one afternoon, as I was walking home from a visit among them, I happened to run into Mrs. Maryk. She said she would give me a lift.

It was a lovely early spring day in Palo Alto. The magnolias had just blossomed, strewing thick, waxy petals across the tarmack that actually crunched under the wheels of the car. When we turned down the Embarcadero, past the Municipal Bowling Green, the air was dizzyingly sweet. Mrs. Maryk said: "Lovely, isn't it? Makes one feel like a girl again."

"I offered Dr. Kerensky a ride to the campus," she continued, all in the same breath, "and do you know what he said? He said: 'Thank you, no!' A man his age. 'It's better for the health to walk,' he said. Imagine," Mrs. Maryk declared with a high squeal, narrowly averting a head-on collision with another passing car, "a man his age . . ."

"Just how old would that be?" I asked, knowing that Mrs. Maryk was also getting on in years.

"O not so old as all that," she replied then, "but you know how some of us are . . . we're very crotchety . . . I would say Mr. Kerensky is a very crotchety old gentleman. He doesn't look at all like a Russian. Haven't you seen him yet?"

I confessed I hadn't.

"Well, we shall have to get you two together," she said.

Three days later I received an invitation to come to dinner to meet Dr. Kerensky on the following evening. Another lady friend of Mrs. Maryk's would also be present, she explained, and perhaps her daughter. Mrs. Maryk said she was planning on fixing one of her special Indian curries. "Lamb, I think," she said. "I make my own chutneys . . . and my own fresh mango ice cream . . . I think you'll like it. . . . Sherry at 6:00, dinner at 6:30 sharp.Try to be prompt, won't you?" she declared. "The maid has to babysit for her daughter so she can go to her high school prom."

My landlady's late husband had been distantly related to the great illustrator Frederick Remington. Life-sized portraits of fierce frontiersmen, army officers, Indian chiefs were the only works of art gracing her walls. She had been a child bride, she once explained, and these were among her many fabulous wedding presents. But it always came as a shock to me, after standing among the verbena in her front doorway, to be greeted by this lovely old matron and then to be ushered past chintz upholstery, fine teak tables with Indian brass pots of mimosa, along carpets from Persia, into the library with its barbarous collection of Remingtonia. When I arrived at precisely 5:59 on the specified evening, I was girding myself for my dual encounter with the Wild West and Kerensky by recalling what a dimly Trotskyite but mostly Stalinoid relative had once declared over pot cheese and sour cream at my grandmother's house in Newark, New Jersey. "Kerensky," this old harridan from *Minskgobernya* announced during a lull in the battle for Stalingrad, "was to the revolutionary movement like an ingrown hair to a colossal boil." I rang the front doorbell. Moments later, this slim little runt in a dark suit appeared at the entranceway. "Who is it?"

"Dr. Kerensky?"

"And who are you?" he replied, rolling his *r*.

"I'm the student from upstairs . . . Mrs. Maryk asked down. Are you Dr. Kerensky?"

"Yes, of course I am," he declared, "and you are . . . Mr. Ermine, isn't it?"

"Elman," I corrected him.

"So? Like the violinist."

"A distant relative," I lied.

"I hear your machine . . . your typewriter sometimes," Kerensky said then.

"Does it bother you?" I asked, oversolicitous.

"Certainly not," the former provisional president declared. He ushered me past him into the Remington room.

"So . . . you are Mischa Elman's nephew."

"Actually," I cut in, "the relationship is quite distant. Something like fifth cousins twice removed. Mrs. Maryk is Herbert Hoover's niece, but Mischa and I are not too close."

"Mrs. Maryk and her lady friend are in the kitchen," Kerensky explained then, without changing expression, "and there is only sherry . . . will you help yourself?"

"Don't mind if I do," I said, filling a pony glass so that it over-flowed the brim.

We were sitting now in opposite chairs alongside the mantel-piece. I was struggling manfully to begin a conversation. Kerensky stared at the little puddle I had made on Mrs. Maryk's teak table: "So . . . you are related to Mischa Elman."

"Strange that I should be meeting you in person," I cut in, "because I was just reading about you in Trotsky's *History of the Revolution* . . ."

It was, of course, just the wrong thing to say. "How interesting!" Kerensky said. Moments later, Mrs. Maryk tinkled her little bell for dinner. Throughout the rest of the evening Kerensky was like a statue. The only kind words he had were for Mrs. Maryk's fresh mango ice cream. He took seconds. But, although the curry was superb, the ladies gabby and charming, I had very little appetite. Suppose he were to ask me again about Mischa Elman? Could I tell him the bitter truth—that our suits had once been mixed up at the dry cleaners? Over dinner, Mrs. Maryk talked about the flies in Cairo where another of her rela-tives had been curator of the Egyptology museum. My chair was fac-ing a giant Remington panorama of a battle on the plains. I found myself totaling up the casualties.

Still another of Mrs. Maryk's numerous relations were the Lees of Philadelphia of whom the great historian Charles Henry Lee was per-haps the most celebrated figure. Early the following morning, I found myself glancing through Lee's marvelous *History of the Inquisition* with vague thoughts of making my peacock into a symbol of post-Siglo De Oro Spanish Jewry, when Kerensky appeared at the head of the stair-well in the small library which Mrs. Maryk kept for her tenants. "Young scholars start the day early," he declared.

"I'm not really much of a scholar," I said, a bit startled.

"What are you doing in school?" he asked.

"I want to be a poet," I explained.

"Do you know Pushkin and Lermontov?" he asked.

"Only in English translation," I lied.

"Then you don't really know them at all," Kerensky announced, commencing to take his leave of me with a spin of his cane.

Two days later we passed beneath a eucalyptus grove on the way to campus. I was on my bicycle. Kerensky was walking.

"Good day, " I said.

"Why do you say that?" he asked, pointing with his cane at the storm clouds which were already glowering over the peninsula.

It was about a month later that I flew to New York to get married.

Upon our return, Mrs. Maryk announced that she wanted to throw me a small party. "I'll invite Dr. Kerensky," she said.

I was up most of the night before worrying over what new *faux pas* I might commit in the presence of the former provisional president. It was truly a Dostoyevskyan evening. My bride slept chastely while I groaned and chattered my teeth like Prince Mishkin. Should I let on that I knew the secret of Simbirsk? Did I dare to say more about my alleged ties to Mischa Elman? Whatever I did, I expected that Kerensky would take his cold revenge by pulling me across the garden by the ear. But, as it turned out, he was gay and debonair, and I managed to keep my distance. Once, in passing, he wished me luck with my lovely bride. The second time we spoke was over coffee when we were all seated in garden chairs listening to Mrs. Maryk expound upon a plague of dysentery she had once witnessed in Mysore. "I have never seen such a bunch of uncomfortable tourists," she was saying. "I doubt if any of those men will ever again promise their wives to take them to the Taj Mahal."

Suddenly I felt the pressure of a hand on my arm.

"*You in the West are in for a big surprise,*" Kerensky was saying *sotto voce.*

"Marvelous," I told him.

"There cannot be any doubt about Soviet intentions," he went on. "Stalin once said . . ."

I nodded in agreement.

Someone interrupted me. "What?" I asked.

"Darling, I think we should get home early," my wife whispered in my other ear.

I waved her away. "What did Stalin say?" I asked.

"Sometimes," Kerensky said, "bitter experience is the only teacher."

"Yes. But what did Stalin say?" I was merely trying to hold up my end of conversation. I heard my wife say: "Please Dick . . ."

"What did Stalin say?" I demanded.

Mrs. Maryk paused in her interminable narration. I felt Kerensky relinquish his grip. "Did somebody mention Stalin?" Mrs. Maryk asked.

"I believe," Kerensky said, rising from his chair, "it is time for my evening stroll."

He went over to Mrs. Maryk, took her hand, and kissed it lightly. Then he turned toward the rest of the company again. "So," he said, narrowing his eyes on me until they seemed to give off sparks, "you and Mischa Elman are related . . ."

". . . and Mrs. Maryk is related to Hoover and Frederick Remington and I don't know who else . . ."

"*You and Mischa Elman . . .*"

"*What about Stalin?*" I asked.

"If the West isn't careful, it will be in for a tragic surprise . . . a surprise to nobody except the West," Kerensky added.

". . . And what about Stalin?"

"The innocent learn from bitter experience," he said.

"Don't you think it's time to say good-night?" my wife added then.

When we were thanking Mrs. Maryk for her hospitality, I saw Kerensky scamper behind the lemon bushes toward the back stairs. My landlady said: "I'm so pleased Dr. Kerensky had somebody he could talk to."

I said: "I wonder why he never finished telling me about Stalin?"

"Probably," put in one of the other ladies, "it's one of those top secret affairs of state."

"Just the same," Mrs. Maryk said then, "I think he was right . . . whatever he was saying." She turned to my wife: "I don't know how I shall replace your husband now that you're going to be living elsewhere. Who will I find to amuse Dr. Kerensky?"

"Why not try Pushkin and Lermontov?" I volunteered.

"Oh," said Mrs. Maryk, "I don't think I'd like a house full of Russians."

That day, in front of Columbia, I asked Dr. Kerensky if he remembered Mrs. Maryk. "Certainly," he said, "she died . . ."

So did Stalin!

And Kerensky, much later on.

YVOR WINTERS, THOM GUNN, AND OTHERS

The other day in the small north shore Long Island town where I live, I ran into a former member of Yvor Winters' Stanford poetry workshop. He is now a retired New York City high school teacher, this chunky, gentle, sad, slow-talking New York Jew who has only just gotten back to writing poems again of some beauty and passion after his encounters with Winters in the workshop thirty-seven years ago.

Oddly, Winters invited this fellow to come all the way from Brooklyn College to Stanford on a full poetry fellowship and then proceeded to savage every poem he ever submitted to the workshop with arguments that ranged from close textual criticism to the ad hominem.

It was a brutal spectacle to watch this Coney Island Keatsian subjected to Winters' unrelenting persiflage. Even though Winters was as often accurate as not, Martin flayed was painful to observe. I have somewhere read of a kind of Oriental demon who gained power over one only as one recognized and feared him. So convinced was Winters of the rightness of his prescriptions that by his overbearing manner he seemed to be trying to discourage my friend from wanting to write anything, even a business letter, ever again; and he almost succeeded. But why? He might just have saved a lot of time and money by sending Martin a letter of rejection when he'd first applied for the fellowship, saying he preferred his Delmore Schwartz sliced thin on rye with a slather of mustard.

At times I was grateful to my Brooklyn friend for being in the class; when he became the target, some of Winters' ire was deflected that might have been directed at me.

Toward my own poetry, "Arthur," as his wife, Janet Lewis, called him, was alternately condescending, with restrained praise for my earnestness and critical of my "Brooklyn ear" and general ignorance of the traditions of English and American poetry, and my absence of reading knowledge in foreign languages, and up to a point he was on the money. If I wanted to be Rimbaud, what was I doing in graduate school?

Trying to stay out of the army, of course. Graduate study gave me a draft deferment. But I also knew I lacked erudition and polish and was often sunk in forlorn reveries. I needed to reach beyond myself through craft and thought and, after reading some of Winter's critical essays and the poems he admired, I believed this powerful and eminent "new critic" could teach me. Winters was not uncharitable: he thought I was probably capable of becoming educated and would make a decent critic, especially whenever I collaborated with him in attacking his pet scapegoats.

It was a small workshop which met in Winters' dingy office, in an atmosphere of fear softened only by his constant production of pipe smoke and methane gas. The walls, as I recall, were empty of decorations except for some old black and white prints, and the atmosphere was gray; Winters wore old gray suits and was heavy, flaccid, sort of grayish. When he was calm, Winters could resemble a large lovable old hound you wished to pet a lot except that you knew he sometimes bit.

He was a great admirer of the poetry of plain speech. He despised mere feckless adornments of language or thought. He maintained that a well-argued shorter lyric of under a hundred lines was superior even to *Hamlet* or *King Lear*, and certainly most novels, as formal expression. He upheld the expository over the dramatic forms, but was himself a bit of a ham, reading even the poets whose works he claimed to despise with a deep vibrato, a monotone.

In the class was a very brilliant young society woman whom Winters much admired; her poems were full of morbidity, religious sentiments, and pain, in latinate blank verse. She later became a nun and to my knowledge stopped writing.

The expatriate British poet Thom Gunn was also a member of that class, and the poet Alan Stephens from Arizona, a tall, dry, extremely reasonable man. Winters admired the writings of both these poets, especially Gunn.

This was Thom's second trip to Stanford. A few years earlier, after military service and study with Leavis at Cambridge, Gunn had been a poetry fellow, like my friend from Brooklyn. (Increasingly sullen most of the time in the workshop, the Brooklyn poet after a while stopped arguing with Winters and stopped producing poems. I bought my first jalopy of a car at a bargain price of seventy dollars from him when he finally had taken all he could bear from Winters and left the university to go back East.)

Like Winters once had been, Gunn was also, I believe, a motorcyclist. Winters truly admired Thom's intelligence and talent with conventional meters and his immense knowledge of English and American poetry. With his reputation as a poet growing here and in the U.K. through the success of *The Sense of Movement*, Thom was invited back by Winters, and he wrote some very fine syllabic poems, some of which appeared in his collection, *My Sad Captains*.

Winters was very gentle in his criticism of Gunn's work. He sometimes deplored obscurantism and romanticism, but he liked Gunn's classical imitations, his feeling for historical subject matter in his poems, his sense of form, and the clarity of his diction. I admired the contemporaneity of poems about motorcycle gangs, his hipness to the vernacular, his Ray-Bans and black, silverstudded motorcycle jackets, and cowboy boots. Gunn's style was restrained flamboyance.

We were both very masked about such things in those days. I was just married to a beautiful woman and would have been shocked to admit I was attracted in any way to a man; Gunn was still not yet out of the closet. If he presented himself at parties, he usually brought along female dates or came alone. When he introduced me to his roommate, Mike, I was naive enough to think they were just simply roommates, not lovers, as I later discovered.

Gunn was slim and tall, with a sharp, handsome, pockmarked face and inky black hair, long sideburns. He was generous in his criticisms of my work and usually kind, and he participated in the workshop as just another member, never put on airs.

He'd served in the Royal Air Force in the north of England and had earlier been to private grammar schools and was pretty much in exile from the decadent English literary scene, having acquired, at times, an American lingo and an American twist smile. He told me once his father was the editor of the *Daily Sketch*, a lurid and sleazily dishonest London tabloid, and he had a younger brother who was a photographer. He seemed in those days to be interested in a courtly romantic way in the young debutante who became a nun, but, when I asked him if indeed that was the case, Thom quickly changed the subject.

There was little that Thom showed in public you could interpret as swish or faggy. He swaggered a little in his movieland leather togs and boots; so did straight poseurs in their rough trade garments. My wife, Emily, also had a crush on Thom, and he never seemed to give her the time of day, I noticed, while seeming courtly.

Once Emily and I were driving through the Mojave Desert in bloom to L.A. and were hoping to take a tour of the Fox Studio lot. Thom happened to be there that day, too, as a guest of the writer Christopher Isherwood, who was also easy with us and outgoing, and in public not so very campy, though with the longest auburn eyelashes I've ever observed on a man.

Isherwood had been hired on as a writer for a Deborah Kerr and Cary Grant movie about a shipboard romance, *An Affair to Remember*. We were invited by Isherwood to lunch in the commissary and then to watch some of the takes. Thom and Isherwood seemed very close. They sat side by side. I thought that was because they were both English.

When I left Stanford, Thom gave me an inscribed copy of *Fighting Terms*. At the time of my divorce this disappeared from my collection and later was listed in the catalogue of a well-known dealer for a good sum of money. Needless to say, Gunn was very hurt that I'd been compelled to sell off his gift to me. I'm not sure that I ever did. Though I occasionally would sell off items from my library, including correspondence which wasn't very personal, to dealers in order to make ends meet, I don't ever recall selling any of Thom Gunn's books. In fact, I have always purchased every new book of his when it appears and quickly read the poems from cover to cover, more than once, in part a matter of brand loyalty, and because I really like to own my friends' books.

We write to each other now and then, but live entirely different lives. When he published his collected essays after the AIDS plague began, I was alarmed to read that Thom had participated with apparently great joy in the San Francisco orgy scenes of the sixties and seventies. His most recent poems in a volume called *Night Sweats* memorialize some of his friends who were victims of AIDS, and, inferentially, make reference in the title and elsewhere to the terrible trepidations of one who, luckily, so far has not yet been infected with HIV.

Yvor Winters was a moralist. He liked poets whose work illustrated his critical exhortations, and they were entered into his lists of bests and worsts. He always ranked his students among the other poets who were publishing as though handicapping horses: Don Stanford, Achilles Holt, Ann Stanford—these Wintersian products seemed to have much better bloodlines than my own. You were praised a lot for agreeing with Winters. Nobody I had previously encountered had been so evaluative. It wasn't very long before I began to feel that every impulse that had impelled me to write poems was counterfeit. I had managed to use graduate school to avoid basic infantry training: Now here I was plop in the mud in the middle of the infiltration course with Winters firing live ammo.

He had been a Hart Crane enthusiast until Crane's behavior as a poet and a person became so problematical. Some say his harsh review of Hart Crane's epic poem *The Bridge* drove the poet into that melancholy which culminated in suicide. I've never really believed this, though perhaps Winters did, for, if he knew of Gunn's sexual orientation, he was truly careful never to be ad hominem in criticizing Thom's work.

Once Gunn and my wife and I were invited to the Winters' house in Los Altos for a steak barbecue. There was good food and a lot to drink. Everybody got a little high, and, after the meal, Winters entertained the guests by acting out on his tiptoes some of the great prizefights of recent years: Louis-Schmelling, Sugar Ray Robinson versus La Motta. He toedanced and swung at imaginary opponents as this contender or that and would stop and thoughtfully indicate just what had been the crucial blow to end the fight and where and with what velocity it had landed on the face or body of his opponent.

I thought he looked a little silly, and so did Winters' wife, Janet, who kept saying, "Arthur, it's getting late. Let's call it a night."

Gunn said very little. He just watched the spectacle of Winters up on his toes with his distending large Johnsonian belly, acting out those bearish fantasies. Were they so very different really from Gunn's gangs of hogbikers riding out into the open countryside in search of speed and grace?

I would have to say I never detected much humor in Winters. He did seem to find it amusing if you made a face after eating one of his home-brined olives or if you had car trouble. He also could be generous in rewarding hardworking students if they accepted certain quid pro quos. Just before I volunteered to do my army service and get it over with, Winters recommended me for the Royal Victor graduate fellowship at Stanford, which was a great honor and quite lucrative, though it meant I would have to take an ordinary Ph.D. in English literature.

Half a year later I wrote Stanford that I wouldn't be coming back. I really didn't want to be one of Winters' epigones. I'd discovered prose and wanted to learn how to write it with vivid efficiency. This was probably a bad error of judgment on my part. If I'd stayed under Winters' protection I might have made a living at some college or university without all the dislocations and stresses I've undergone. But I was always much too frightened of Winters and knew I lacked Gunn's international reputation, which sometimes protected him from the old man's savagery. I didn't think I'd be able to hold my head above the water.

Come back, memory! What did he do and say that was so intimidating? Was it his claim that he'd sparred a couple of rounds with Jack Dempsey? My own father used to boast to me of biting off a man's ear in a street fight.

Winters had lived a solitary existence before coming to Stanford. He'd done exemplary things like teach Navaho school children, and, apparently, driven himself quite mad at one point. When in his cups he would blabber about the corrupt East Coast literary establishment and how he would never teach at Harvard even if he was invited.

His patriarchy often seemed lugubrious; he would often have tears in his eyes when elucidating all my failings. He never quite said he was infallible, but I can't recall him disclaiming otherwise. This made me all the more stubbornly ignorant and ornery; I kept looking for exceptions to his pronouncements, flaws in his reasoning, my constant rejoinders to his critical remarks being "Yes, but . . ." which is how students say, "Go to hell!" politely.

If you constantly disagreed with Winters, he wrote you out of his cabal, his conspiracy against the poetry establishment. You became one of "them." Winters was actually able to make you feel your inept poems were high crimes and misdemeanors, treasonable acts. He would raise his voice in anger and tremble and attack you where he knew you to feel weakest and most insecure. In his thrall we were stripped of the necessary autonomy of error. Hardly the way to encourage creative experimentation, such as one might expect from a workshop.

When I got to know Winters' publisher, Allen Swallow, he seemed brave about riding around on motorcycles but just as fearful of Winters as I was.

Once, some years later, I reviewed a book of poems by Winters' protégé, J. V. Cunningham, the epigramist and scholar. Cunningham was a big drinker and an avid horseplayer, and he came to New York and made an appointment to see me because he was very pleased with what I had written about his poignant book of poems *To What Strangers, What Welcome?*

Cunningham seemed very friendly and agreeable, although he was not pleased to drink slivovitz, which was all I had to serve him. I'd read the essays Winters had written about his former student, and it was hard to recognize him in person or in his latest poems as the scholar-poet-wit celebrated by Winters' hyperboles. He seemed quite modest about himself, and observant, and careful. I inquired if he thought his old friend's hyping of his poems accurate.

"Oh, that's just Arthur," Cunningham said. "That's not really the way it was. When Arthur would get an idea about you, you more or less were stuck with being like that. I never thought of myself as a Wintersian. I've always been in too much personal disarray."

When Malcolm Cowley was at Stanford, Winters refused to hear him read his poems because of some antique literary quarrel of forty years' provenance. He was perhaps justifiably frightened of Robert Lowell when he came to visit and threatened to pitch a tent on Winters' property in Los Altos.

(I bumped into Gunn on the streets of New York about ten years ago. He was leaving the offices of Farrar Straus off Union Square at lunchtime. I don't think Thom recognized me at first, which was appropriate, since I had never really recognized who he was when we were at Stanford together. Then, after a moment, he acknowledged in the presence of his companions that we did indeed know each other and greeted me with shy warmth. Some weeks later I wrote to his Cole Street address in San Francisco that it made me happy to know he was alive and well.)

When he was old and sick, Winters wrote to tell me he thought I was a fool for not having continued in graduate school. I never sent him any of my novels to read because he told me he no longer cared to read novels. He lacked the time. Once I asked him if he admired Dostoyevsky. Winters said he would not read any more translations, so he didn't really know what he thought of such books.

Some years ago I found some early Winters poems in a quarterly in a used bookstore. These were the poems he later said were "associative twaddle" and repudiated, as he came to write contemporary imitations of Ben Jonson and Fulke Greville. They seemed to me very beautiful and very original evocations of certain mental states in fluent vers libre, similar to Cunningham's procedures in *To What Strangers, What Welcome?*

When the poet Louise Bogan came to Stanford, Winters and Janet Lewis were her generous hosts. He confided to the class that he felt sorry for the life she was compelled to live as an exploited single woman in New York, but thought her poems "beautiful and not overly emotional."

Yvor Winters seemed even more afraid of his emotions than I was, and he wrote himself out of the contemporary canon. This took courage at the start of a career and enabled him to survive as an academic. He seemed to wish the same for any student whom he could influence. He was often intimidating, usually insightful, and occasionally lucid, astute, intuitive, brilliant, and imposing. But who was he trying to persuade? Ignoramuses like me? Himself? Others? We were all enlisted in his campaign against the false coinages of modernism and literary madness, his tight quatrains sometimes arguing against his own moral exhortations:

> A poem is what stands
> when imperceptive hands,
> feeling, have gone astray;
> it is what one must say.

I now know how dismaying it can be when what one must say leads one away from reasonable statements. "What one *must say*" has also influenced my writing, though I avoid quatrains and still admire what I think of as Dostoyevsky in translation.

Here is a poem produced by my "Brooklyn ear" I call "Daybreak":

> In the morning under certain
> trees the light is orange
> and the smooth channel pinks the
> marsh in places where it is the lightest shade of blue,
>   or purple. You
> sleeping on have never seen this just as I, perhaps, never
> have known how to sew the seam
> in my trousers when others could, or
> where to look for a grammar of nuances;
> if one can say in Old French
> I open the window in order to see
> the forest. But contradictories
> exist when, as it happens,
> we are both so very frail to judge
> what we cannot fail to know, but lovingly.
> But in the mornings trees also
> thread their lights on the grass and the
> channel warms under sunfires slowly
> like a ribbon of wet glass.

ALDOUS HUXLEY

He was tall and thin, and very pale, and handsome, with ravished good looks when I knew him, and, it seemed, very close to blind. He would peer at manuscripts, but it was not clear if he was reading them. In the classroom his voice was weak, though plummy at times, and did not carry very well. I seemed always to be leaning forward across the table in the Jones room to hear his words. Many years his junior, his pretty wife Laura, I was told, would be reading our manuscripts to him. But it was not clear whether this was a problem of eyesight or ennui. He told me once sad stories by young writers on the cusp of life depressed him.

I remember him asking my friend William Wiegand repeatedly what he could find out about the sewage disposal system of San Francisco. How did it function? What did it produce and how? He seemed at that point in his life much more interested in ecology and the purification of waste products than in literature.

He claimed to like something I wrote once and gave me some good practical advice: I should hire somebody to go over the spellings in my manuscripts. "Even as misspellings," he pointed out, "your versions are preposterous."

At that period Huxley was interested in LSD. In the environment of Palo Alto so were a lot of others, friends of Ken Kesey and the Grateful Dead, who hung out in the vicinity, and Richard Alpert (a.k.a. Baba Ram Das), the son of a former CEO of the New York Central Railroad, who, confronted with the bankruptcy and takeover of his railroad, committed suicide. Huxley seemed to shy away from encounters with such people. Whenever he was asked in class about his interest in hallucinogens he recommended to would-be experimenters that they have monitors present at all times.

He would talk a lot about artificial intelligence, but also about De Sade and also faux naive poets such as the English romantic Clare, for whom he seemed to have a fondness. I once complimented him on his screenplay of *Pride and Prejudice*.

"I tried to be civilized," he pointed out, "but it was done for money."

I don't think he ever had much to say about student manuscripts except to wish the writers godspeed and good luck. He certainly never tried to discourage anybody.

There was a gifted young woman in the class who looked a lot like a witch. Her stories were very strange, illogical, but moving. I don't think she ever had a career. Huxley admired her. But I don't think he really approved of the teaching of "creative writing," like so many English persons, and he always took a hands-off attitude toward her work and to critics in class who took her on for being vague or gnomic. He seemed to be very content presenting himself to us as a monument of seriousness and curiosity and probity. We were to learn through emulation of his qualities of mind, which he would occasionally expose in soliloquies.

I found being in his presence inspiring. Though he wrote in a more or less traditional manner, he didn't seem to have any idea he wanted to impose on anybody how fiction should be written, what was taboo, and what not. With him as audience I found myself writing scenes which I would later work up as stories, and when I later read his *Devils of Loudon*, I became aware of the possibilities of historical writing and of his true erudition and humanity.

I had a far different experience with Wallace Stegner. He was a very handsome, well-groomed, charming man, lived in comfortable affluence, rode horses, was usually gentle to his students, though all the time I sat in on his workshop I felt like a misfit. I was reading Dostoyevsky; he admired Scott Fitzgerald. I looked like a psycho; he tried to appear sunny. He could discourse on Percy Lubbock's distinction between round and flat characters; I was looking for a subject other than myself and my family, and I had nothing much good to say about either.

Stegner treated me with the tolerance one usually bestows, albeit fearfully, on recently lobotomized child molesters. I jabbered too much in class about all the Russian writers whom I admired for being, among other things, uncouth, and somewhat humorously melodramatic, such as Gogol and Dostoyevsky, just as it was in my own household when I was growing up. Stegner seemed to demand a less intrusive authorial professionalism that I could only imagine myself achieving much later in life. Like Yvor Winters, he seemed hostile toward and suspicious of people from New York and found their interests lacked gentility, were sleazy and unappealing. He never was unkind to me, but I was aware that nothing I wrote could possibly please him, and when I had to submit a short novel, *A Coat for the Tsar*, for my master's thesis, and he was required to approve it, I had the distinct impression that he found the whole enterprise extremely distasteful, though he agreed to pass me with some distinction.

Maybe my mistake was to write about Jews and without a hint of Christian charity. My characters were a loathsome bunch of self-haters and operators. Stegner was not wrong about *A Coat for the Tsar*. It was a cooked-up piece of Eastern European *shtetl* hokum I had put together in a few weeks with the sole intention of going from point *A* to point *Z* in a continuous third-person narrative. That it had all the authenticity of a Taco Bell comestible is one way of putting it, but quite another way would be to recognize that I had, indeed, gone from *A* to *Z*, without faltering, and along my route had managed to depict a few recognizable human interactions.

Not too bad, really, for a novice at fiction!

TILLIE OLSEN

Sometimes on winter nights
we've sat beneath the
same red moon, you
on your Coast, and
I on mine, aware
 this loony world has
importuned another
human soul, and offered
in her place the standard
rascal. The standard
for a rascal won't improve
Tillie, though hope
endures. You taught
me that—how thunder
along the interstates
between us now can rock
undreamt of infants
in their cradles.
Sudden temperature inversions
move toward Spring
 even before Winter. If
daisies are premature, so
is the next big ice age.
You are still with me
now across a vast indifferent
middle distance, and,
in Time, I send
out this emanation
from above my Sound:
Work, struggle, joy,
You taught me these,
and gave us common ground.

I wrote this poem nearly a decade ago for Tillie Olsen's seventy-fifth birthday. I think it's probably truthful to my feelings about Tillie, whom I've known more than three decades, ever since we were classmates together in Malcolm Cowley's creative writing workshop at Stanford University. My calling us "classmates" is misleading, as Tillie was already an accomplished fictionist and a subsidized Stanford Writing Fellow, I a callow tuition-paying refugee from the East Coast, *just out of* college. As an artist I was still in diapers, considerably less mature than I should have been, and Tillie, a wife, a mother, a grownup woman. Mr. Cowley was also a little less than mildly encouraging about my manuscript submissions. He was truly knocked off his shoes by Tillie's stories, "I Stand Here Ironing," and "Hey Sailor What Ship?" which she read to our astonished class, as were most of that same class, and, later, most literary critics and readers, when the stories were finally printed in magazines and books a few years afterward.

As good as I thought Tillie's writings were, I was a little annoyed that I had found, as we used to say on the basketball courts of Brooklyn, a "ringer" in the class where I had gone for help with my writing. (This was, as I now know, a very commonplace delusion of novices; such "unfair competition" is, of course, stimulating to the novice, the true outcome of talent and effort, which I was only just beginning to perceive.) I thought Tillie's appearance in the class made it next to impossible for me to get Cowley's attention because he was so preoccupied with helping her. Cowley was arranging for Viking to look at one of her manuscripts and recommending her to the Ford, Rockefeller, and Guggenheim foundations for grants. In view of the hard labor Tillie had done for twenty years as a bookkeeper and a secretary and the wife of a leftwing trade unionist with employment problems, this all seemed like long overdue reparations and justice for one whose performances as a reader and achievements as an innovative writer of stories were stunning. But—what about charity for me? I crankily observed back then.

I can remember complaining to another classmate that Cowley kept his hearing aid turned off for everybody except Tillie. "I don't blame him," the fellow said.

One day I read the class my story about a college love affair between two middle-class Jewish kids in a rundown flat in upper New York State during a cold winter. It was called "Isaac and Sonia," and it was as funky and sensate as I was capable of making it. Cowley and most of my classmates were not very happy with the self-conscious ethnicity of the story, but Tillie had some praise for me and afterward invited me to a campus hangout for a cup of coffee.

I blush now to say that I was naive enough in those days to believe I was having a rendezvous with a beautiful woman, for Tillie was extremely handsome to gawk at, with her strong, dark, chiseled features, olive skin, and her heavy black helmet of hair.

Seated across the table from me in a wooden booth scarred with hearts enclosing initials and Greek fraternity logos, Tillie talked to me with great care, and concern, an almost maternal solicitude.

She once again praised my story for being raw and truthful up to a point, and then she criticized it, quite gently, because it lacked a social perspective, was entirely private and spoiled-brattish, and just a little hard on young women.

She gave me a list of books to read. Zola and Tolstoy and Edith Wharton's *Age of Innocence*, Jack London's *Martin Eden*, and *Sister Carrie* are the works I remember now.

Then we talked about our very different lives.

Tillie told me over coffee that first time that Jews were not the only oppressed and that she herself was part Jewish and part native American. She'd never gone to college because she'd been involved in the "radical movement" and educated in the "school of life," as I think she called it; she'd been writing on her own many years while holding down ill-paying jobs and raising a family. She told me her family name was Lerner and that she'd once published some things under that name as a young woman and had even won a prize. But she now felt the necessity to work full time, and Cowley's interest in her work and the Stanford fellowship had given her some hope that she would never have to go back to the same drudging existence again.

Tillie's career—a word she would probably never use—seemed difficult. I was nevertheless envious of her close, warm family life as she depicted it for me, the realities of a struggle for more than mere economic gain. My story was certainly skimpy by comparison: I was the unloved child of a successful New York real estate attorney and his unhappy wife. I'd been briefly involved with leftwing intramural politics in high school, having been recruited for my alienated stance by the YCL, briefly, and once the leftist Hashomer Hatzair Zionists.

It was midway through Eisenhower's presidency, the Khrushchev era, and my next door neighbor in my Stanford rooming house was Alexander Kerensky. Old men ran the world and discouraged the young from stepping out of line. I was just very cynical about almost everything, like most college students, especially about the prospects for political action and social justice.

Tillie advised me, if I could possibly bring myself to do so, not to be so cynical. It was harmful to my writing and to me as a person, she said.

"I can tell you have a good heart and are afraid of your feelings," she said. "Well, you needn't be. You won't come to harm. But don't hurt other people with your words, Richard. You needn't. You probably have a lot more to give than that."

When we parted I felt embarrassed for my involuntary blush and my stammer, leftovers from my pose as her would-be seducer, but also reassured by Tillie's kind words.

We met a few more times like that during the semester, and she was always caring and affectionate toward me, with just a touch of chastisement added on, so knowing her as I did became important to me.

When I left Stanford for New York and later was required to train as a soldier, I continued to write to Tillie, and she always wrote back, suggesting books I should read, such as Paul Nizan's powerful novel *Antoine Bloye*, which I later got Monthly Review Press to publish in English from a xerox of a Soviet edition Tillie had passed on to me. She would send me words of encouragement when I sent her poems, or she would send me quotes from Whitman's *Crossing Brooklyn Ferry* poem and from some of the other great writers, and even their pictures she sent to fix to the wall above my eyes when I wrote, as she always did, I later learned, carrying about with her a small trove of such pictures and quotes to make a kind of altar piece wherever she would sit down to compose. Tillie also was consoling about my difficult and unhappy first marriage, and, though critical of my wife, sympathetic with the plight of a talented woman who had chosen the wrong mate and was surely suffering, too. And once or twice when her fame was increasing she flew to New York to see Cowley, and she looked me up, and we took long gabby walks through the city together, across the Brooklyn Bridge and through Central Park.

When Tillie's collection *Tell Me a Riddle* was first published in a small edition by Lippincott, I think I was for a brief while its first and only reviewer, for I convinced the *Commonweal* to allow me to write a *small* enthusiastic notice, which was not awfully well written, as I was new to literary journalism. Tillie was grateful for the publicity but critical of some of my assertions.

It was through Tillie also that I reencountered my old Stanford acquaintance, the writer Hannah Green. One day as we stood admiring the arcing bow suspension of the Brooklyn Bridge from the ground level near the ferry station on the Brooklyn side, and I was feeling a little down, Tillie suggested I "look up Hannah," who, she said, was in the city and "in need of a good friend." I took her advice, and some days later Hannah and I took coffee together. Hannah and her husband, Jack Wesley, the painter, have always remained dear to me from then on.

Once when Tillie was a visiting professor at Amherst she sent a "brilliant young" (her words) Amherst student to visit me and interview me about writing as a career. As I recall, I recommended that he go on to law school and continue to write, in his free time, for I was having a hard time keeping my life together without a decent-paying job. That was just after I had published *An Education in Blood*, an ambitious novel I still think well of, which went nowhere.

The young man Tillie sent me was cool, smart, very polite, and very attentive, and he said he wanted to be a lawyer and went on to practice law and write quality best sellers. His name was Scott Turow.

Tillie made me reread Whitman and read Thomas Hardy. She showed me passages of Henry James I would not have noticed on my own, and she gave me a long list of books on war and peace and social conditions—Russian, American, German, Philippino—to which I still refer. She was an excellent teacher and a fine critic, and occasionally she had kind things to say about my own work. Her copy of my novel *The Twenty-eighth Day of Elul* was crammed with so many little blue slips of paper containing notes to herself and to me, when I once had a chance to look at it, that I was impressed that she would take anything I had written so seriously.

Tillie's growing fame and increasing involvement with the burgeoning women's movement made it harder to sustain our little intimacy. I heard her read the entire novel *Tell Me a Riddle*, which took a couple of hours, to public audiences more than once, and sometimes I found the adulation she received from her increasingly female fans a little trying. She seemed to believe that she could command an audience to remain attentive to her works and her ruminations for as long as she chose.

One of the covert assumptions of Tillie's book on why writers become silent is that such a courageous enterprise, particularly for women, requires the same support system other people in less demanding callings are apt to have, but in fact they have very often endured with much less. Tillie had experienced certain deprivations far too long, and now she was enjoying having fans, a public, and a real measure of support.

I kept asking how she found the time to write new work if she was so politically involved and so much in demand for public appearances. She seemed to find it hard to keep away from the rostrum and the microphone, and she was commanding large (and much needed) fees for her appearances. But she'd just published *Silences*, which was a sort of album of how writers lose the *will* to write, and I wondered if she was being similarly affected. Would she ever finish a long-talked-about novel?

In one of the little magazines I read a powerful novella about two men traveling through the northwest woods by car. She called it *Recqua*, but when I asked her about it and other new work, she changed the subject.

The second time I heard Tillie read through all of *TMAR* was a hot night in the city, and the audience was uncomfortable and restless. I suggested she should have chosen shorter works. I quoted back *Brooklyn Ferry* to her: "It is not upon you alone the dark patches fall. The dark threw its patches down on me also." Once Tillie and I found ourselves together for a while at the MacDowell Colony, but Tillie kept pretty much to herself, and so did I. We exchanged notes but were otherwise occupied. I can remember scribbling to her: "I too knitted the old knot of contrariety: Blabbed, blushed, resented."

Another visit took place when I was on assignment in San Francisco and Tillie had me up to her flat on Laguna Street in a well kept up working-class project building in a neighborhood that nowadays would be called multicultural. She served me green tea and told me many of the people she lived among were longstanding friends and allies. Afterward we walked through the neighborhood, which, as I recall, abutted the Filmore District.

When I heard that her husband, Jack, had finally found employment as a professor of labor history at a college in the San Francisco area and was a much-loved teacher, I wrote Tillie to send Jack, whom I'd only met once but liked, congratulations. When Jack died, I wrote to her again. I wrote that poem for her seventy-fifth birthday album at the invitation of her daughter.

She was then living part of the year near Santa Cruz and was very close to the poet Adrienne Rich, whose writings had always seemed to me manufactured. I had not liked her exquisitely shaped early poems when they'd appeared with mine in the early *Paris Review*, and I was no great fan of her powerful hectoring poems of political engagement. Whenever certain poems on adult love and childbearing reminded me of my mother's depressing vision of human relations, I used to shut the book and take the dog for a walk.

I've never felt that way after reading Tillie's works. She has powers of evocation that are always generous. The opening chapter of *Yonandio* evokes childhood (and motherhood), even as I recall again, reading this, that the mothering I received wasn't always enhancing to my young life. Tillie writes beautifully about men as well as women. She never settles for polemics. But she can be harsh toward those she regards as backsliders. My experiences in Central America convinced me that revolutions needed critics or they would reward their errors and abuses by consolidating their hold on the lives of those who helped them seize power.

Could Tillie agree to that? Frankly I don't know, but I suspect she would call me cynical. In her tiny elegant handwriting and in her letters, sometimes addressing me as "Dick," a nickname I have never favored, she might press her strongest political criticisms obliquely. "Don't confound these efforts to change the lives of working people by recalling the disappointments visited on you in childhood."

I can often hear her voice as I write my poems and stories, and I imagine it is usually in minor disagreement with my efforts to invent love and provoke laughter, so that I have to turn away from the sound with a squint and a frown and shut it off from my hearing. Nowadays Tillie Olsen is a major cultural presence; her works are taught in schools, and her importance to other women writers is undiminished. I still have great anticipation to read any new work she will ever produce, and even if that never happens again in her lifetime, I can never forget her great kindness toward me and generosity when I was just starting out, and the fact that she helped educate me, and at times sustained me with encouraging words and gentle criticisms and thereby enabled me to survive.

DAN JACOBSON

I got to know Dan Jacobson my second year at Stanford when he was a writing fellow and I was on scholarship. Like Tillie, Dan was one of the class "ringers," banned in South Africa, well-published in England, and even, I think, in Israel, but still hardly known here, as he wrote short novels of seriousness with thus far little commercial promise. I was very impressed with his gentleness, his broad, flat South African accent, and his powerful stories about race, such as *A Dance in the Sun*, on which he was then working.

One day as we were walking out of Wallace Stegner's class I fainted; it may have been the heat or forgetting to eat. Dan looked after me until I was able to drive myself home again.

He'd brought his wife and two stepchildren with him, and we sometimes socialized. They were short on funds, and he was writing a lot for very little money for English weeklies and very occupied with his own affairs, but he once agreed to read and annotate one of my manuscripts, and I learned a lot from him about being precise and lucid.

"It's important to be clear," he told me. "It's one of the things I'm trying for all the time as much as anything else. You can't expect the reader to guess. You need to try and be more lucid." He was right, of course; in those days my prose was rich in intentions and gruesomely sloppy in performance.

Dan wrote a nonfiction book about his California experiences, *No Further West*, which was a very engaging celebration of the new societies of the West Coast of malls and freeways and tract houses. It went against the prevailing anti-American stance of the British Left and was not popular. He seemed to regard California as having the weather and topography and affluence of South Africa, but, being a more innovative society in constant evolution, there was not quite such virulent institutionalized racism. (He, of course, had not bothered during his stay in California to visit Watts or Pacoima or some of the ghettos of Oakland and San Francisco.)

He had studied with F. R. Leavis and was, consequently, very intrigued by Leavis's dour contemporary at Stanford, Yvor Winters, with whom I was studying. Dan admired Winters' quest for rational content in literature. So did I, I thought, but Dan saw Winters' limitations more quickly than I. A man who found fault with Yeats? Imagine . . .

Dan was also then a person of great intellectual curiosity, sufficiently intrigued by vernacular writers such as Twain and Henry Miller to write fine essays about them.

I was very admiring of Dan as a craftsman, and when I left California we kept in touch. My first wife, Emily, and his wife, Margaret, collaborated on a couple of children's books about bears and spiders which were published and sold decently enough. I was even able to help Dan arrange a second year in the States, teaching at Syracuse University, through my old professor, Donald Dike, who was always a good friend to new writers. By now the Jacobsons had a third child, and they were somewhat more prosperous. One of Dan's stories, "The Zulu and the Zeide," was made into a Broadway play, and he was beginning to write for better-paying publications. We named our daughter "Margaret," in part, after Margaret Jacobson, who was also very earnest, and gentle, and sweet to my wife.

Dan in those days was small and slim and sweetfaced, with thin hair and a nasal, flat intonation. If angered or excited his voice could grow thick and distinctively South African–Jewish; he also spoke a little Afrikaans and had once learned some Hebrew from *cheder* and a later period spent trying out an *aliyah* to Israel. As with most South African Jews of his day, the family was originally Lithuanian, and, in truth, if Dan had worn a *streimel* and sidecurls, he could have easily passed for a highly intelligent student of the Gaon of Wilna.

Though I gather he has lately become very British, after living for so many years in London, he seemed to wish to uphold in those days a distinctively South African nationality. Although he was angry that some of his books were not permitted to be published or distributed in his motherland, he was not always at the barricades calling for revolution. He seemed to despise the xenophobic Boers and their closed-mindedness and could no longer abide living in South Africa, but he also believed the Boers' sense of grievance—though misguided and cruel—sprang from a genuine history of oppression and the poverty of their experience. On the wall above his writing desk was a photo of his father riding to war in a Boer hat in the Karoo.

The last time we were together, he asked me to invite his old friends from Cambridge, the Podhoretzes, to dinner. I really took a dislike to Midge and Norman for dominating the conversation. They were full of backbite and gossip, and Dan's closeness to this couple made for a strain in my relations with him. His editor at MacMillan had us to his house during another Jacobson visit, and this man's wife, an English woman, as I recall, spent most of the evening imitating Zulu throat clickings and flirting outrageously with the other women. A few months later that same editor committed suicide.

I introduced Dan, along with Harvey Swados, when they read together at the Ninety-second Street Y. His story "Beggar My Neighbor" was very moving to me. With compassion and intelligence, it seemed to be suggesting some of the fearfulness Podhoretz wrote about in his race-baiting essay, "My Negro Problem and Yours." Dan's story was not at all racist. He was trying to depict the hungry poignancy experienced in South African childhoods lived on either side of the divide of race. Nevertheless, whenever he came to the States, Dan wanted to socialize with this odious pair of sharptongued arrivistes, and, if I wanted to see him, it would almost have to be in their company. I tried to keep my distance.

We continued to write letters to each other for a while, but then my first marriage ended and the friendship evaporated. In one of his ultimate letters to me Dan said he understood my need to have a life separate from my wife, but he hoped I would not be cruel and hurtful to Emily, which was good advice, though not so easy to accomplish.

Recently Dan communicated with me again after I sent him a copy of a book of poems I wrote about, in part, California in the fifties. Dan sent thanks along with a copy of his novel *The God Lover* and remembrances and regards.

He's still a very serious, earnest, and fine writer of tales which are increasingly like those in the Old Testament. Everything is set down in simple, lucid language through a concatenation of catastrophes and resolved like the word of God. I miss the humor of the early novels about Jewish diamond smugglers (the *Price of Diamonds)* and down at the heels British Bloomsbury types, which sometimes I too would encounter when we were together. Whenever I read something new of Dan's nowadays I know this is going to be an unrelenting representation of the hazards of moral human beings, a matter of conscience and the free will, and sometimes all this seriousness seems overbearing. As writing, it seems only half the story of human lives— joyless, like a man making his quietus—so entirely remote from Golders Green and Hampstead Heath, where he's ensconced himself all these years, that I wonder if my old friend ever permits himself to express a happy moment unmediated by conscience.

DAVID LAMSON

David Lamson was not the usual sort of resident of San Quentin Prison's death row; he was college educated, and from a middle-class family. His sister was a prominent physician in Palo Alto, California. He lived on the Stanford University campus, played regular bridge with members of the Hoover family, and was employed as sales manager for the Stanford University Press. When he discovered the gory body of his wife, Allene, with the back of her head smashed, in the bathroom of their small house on Salvaterra Street on Memorial Day, 1933, after coming in from a spell of yard work, Lamson became the only suspect of the Santa Clara County Police. He was tried and convicted of first degree murder and sentenced to death by hanging at San Quentin.

When the verdict on Lamson was overturned by the California Supreme Court some thirteen months later, he was released and never retried for his wife's wrongful death, which Lamson maintained all along had been accidental, caused by a fall in the tub, or else was the work of a prowler. Free of his confinement in prison, Lamson was unemployed and the father of a two-year-old daughter. During the next couple of years he wrote and published *We Who Are about to Die*, a memoir of simplicity and originality about his time on death row which remains one of the strongest first-person prison books I have ever read.

Published in 1935 by Max Perkins of Scribners, despite the objections of others on the Scribners editorial board, after a lengthy correspondence with Lamson and with his major supporter in the Stanford community, the poet and critic Ivor Winters, *We Who Are about to Die* is, like much of the most convincing nonfiction, the performance of an amateur, a man compelled to write by the freakishness of his experience. Appalled by the concatenation of events which led to his arrest and condemnation, Lamson survived his confinement by making notes to himself for a book.

When it was first published, *We Who Are about to Die* received considerable attention. The book was sold to a motion picture company and bowdlerized beyond recognition. Sales were boosted by a nationwide broadcast of Alexander Woolcott, praising Lamson's humanity. Though his *temoignage* did not remain in print for very long and was, to my knowledge, never reprinted, it established Lamson as a professional writer. For a decade or more he became a very successful writer of Western pulp short stories for magazines such as the *Saturday Evening Post* and *Colliers*, most set in and around his birthplace in Wyoming or California's Antelope Valley where he had moved and eventually remarried. After many years in this remote part of California he moved back to Santa Clara County and went into the air taxi business, and died in Los Altos more than a decade ago.

What is most striking in this memoir of a man condemned to die for a crime of which he claimed to be innocent is how little attention Lamson gave to the circumstances of his own conviction, not arguing his case but summarizing it briefly, and how much space he devoted to the cases of others, and to prison life among the condemned. Lamson is almost as compassionate toward others in his situation as Chekhov was among the prisoners of Sakhalin Island, as though the fates of these others had never for one moment been what he could expect for himself. He was convinced that though some of his mates on death row or elsewhere in prison were unpleasant, evil, or guiltier than he, many were not, and most were "people" like himself, fearful and desperate.

He arrived on death row with all the standard prejudices of the Wasp establishment of his time against Orientals and blacks, and other ethnics, and left befriended and befriending and angered by a system of punishment without the resources to truly educate or rehabilitate its inmates. The postscript to Lamson's memoir contains a lengthy sociological analysis of the inmate population and costs at San Quentin for the year 1934 and a plea for genuine education and rehabilitation.

From my vantage point Lamson's polemics on prison reform seem less impressive than his personal witnessing of his life on death row, and his accounts of his neighbors, many of whom were hanged during the time he was an inmate, or in the time thereafter. Of three young black men he encountered toward the end of his stay, he writes, "There was about them, that first day in the yard, an air of bravado, of hardness, of swagger that seemed to mask a sick grey fear."

In a similar vein he writes of his own first encounter with San Quentin:

> In some ways it is like a city, or like a large university, or like an armed camp; and sometimes it will seem altogether like some

one of these things. But most of all it is like a prison, and that consciousness is never far from you; if it rises from you a little as fog rises, something is sure to happen to bring it swooping down again, to make your eyes wary, your ears alert, your nerves tense, your manner casual with caution that conceals caution. Convicts and guards alike carry this mark of prison upon them: an alertness that veils itself, a fear that is more terrible than the alert fear of wild animals, for it is a fear of fear.

San Quentin has no doubt changed a great deal physically and administratively since David Lamson's stay there more than sixty years ago, and many of the routines may have also changed, though probably not the deadening sense of wasted time, nor the strange cordialities of guards and guarded which Lamson so accurately depicts as ways to circumvent the brutal force always available in such places. During Lamson's stay there were prison breaks and regular cautionary firing of machine guns from the towers surrounding the main enclosures. Prisoners who strayed from where they were supposed to be were warned back with whistles first and then rifle shots. Recounting these incidents Lamson is stoically understated. A freakish hunting accident with his own rifle in Wyoming during his adolescence had resulted in the death of one of Lamson's friends, but his prison memoir makes no reference to that event. It became the circumstance of a second published, though unsuccessful, novel, *Whirlpool*.

As in many prisons today, San Quentin prisoners in Lamson's time were expert at forging and concealing knives and homemade guns from various implements on hand, and there was a considerable traffic in contraband of all sorts. All this Lamson records, in his accurate, civilized, and somewhat off-handed manner. He tries to show respect for all the inmates, who could manage to remain human-seeming in a hostile and inhuman place. It's his conviction that inmates had to rebel against their confinements which were often unjust, because they were innocent as charged, or else too harshly sentenced, and that the guards had no other recourse but the use of force when confronted by such rebellions. He writes: "Guards are people. Convicts are people. When guards and cons are put together under certain conditions a certain situation will inevitably follow . . . it is forced on them by those who are responsible for the conditions.

"Hence I say that the responsibility for every instance of prison brutality, of riot, insurrection, escape and bloodshed, rests squarely with the people of the State—with society."

Yvor Winters had tried to convince Max Perkins that he should be allowed to write a book about the "injustice" and flagrant disregard for the truth in police work on the Lamson case. There's an extant manuscript of some thirty pages in the Scribners files at Princeton and lots of correspondence. Perkins believed Winters lacked the authority to write such a book. When Lamson's book was published, Winters compared *We Who Are about to Die* to Richard Dana's account of conditions in the U.S. Merchant Navy in *Two Years Before the Mast*. This was apt indeed, as both these men of solid middle-class backgrounds achieved a measure of human solidarity with hard-pressed men of far different social classes through their ordeals, and both—once released from such captivities—produced only such accounts as were true to their experiences before going on to lead other lives.

Lamson's subsequent short story writing was tailored to the market of his day, and as that market declined, or he perceived that it did, he went into other work and wrote little, if at all. He had been a writer of humorous light verse in college, and an amateur actor, very much a man of his time and class, who had married a pretty girl of similar background at Stanford, the executive secretary of the Stanford YWCA. Nothing in Lamson's background prepared him for his prison experience, its starkness, and the fearful verdict that awaited him there eventually. He'd had vague literary ambitions and a callow air of cultivation. Abandoned by most of his respectable Stanford social set, but convinced of his own innocence and supported by able appeals lawyers and a few staunch supporters such as Winters, Lamson's sister Margaret, and the popular novelist Kathleen Norris, a Palo Alto resident, he remained calm and observant and rarely seemed to lapse into self-pity. His strongest emotions were held back as he observed himself becoming a part of the routinized life of the "joint," but he occasionally allowed himself to experience small moments of intense painful recognition as when, after wake-up, he found himself staring out at the landscape of the prison farm from the window of his "stone cave" of a cell:

And that is a strange sight to see from a prison cell, I think—the green hills, and black and white cattle grazing beneath the great live-oaks. There is something strange and a little bitter in all sweet pastoral things seen from a prison cell, whether the pleasant pastures beyond the wall, or the garden with many colors, or the seagulls drifting and crying overhead, or even the little sparrows and wrens that flutter and chirp in the prison yard, and build their nests in the crevices of the wall. For all of these things fit oddly with prison, and with you being in prison. In that word—prison—there is only stone and steel and wall and pavement, not the earth and the free things of earth and sea.

Sometimes a man's addiction to the ordinary, to his own ordinariness, is his best defense against willy-nilly impulse when confronted by police lunacies or the harsh and punitive irrationalities of the state. Why are we fascinated by tales of such confinements? By accounts of Robinson Caruso, or the French prison memoirs of Devil's Island such as *Dry Tortuga*? They tell us about our own capacities to remain human and enterprising under the most adverse conditions. They remind us of our most fundamental human resources—intelligence, imagination, the ability to experience ourselves and others in solitude and time without falling into madness. It's a fate we all dread and somehow relish and anticipate at times, like being on the dole or fighting in a war. A way of testing ourselves apart from the sometimes invidious views of others and our more social selves.

In prison David Lamson remained ordinary and heeded the advice of other inmates and his keepers to "take it easy." As soon as he could after being released from prison he left Santa Clara County and the life he had once led and found a life for himself in nature, on a ranch, in the Antelope Valley. But in the minds of some he was never exonerated. He maintained that a freak accident had occurred, whereas some, guided by stupidity or malice, believed differently. That's why I was astonished when I found out through Lamson's former literary agent, Leah Salisbury, that he'd moved back to Santa Clara County.

I was then doing preliminary research on a book about the Lamson murder trials which I regarded as a prime example of American vigilante justice in the thirties. Lamson was perceived by his jurors as a Stanford swell, a cut apart from the mob who'd been inflamed by publicity to judge him. He was convicted on salacious rumors of adultery and entirely circumstantial evidence during economic hard times, a time of violent agricultural strikes throughout the Santa Clara Valley. A little while after Lamson was removed from the local jail, vigilantes broke in and removed three union organizers and lynched them. I thought if any wrongful act had occurred it was clearly unpremeditated, that Lamson had, in turn, been wronged by ignorant and overly zealous policemen, a ruthless and demagogic prosecutor, a jury infuriated with envy on the cusp of that economic downturn and bitter failed hopes.

A little while after I heard from Leah Salisbury, David Lamson himself broke a long silence and wrote me a short, careful letter to ask that I not write such a book about his trial. He was making a request. He clearly knew he had no legal right to demand such of me. Lamson said the death of his wife had happened more than three decades before. He had a new wife and grandchildren in and around Palo Alto and simply did not wish to relive such an unhappy event with them and saw no need for it personally. He simply asked me to be compassionate and desist.

I have never been sorry that I agreed to do what Lamson asked of me. When, much later, I published my novel, *An Education in Blood*, it was clearly a work of fiction, set in a different part of the state, and inhabited by characters who had no real resemblance to David Lamson.

In a sense, David Lamson forced me to invent my most ambitious fiction, and I allowed him to keep his privacy that was so awfully and flagrantly disturbed by the police investigations and publicity surrounding his first wife's death.

I have no personal knowledge that Lamson was anything but an innocent man, cruelly deprived of his liberty by hasty official judgements, but I have often wondered, if he had been guilty, could he have written so carefully and well about prison in *We Who Are about to Die*?

The allegations against Lamson were that in a moment of rage he had struck out against his wife who was in the tub and brought about her fatal injuries. Such moments of rage have occurred all too often with husbands and wives. We're probably all capable of such rages, and afterwards there is remorse, which often takes the form of a heightened awareness of the ordeals of others.

"The stare of a crowd at an accused man, or a convicted man," wrote Lamson of some mates who were being escorted past his cell in manacles, "is terrible, because it has in back of it no intelligence. It is stupid, bestial, inhuman, eyes glassy in white pulpy faces and below the eyes mouths a little open. The eyes never flicker, never waver, never move. There is no light in them. . . . The faces are masks more horrible than devil masks, whose terror lies in the total lack of any expression save the expression of dumb staring."

Forced to recall his own moment of public scrutiny at the time of his arrest and arraignment, Lamson writes that the mob's bestial staring "shakes your faith in humanity, in the excellence of the human race."

It's my hope that in the years he had after prison with his new family some of that essential faith in others was restored to David Lamson, and one indication that it was may be his writing and publishing *We Who Are about to Die*, which tries in serious and intelligent ways to humanize the experience of those who have been condemned by society. It was because I was so moved by the sobriety and decorum of Lamson's book and the trust he was bestowing on me through his letter that I willingly acceded to his request for privacy which was truly a fictional request because memories in Palo Alto endured and he had deliberately returned to the scene of his most awful humiliations to plead with me and others to be forgotten once again.

There possibly may have been brief explosive moments in Lawson's life, but these were not his total life experience, and, after so many years, he seemed to know that certain harmful personal injustices could no longer be rectified through publicizing them, as I had intended. From all accounts, Lamson remained a careful man, a gentle self-effacing person. His own account of his worst ordeal, though, should be back in print, as a memorial to his solidarity with others, even less fortunate than he was, who were condemned to be executed.

BASHEVIS

Isaac Singer used to call my old high school friend, who sometimes visited his flat with me, the "Professor." This self-taught scholar of Jewish history and Yiddish was a gentile, a bit formal in his manner, and a literary conservative, preferring the writings of Peretz and Singer's older brother, Israel Joshua, to Bashevis's "modernist" evocations of the demonic.

In conversations with Bashevis, Singer's nickname for my friend sometimes made him blush and stammer, and seemed aimed to do precisely that, as Ronny was a little pompous as well as unsure of himself, and also unemployed at the time, living on hope and fear. Bashevis was criticizing my friend's booklearning, his seeming naivete. With a certain formality, however, Bashevis always called me, who had far less booklearning, "Mr. Elman," even after I had written reviews of his books for *The Nation*, *Commonweal*, and the *New York Times*, had interviewed him in *Commentary* and for the United States Information Agency, and wrote a profile of him for *Holiday Magazine*. In those days I was young enough to glance over my shoulder metaphorically whenever he called me "Mr. Elman" to see if my father had just entered the room.

When I first got to know him well in the early sixties, Bashevis was living next door to the Walter B. Cooke funeral parlor on West Seventy-second Street off Columbus Avenue and sometimes pretending to be as shy as the wolf in *Goldilocks*. He was still hardly known beyond Yiddish literary circles but seemed, in retrospect, to be anticipating larger renown, a profound change in his circumstances through the adulation of certain young American visitors like me. Every word he spoke that first day was poised and apt, a parable for literary treasure hunters. "Whenever I see a hearse parked outside," he said as we entered the flat, "I think the angel of death has been patient long enough. But in a city like New York this angel is truly overworked. He has such a busy schedule. There's a death everyday around here, and sometimes I think they're all my Yiddish readers."

Without seeming ancient, he sustained an illusion of frailty, this acute but diffident man in his fifties standing in the sunny front foyer of that spacious flat while proposing so many ironies about his literary situation that I was enlisted almost instantly to his cause solely on the basis of ignorance and ambition. It would be Singer and myself against the *goyim*, I thought—the likes of T. S. Eliot, for whom anti-Semitism was a matter of literary aesthetics. Why couldn't a Jewish writer be a great artist? Singer was. But Singer soon disabused me of believing we could ever be allies for the same causes. My choosing him to emulate didn't necessarily reveal great discrimination on my part. "Do you believe in ghosts, Mr. Elman? I don't necessarily believe in the otherworldly," he pointed out, "but I don't disbelieve. That's another matter entirely. Some people are just very gullible, and you remind me of one, a person I knew in Warsaw. A certain friend was maybe just a little like you. A certain Tronk. You could be him, or then again like somebody else entirely . . . a free thinker, like you . . ."

I protested that I hardly knew who I was at all, but I was trying very hard to learn by writing a lot.

"You shouldn't try so hard," Singer said. "Young people don't know how to be happy. It so happens the torments of this world are as nothing compared to the next."

I was tempting him to see me as the fool, and it couldn't be helped, since I persisted in admiring him so much.

"Maybe you should go back to school," he once observed, "and study for a profession. It's hard to be a writer without gifts."

Here he was, the great Yiddish master in a city where Yiddish was dying day by day, and he still wrote a column for the *Forward* in which he confessed he sometimes had to invent from the whole cloth recollections called even then his "Memories of Warsaw," but when he looked at me it was through the murky prism of my own shoddy faults. "I only want to be of help to you," I told him, which was a lie, as we both knew. If his works were suddenly finding him a new audience in English through the translations of "Americans" such as Isaac Rosenfeld and Saul Bellow, Bashevis claimed he was still pretty much in the dark about who was who in this America where he'd been living since the 1930s. I could maybe be his guide. For example, was this Mr. Saul Bellow, he asked, so important?

Behind Singer's back his writing space was closed off by uncurtained glass doors. He wore the same severe costume every time I visited: a pair of dark suit trousers, a stark white cotton dress shirt, and plain black shoes, but there was nothing ordinary about his pale face or deportment. Often his pet parakeet would be perched on the dome of his quite bald head when he came to the door, and his smile was always winning and friendly. He took you in with it and got your measure, and offered you a seat, and was easy in his discourse. His English was fluent but heavily accented, he had a white fringe of hair about his ears, the blue eyes were clear and quick with scrutiny, and the smile ironic.

"I used to have two such little birds," he announced. "It was also an arranged marriage, and it worked for quite a while. They would fly around the flat together like lovers. But my wife one day left the window open, and in a city like New York such opportunities can be devastating to even the best arranged marriages."

Almost from the first Singer loved to talk about women and sex, "though not like certain Polish officers," he would protest, and especially out of hearing of his wife, Alma, who worked days in the Better Dress Department at Lord and Taylor. Bashevis also loved flirting with the young women I brought along to visit with him and asking them impertinent questions such as, "Do you sleep with men? Are you a virgin? Do you have any women friends who still are?" He was coming on to these vivacious literary admirers, but he was also gathering information for his fiction about an America he kept from himself at some remove.

Whenever I interviewed Singer, he always, in turn, interviewed me. I asked about his reading of Flaubert and Dostoevsky. He wanted to know why, in an America of boundless economic opportunities and comforts, the son of a successful Jewish real estate lawyer would want to be an impoverished writer. He always made sure I understood that he believed in *good* and evil. From a very poor Jewish family, a religious background, he was nevertheless not the usual sort of self-denying Puritan but very interested in erotic experiences and temptation. Singer said he truly believed in the temptations of the Evil One. They were real and vivid to any sensate being. When we met he was still barely managing to get by in New York, in part because of the lingering effects of his departure from Poland, all those griefs and dislocations, and also because of his threadbare Bohemian manhood in Warsaw and New York as a literary journalist. America was so strange, for that matter, the Evil One always so present here too. Was that why Singer always looked like an atoning sybarite? He always dressed in those stark blacks and whites, with maybe a navy blue tie, even during the heat of summer.

Once we met for lunch at Steinberg's Dairy Restaurant on Broadway, on a sweltering afternoon, and, when Bashevis arrived like a professional mourner in his dark suit and tie, I wondered how he would respond if I were to give him a gift, a T-shirt with his customized logo, or a gaudy Hawaiian cabana shirt. The interior of the restaurant had stainless steel portholes sunk into the walls, resembling the second-class salon on a prewar ocean liner crammed with immigrants. Conversations were hushed, only the waiters animated. That day Singer made it clear that he was not so standoffish as he appeared. He talked with an extravagant intimacy bordering on indiscretion about the estranged wife of a famous poet who was assisting him in translating some stories. "It so happens she is very wholesome and good looking," he exclaimed, "like certain first ladies of the Warsaw theater. So fair and still pleasingly voluptuous."

Then he told me about all the affairs inside the restaurant that were being carried on over lunches of *tschav* and mushroom barley soup by various middle-aged ladies and their escorts, though Bashevis ate very sparingly in my presence that day, as he almost always did. "Like a bird is one way of putting it," he suggested. "Maybe you thought they come here for a glass of tea with a handle," he added, suddenly.

I'd come to see him that first time with my friend, the journalist Joel Blocker, after reading his brilliant collection of stories *Gimpel the Fool*, to declare myself his devoted protégé, but he was not quite interested in me as that, and my Yiddish was much too rudimentary; it would be of little utility in translating his stories. I came looking for a master, and what I got was his imitation of the *Evil One*.

"It's very good of you to praise my work," Bashevis said, and shrugged and handed me a copy of *Partisan Review* with a new translation of one of his Market Street stories. I've since learned that Singer's Gimpel was not to be interpreted as a fool at heart, but was wise to remain gullible if he was also to remain truly loving to his unfaithful wife, but in those days I felt pretty much like a fool every time I opened my mouth in Singer's presence.

I also probably needed help with my writing, if I had any talent at all, he seemed to be inferring, and I certainly needed a different father, but Singer never for one instant permitted himself to act in *loco parentis* with me except to reproach me when I later left my first wife. If I ever had a literary career it would surely have to be without his help. Singer was simply hopeful that I could be helpful to him as an enthusiast. I reviewed books once in a while. Perhaps I might review one of his, if I liked.

He really wasn't a celebrity yet. When I later circulated stories I'd helped to translate among magazine editors, most had never heard of him. When Joel Blocker and I conducted an interview with Bashevis that was eventually published in *Commentary*, we did so only after we had considerable difficulty convincing George Plimpton of the *Paris Review* that he should consider the piece for that quarterly's famous series of interviews with writers. After holding onto the piece a couple of years, it was Plimpton's considered opinion that Singer, who was now beginning to publish widely to astonishing notices, was still not worth the same attention he was lavishing on James Gould Cozzens and Isaac Dineson.

At the time I was working as an interviewer and producer at WBAI, a noncommercial radio station, and, when I asked Singer to read from one of his stories on the radio, he did so graciously, but he did not wish to be interviewed by me on what he'd heard was "a Communist radio station."

Fairly early Singer asked me if I was a believer. When I replied that such questions didn't really interest me, Bashevis responded, "Nevertheless, such questions are important. One chooses to believe or disbelieve. Are you a Socialist?"

I said I thought I probably was something like that.

"It's a sin," he replied, "choosing to disbelieve." But he added, flatly: "It's not surprising they call the Jews a stiff necked race." One of the first people Bashevis introduced me to was his editor, Cecil Hemley, of Noonday Press. Cecil was a stocky man with a high color who smoked too much, had a little trouble breathing, and always seemed to be in a rush.

He wore baggy old gray suits and sweated a lot, and when he died of a heart attack Singer seemed bereft. A gifted novelist and poet, Cecil was devoted to Singer. He seemed to drop by every day on the way home from work, and he was very pleased to meet me with Blocker. He seemed to have high hopes that our enterprise on behalf of Singer's reputation would justify his efforts for the writer at Noonday. When I finally reviewed *The Magician of Lublin* favorably in *The Nation*, Singer didn't comment on my notice of his work, but Hemley sent me a generous personal note.

Singer, who foreswore meat and strong drink, sometimes served us tea and dried fruits in his flat, or cold cherry pop, and once in a while his wife would bring home pastry and other sweets for the guests. She was a handsome blonde who spoke no Yiddish. Legend had it they'd had a passionate affair some years back, and for Isaac she'd left a professional man and grown children in the suburbs.

She was never very forthcoming in our presence and used to stay in the bedroom or the kitchen most of the time when Bashevis had visitors. Once though, when I asked him about Dostoevsky, after he'd confessed to having translated *The Possessed*, while still in Warsaw, into Yiddish, Bashevis would not speak about that Russian writer except to say he no longer read "such books," until Alma Singer interrupted from the next room.

"Tell them the truth Isaac," she said, "about how you used to love Dostoevsky."

Bashevis seemed to grow quite annoyed with her. "Alma," he said, "when you write a novel and they'll come to interview you, you'll tell them about Dostoyevsky and Jacob Wasserman both together, but they are here to interview me, so please, Alma, don't say another word . . . not even about Sholem Asch."

Afterward he was smiling, as if his seeming exasperation had been a game they played regularly, but she was silent for the rest of the evening. Was she also resentful? Showing me to the door when Bashevis went off to speak on the phone with a copy editor at the *Forward*, she told me I was to come again for tea the following Sunday and bring my wife, if I liked.

Isaac and I never really socialized. We were friends only within limits, though he used to use that word sometimes when I dropped by with a newly published review I'd written of one of his books. How can you be friends with a man who holds you in sure contempt for wanting to be more like him? His experiences were so distinct from my own that it was amazing we could even communicate about his work. We spent a lot of evenings together, with others, and sometimes tête-à-tête. Singer enjoyed my admiration and wanted my esteem to serve his purposes, but he did not regard himself as similarly obligated, and I never blamed him for that in those days. I felt I could be a student of his every mood and gesture. If he was also giving me some of his free time, as he surely might have maintained if I'd ever protested his treatment of me, that was surely the sort of education I could not get from any other sources.

He was a European; he was a Jew and entirely unassimilated, unlike Hemley, and Blocker, and myself. So much of what he represented had been turned to ashes, though not Singer, who had escaped that fate to be my teacher, not only through his writing but through his conversation about his life in Warsaw, his friends and lovers, though not about the child of love he'd abandoned to escape to America; I was to learn about him elsewhere much later when I read *The Family Moscat* and about the child's mother, a Communist, Singer's former mistress. Sometimes when we walked together on the Upper West Side, Bashevis claimed to want to talk only with the pigeons.

"The Cabalists believe birds are the agencies of human souls," he once assured me, "and they are sentient beings, just like you and I."

His "you and I" was flattering, and it was a first. Bashevis never complimented me except in odd ways: "You have good color today." I thought that was because he did not really enjoy my company or my conversation. He also had nothing good to say about any other writer I claimed to find interesting. Jean-Paul Sartre was not "a good writer," he told me when the Frenchman was awarded the Nobel Prize, and "Babel was a Marxst until it killed him."

It's probably no accident that living in the middle of the city I chose to write my first extended fictions through various central European mouthpieces; there were in such books such as *The Twenty-eighth Day of Elul* parodic elements abstracted from the careful, accented speech of Bashevis.

Isaac Singer never bothered to read those books, even when some years later they were published and well reviewed. He claimed not to read any of his Jewish-American contemporaries and certainly not the writings of young "sociological Jews," his way of referring to writers like me. When asked to name some living writers he admired, he'd mention Henry Miller and the man he called "Petrakis," a Greek-American from Chicago who had written flatteringly about his work.

Singer claimed to detest the belletrist Maurice Samuel for mistranslating and bowdlerizing *The Family Moscat* when it was published unsuccessfully by Knopf in the early fifties.

Other literary journalists he actively disliked were Maurice Hindus of the *Times Book Review* and the critic Irving Howe. Howe's sin was that he read Singer's writing as a Socialist, according to Bashevis, and a Marxist materialist, seemingly invulnerable to the temptations of the Evil One, and didn't know what to make of the master's constant evocations of imps, demons, incubuses, succubi, and dybbuks.

Singer really pretended to keep to his own world and occult fantasies, but he was always glancing over toward the rest of the talent in the big American room he now shared, especially if they were writers with larger reputations than his own. Once we spoke of Robert Lowell's *Life Studies*. "A *meshuginer*," Singer told me. "Crazed is what Cecil told me. Have you ever met this poet? Cecil says he gets very violent just like Essenin."

"This Norman Mailer," he said another time, "he's just crazy too, isn't he?" As if that said everything there was to say about such a protean genius of obsessive self-advertisement and real talent. It certainly seemed to cover a good deal of worldly curiosity and envy. He once described himself to me as "hidden from sight on the Upper West Side next door to a ritual bath, a man who goes to Miami Beach in the summer because I have such a bad hay fever," but he was never so unworldly not to take note of each new upsurge in his growing literary reputation. Whenever a favorable review of one of his books appeared he'd ask me the same questions about the reviewer: "Is he a famous writer? Is he well regarded?"

I can remember how proud he was of the fan mail he got from Edmund Wilson, hand-scribbled in Yiddish, which Wilson had taught himself in order to express his admiration for Bashevis. "This Wilson, he said, "he's not such a nice man, and he was married to Mary McCarthy, and she was a great beauty, I heard, with the appetites of Catherine the Great, but Cecil says he is also an important critic."

"Very," I affirmed.

"Do you know him?" he asked me. "Is he a nice man?"

I shrugged.

"I'm sure he isn't really so nice," Singer said, "because he drinks so much, but he's influential, and he's teaching himself Yiddish like the Professor, your friend. I don't have to be his friend, but I am truly grateful."

If Singer was really not the Evil One, he was certainly not a nice man, I learned to my increasing dismay during the course of my weekly visits. I had also gotten somewhat involved in the peace movement and civil rights agitation. When I mentioned my admiration for the courage of people who were putting their lives on the line in the South, he told me, "A Jewish boy like you [I was then in my late twenties, or early thirties] shouldn't try to help the *Schwartza* because these blacks are all anti-Semites and they hate Jews just like everybody else of their class."

The longer I knew him the more I saw him as closed off, harsh, ruthless, manipulative, cold. He was determined to have it both ways, to blaspheme and sing praises unto the Lord, unlike his straighter, more liberated brother, so that he was both the empathic teller of love stories about women and men and a world-class misogynist who believed women were to be used by men as their playthings. He confided to me once, presumably from experience, that many Communist women were "nymphomaniacs." He teased me that he personally liked to go to bed with two women and "to watch what they do with each other, if I can. Women have no shame," he confessed, "and there's no sin to it in Talmud or Shulchan Aruch. What women do together is just like playing . . . fooling around . . . whether it be Miss Susan Sontag or that Frenchy, Colette."

On the other hand, he took great delight in a correspondence he had with a Yiddish-speaking nun, a convert named Sister Muriel, in Minnesota.

When my first child was born, his wife sent my wife a layette blanket. Singer said a man's children were like good deeds, "good deeds and bad," he added.

Four years later when my wife and I were close to separating and I let slip the confidence that I was having a love affair with another woman, Singer was cold and cynical. "You shouldn't expect sexual bliss in marriage . . . that you have with other kinds of women." He became increasingly moralistic. "A Jewish husband," he went on, like my own mother, "should behave more sensibly." This from the admirer of Knut Hamsun's ecstatic Pan, the author of that passionate lovestory *The Slave*.

It was now 1969, a year of revolution. At thirty-six I decided that I had outlived any further usefulness to Singer and it was just as well, as I had my own life to lead, a talent, my own needs. I wasn't going to be Bashevis's epigone any longer.

I was teaching at Columbia when Erica Jong, until recently a student poet, published *Fear of Flying*. Singer wanted to know "what kind of girl could she be to write such a book?" It seemed he wanted very much to meet Erica. I told him I thought Erica was presently involved with Alfred Kazin. "A sullen old billygoat like that!" Singer exclaimed. "Tell me please, is he such a good writer?" Impersonating the Evil One is a knack one can easily acquire. I kept silent.

Around that time Singer published a children's book about his growing up in Warsaw, a spinoff from his journalistic memoirs of his father's rabbinical court, and in it he made the remarkable statement that there were no slums or antisocial behavior in the poor Jewish neighborhood in which he'd grown up. He'd only recently been mugged in the elevator of his apartment building, and he was feeling very bitter toward the New York underclasses, but his statement was both ridiculous and untrue, even in terms of what he'd depicted in his earlier fiction, and I went after him in print for being a bigot.

We only spoke twice after that. I was on a train a few years later going upstate, and I turned in my seat, and there was Bashevis sitting with a woman even younger than Erica, and they were deep in conversation. I'd just come through a difficult time, and I was in a forgiving mood and went back through the car to shake his hand and say hello.

Bashevis pretended he didn't know why we'd ever been estranged and treated me with the uneasy joviality that one uses in confronting a recently released mental patient.

"You look healthy," he said, as he introduced me to his young companion. She was his assistant, he assured me, at Bard College, to which he commuted once a week to give classes.

"You never come around anymore," he said. "Why not? Have you not been feeling well?"

To all of which I shrugged and nodded cheerfully enough, without giving him any assurance that I was ever coming by again.

When my associates at Bennington College's summer workshop asked me to invite Singer to visit, I reluctantly agreed to call him in the city. Bashevis was curt with me. The honorarium was much too small, he said, which was fair, and nowadays he summered in Switzerland or occasionally went to Israel to see his son. He was simply not available. I didn't quarrel with Isaac about that. I was prepared to say goodbye and wish him well, but I wondered what Singer wished for me, his old promoter.

"I do understand," I said. "And I'm sorry you can't come. It would have been nice to hear you talk again."

"You should see my new book," Singer said. "Many of the stories were published in the *New Yorker*."

I said I was aware he was publishing there.

"Are you still trying to be a good writer?" he asked.

"Not like you anymore," I said, and hung up.

Some months after that Bashevis was awarded the Nobel Prize for literature and I was very pleased and proud that we had once been associated in any way. I was also moved and amused by the address he made in Stockholm which was in praise of the Jewish joke and his *mameloshen*, the Yiddish language. I thought I'd contributed something to Bashevis' worldwide elevation, and when I reread many of his books I was pleased that I still admired some.

When my friend the Professor became Bashevis's official biographer I was a little astonished and upset. They'd had no liking for each other at all, and my friend had always been a man of great integrity; I wondered why Ronny had agreed to write the life of a man whose work he disliked.

Then I found out that Singer had lost his memory and was in seclusion in Florida waiting to die, and that my friend was also dying, and I wondered if it was the sad truth of dying that had somehow brought these two antagonists together again. Within months of each other they were gone, and that biography was never completed. I thought then desperation over my own career might eventually lead me to try to write about my time with Singer, but I didn't choose to do so, preferring to write more fiction and poems (still trying to be a writer, Singer might have said), and then another biographer was chosen, and I thought I would not have to write anything about the pain of my encounters with Singer's misanthropic genius ever again.

It's hard to write about being disabused of certain important admirations. Such humiliating reconsiderations are the loss of hope, and such losses always mean I am that much closer to my own death when time will intervene and waste away my cares until they all seem petty and misguided.

That time when I came to visit my latest "master" in his flat and he greeted me with a parakeet perched on his bald head was more than thirty years ago. I always used to be afraid that if Bashevis ever read something I wrote he would scorn my evident lack of genius. His own dying allowed me to escape such ridicule and obliged me to continue my struggle.

WILLIAM BRONK

William Bronk's book of poems *The World, the Worldless*, published by George Oppen for New Directions, was sent to me by Wilfred
Sheed, then literary editor of *Commonweal*, for an omnibus review of the
fall books of poetry. I'd never heard of Bronk, but I was taken with the
originality of tone in his work, the artifice, and I convinced Sheed to
allow me to review the poems alone in a thousand-word essay.

In discovering Bronk's poems more or less on my own, I found
much to praise. I called his writing "the ornament to it's own honesty"
and pointed out that one of his themes was how "naming things"
gives them "shapes which tyrannize and imprison our perceiving of
them," and I repeated the questioning lines in "Ignorant Silence in the
Center of Things": "*If we could talk, could hear each other speak.*"

My essay was, I believe, among the first serious considerations
his poems had received from reviewers; he was so far removed from
the literary world of reputations coined and slandered that he confessed to me he was surprised to have received any notice at all, and
very grateful, as I later learned, when he wrote a handwritten note
from Hudson Falls, New York, forwarded by the *Commonweal*, that he
would be in New York in a couple of weeks, before setting out on a
winter holiday to Egypt, and could I meet him in the Algonquin Hotel
bar for a drink?

The figure who greeted me that day in the bar was certainly different from the country man of homely diction I imagined Bronk would
be, the man who wrote of living "in a hogan under a hovering sky," or
of painting an old house yellow. This tall, somewhat somber but well-
turned-out fellow, in his late forties, in a teal blue double-breasted business suit with a maroon foulard tie, was waiting for me in the small,
dimly lit bar. He wore glasses, and his eyes seemed full of light. Up
close his face was large, with strong features and thin lips, a gauntness
masked by florid cheeks and a generous jaw. A soft enough glance,
though, after a while with which he eyed me for some moments, and
then introduced himself as "Bill . . . Bill Bronk."

I was to be befriended that afternoon, and from then on, learning simultaneously and with only apparent contradiction, how devoutly Bill held to his public manner of small town businessman, quite apart from his real life as poet in zip code "One Two Eight Three Nine" in his collected poems, *Life Supports*.

His family were from the original Dutch settlement of New York, when the Bronx, he informed me, was commonly called "Bronk's farm." They'd settled then in Albany near Selkirk and New Baltimore, were farmers and shipwrights, and then moved further north along the Hudson Valley. Bronk quickly told me he cared little for such a family history, but still ran a family coal and wood products business in Hudson Falls where he had been raised, and lived with his aging mother in a large mansion, in a residential part of town, which had been built by his father for the family when Bill was about two. He was a bachelor, a fairly solitary person, though a patron of the Lake George Opera Company, the Hyde Museum, and other cultural institutions in Washington and Warren counties, and would be taking his annual winter vacation abroad presently with his sister, Betty, who was single and resided in Greenwich, Connecticut.

Like Conrad Aiken, the author of *Senlin*, a book Bronk had admired in college, he drank real cocktails, manhattans or old fashioneds or martinis, I can't now recall which, and when he ordered the same again for me, had me pretty tipsy rather quickly.

He kept asking me about my own interests, as though wondering what the source of his good fortune was, but I had little to tell him except that I was struggling to survive with a wife and child as a freelance literary journalist and that I would shortly be publishing a novel with Scribners, which I would have them send on to him.

When Bronk finally read my novel *The Twenty-eighth Day of Elul*, he was moved and, I think, surprised that my ambition was somewhat larger than I'd let on. He told me he didn't read much fiction but had read my novel with fascination and sadness. He also said he had been invited to give a reading at a university because of my review and again pressed me to visit him.

Bronk's friendship from the start was always generously bestowed and nonjudgmental. When I told him of domestic unhappiness, he seemed accepting of me and did not demand to know all the details. He simply cautioned me against taking advice from "well-intentioned strangers."

To get away from the frictions of that rapidly deteriorating first marriage, I started to visit Bill a couple of times a year, every fall and spring, in Hudson Falls. We'd take walks together along the old feeder canal towpaths of the Champlain Barge Canal, and he'd prepare me sumptuous meals, and we'd talk a lot, mostly about his writing.

It was not always easy to measure who was lonelier in those days. Bill used to call me teasingly "an outlander . . . a city boy." Listening to the robin chirping in the chinaberry tree or walking with him in the woods just beyond town was a new sort of education for me, as he named and classified certain growing things and had me taste wild plants like fiddlehead ferns. He also encouraged me to get off my high horse and chat with some of the locals. In warm weather we'd take dips in the local feeder near a lock called "Barney Caine," the obscure name of which was the subject of a poem Bill wrote once. Whenever I mentioned other writers or that literary world from which he'd deliberately managed to keep apart, Bill became edgy, sometimes cranky, a little censorious.

It was because of my friendship with Bill that I started writing poems again in the midsixties, a full decade after my experience with Yvor Winters at Stanford, and they were mostly haphazard efforts, free of Wintersian strictures. When I taught literature at Bennington College I would often drive across the rolling landscape of Washington County to Bill's house for a drink and a chat. There would sometimes be other friends visiting: the painter Herman Maril and his wife, Esther, from Maryland, or Gene Canadé, who worked for the UN in Paris but was also a fine artist and engraver. Bill owned a collection of paintings by Maril and Canadé and by Canadé's father.

Bill's family business was not doing much better than my marriage, but he kept the business open a long while for the sake of his mother and sisters, who derived some income from the estate, he once told me, and for certain of his old employees, he also said. Often, when I visited him in that vast wooden shed where he kept a big desk surrounded by his inventory of boards and sash, he'd be writing a poem in longhand, while outside, in the yard, his few remaining employees filled fewer and fewer orders.

The winters sometimes seemed especially hard on Bill. He had some childhood friends in and around Hudson Falls and some young and old aspiring writers who sometimes visited, but he kept pretty much to himself, his mother going off every winter to St. Petersberg, liberating him to isolation. "Big houses alone are nice," he wrote me once after a bout of despair. "You can scream and nobody is bothered."

Bill didn't drive a car and usually walked to work, the supermarket, and the post office. He cooked for himself and shut off rooms in the house, burned newspapers along with coal in the coalstove, and wrote, and read, and listened to music on the radio. Aside from his childhood friend Laura, whom he saw every Saturday night when they took in dinner and a movie together, and spoke with at least once a day, and occasional visitors such as myself and Gil Sorrentino, his publisher; Jim Weill of the Elizabeth Press; or Cid Corman, on a stopover from Japan, who'd published Bill's first book of poems through Origen Press and with whom there was later a falling out, Bronk was alone a lot. The local high school kids did chores about the house and were drafted as company. He could get quite melancholy. I was then living by myself in the city, but Bill resisted visiting me. He developed emphysema and had to give up smoking and do loud breathing exercises which made him sound like a barking seal when we walked together in the woods.

I'm looking at a holograph of four liners from the seventies in which Bill wrote to me: "If we are asked how we shall live in the world/it doesn't ask us. It lives us as it will/or else, no matter, leaves us alone."

"There are houses hanging above the stars," wrote Conrad Aiken in "The Morning Song of Senlin," "and stars hung under a sea . . ./and a sun far off in a shell of silence/Dapples my walls for me."

Spring really comes late to the upper Hudson Valley, but by mid-March Bill's mood would improve. He'd attend chamber music concerts by a local quartet, begin to plan another garden, go trekking for pussywillow branches and, later, morels, and await the return of his mom with trepidation and relief. Caring for her broke some of the isolation and gave him something to do, but it also placed limits on his visitors. Mrs. Bronk was a former Republican committeewoman. Well into her seventies, she drove herself about the area in a large late model Chrysler and was hard of hearing, a little intrusive about some of Bill's company, a difficult woman. They did not seem to share many values.

Bill always remained dutiful. He kept the house and attended to the necessaries she could not herself fulfill, especially when she became an invalid. Often on pleasant afternoons he'd commence long walks in the countryside around Argyle, in part to be away from that domain. His poems of that period exclaim on the gentleness and brightness of October light and the persistence of desire, the beauty of two lovers leaning toward each other like a pair of young trees.

Those were difficult but productive years for Bronk. He turned out poems and collections of poems, sometimes exclamatory—"O Jesus Christ that light"—and sometimes ruminative and elegant—*That Tantalus, To Praise the Music, The Empty Hands, A Partial Glossary on Costume as Metaphor,* and a volume of prose poems meditating on some cultural assumptions that helped construct the Mayan sites of Central America, which he'd been to visit with his sister during another brief winter vacation.

We kept up a regular correspondence over those years, exchanging books as well as thoughts and gossip and poems; I don't know whether any of my stuff is in what Bill generously donated to Columbia University a few years back, but I hope not, as I always scribbled in great haste in between other things and didn't consider myself a literary correspondent like Olson and Creely and some others Bill once knew well. Though I was always welcome to visit him, I rarely did, as I was much too busy with mucking up my own life. The more I knew of Bronk's isolation, the less attractive it was to me as a choice for how I should try to live, but I always knew I had a caring friend who would welcome me and look after me no matter how frayed my condition was on arriving in Fort Edward by the afternoon train. When my oldest daughter was in boarding school in Lake Placid, I always used to stop off at Bill's place and sometimes slept over. When I would bring Margaret away from school for a home visit, Bill and his mother would cook and bake all kinds of treats for the two of us. Bill once prepared a savory stew for me he called "Brains and Balls," and that's what it turned out to be, in fact, brains and "prairie oysters," seasoned with carrots, mushrooms, and parsnips, as I recall.

Bill was now acquiring a major reputation, and many came on pilgrimage to Hudson Falls to meet him, interview him, secure poems from him for their publications, or to ask him to read. It was characteristic of Bill's come-hither stance toward the poetry world that he most often steadfastly refused to read with others, regarding some such invitations as slights. He was still very sensitive to slights and did not easily forget insults, whether real or imaginary. He was convinced he had been overlooked a bit because he had never engaged in literary logrolling and confessed to me once that, when his first manuscript of poems, "My Father Photographed with Friends," was judged only second best by Auden, who awarded the Yale Younger Poets Prize that year to Adrienne Rich, he withdrew the manuscript from circulation for nearly twenty years and never really forgave Auden.

Bill had briefly visited at the experimental Black Mountain College and there rediscovered tastes and friendships with Creeley, Olson, Jonathan Williams. He'd also taught English for a while at Union College in Schenectady. He'd lived in Greenwich Village among artists and experimental film makers such as Shirley Clarke but had always kept somewhat apart from New York Bohemia, and for that reason, perhaps, life in a small town upstate remained his preference. He once informed me his neighbors allowed him a freedom he could not easily have elsewhere.

"I could do almost anything here short of murder," Bill told me in his droll baritone, "and people would just say, that's Bill, is all. It's his way. But you being an outlander, if you cross the street wrong a whole lot of people would be after you."

My relationship with Bill continues. I try to go up to see him once or twice a year, and we just sit and chat, and kvetch a little about getting older. Bill's a lot less hail than when I first knew him, is a little hard of hearing; he no longer cooks elaborate meals or drinks alcohol or keeps up the spruce appearance of the house, no longer takes long walks.

In the midseventies when I lost my job at Columbia I lived for about a year in nearby Fort Edward to save money, inhabiting an upstairs flat rented to me by Bill's friend, Laura. Through no fault of theirs I was lonely and quite miserable most of the time and ended up hospitalized at the Glens Falls Mental Health Infirmary where Bill arranged for me to receive treatment that was gentle and respectful. (Bill's befriending the down and out has often caused him regrets. One itinerant visitor to Hudson Falls, another literary gent, may have ripped off the family's heirloom silver) .

It was while I was living in Fort Edward that I came to behave as a "trickster" and wrote the first of my "Little Lives" of the people of Washington County, which later appeared as a book under the pseudonym "John Howland Spyker" and caused a small local scandal. I came by the perverse idea for such a book from the names on tombstones in the nearby cemetery where I sometimes went to walk and by overhearing my landlady gossip on the phone below me. In a house with paper-thin walls and ceilings, she would gossip every day at noon with Bill, or certain other old friends, about the obituaries and marriage announcements in the Glens Falls *Post Star*.

As I recall, they'd go over the person's entire history and various involvements from memory and then were either bluntly dismissive, or mildly nostalgic, amused, appreciative, anecdotal.

I figured this wasn't the *Popul Voh* I was overhearing but good, plain, old-fashioned jive and gossip, and I could do that as well as anybody. When my book of brief personal histories appeared I had already left the area and lots of local people thought Bill had written it. They were cross with him, and he with me. That all got sorted out when astute John Leonard, in a review in the *Times*, revealed I was the author of those scurrilous pieces. But, if my literary reputation in that part of the country still looms larger than elsewhere, it's because Spyker and "Little Lives" still have notoriety in Washington County. Every so often I get a piece of fan mail forwarded to me from some local person who feels I have conveyed the essential truth about life in the upper Hudson Valley.

Bill has never really been happy about my writing about his county. Though I would have to classify such works as fiction, I also can't deny there was a basis in local legend, if not hard fact, for some of what Spyker alleged. On our walks Bronk was always pointing out various local types to me and recounting their histories: a philandering professional man who inseminated all his patients, a former war hero, a prison guard, a cellist with peculiar tastes. He's always shown a gentle acceptance of his neighbors so very different from himself in so many different ways; he was never smart-alecky about their lives. In a recent poem, "Outdate," he writes:

> The streets and houses look as If they were based
> on old photos and weren't real. They've brought
> new people in. When old ones meet uptown
> we look; we ask each other how we are

A silence fell between us when I left the area. I had fallen in love with a woman I met on the train to New York whom I later went to live with and married. Bill seemed to think of love as charming, if not essentially self-referential. "Loving you is love," he began a poem, "but is not you./Knowledge of you is knowing but not you."

I think Bill felt I had been somewhat unappreciative of his and Laura's efforts to help me get through a bad time. Eventually he may have been relieved that he no longer had me to look after. We continue to correspond, and I have also written more about Bill's writings. I don't wish to repeat any of that here, though he seems to me to be a truthful and wonderful poet of the American language, as original as ever, and he continues to produce elegant and beautiful and startling short poems that often interest me, even though nowadays, as he has confessed, he writes them out in his head while shaving in the morning.

Ruminating on Proust for a recent collection Bill wrote:

> The way Swann, his whole life, loved
> Odette, and she not even his type, is the way
> Contrarily we, each of us, love,
> In spite of natural inclinations, our lives

Some years ago when he was fifty-six I tried to sum up Bronk's importance for me in a poem called "October Visit."

I love Bronk for his poems, and crowy lawns,
his white and yellow cakes, and old canals.
He is going from me I feel I don't know where,
Fades like October light, so gently.
He leaves his chilly afterglow, as when we climb
the wooden porch steps to enter his gloomy old house.
0 gentle guide go slow . . .
Believe you are not alone in all this bright October yellow.

Bronk's voice when he reads reverberates like Charley Mingus' bass in the low registers from his ruined chest. Usually he speaks softly, often with a pout. In Copan, in the silence of a vast mahogony forest, I heard his voice as I struggled with reading translations of the Mayan glyphs.

I think of Bronk visiting New York once and coming downtown with me to the poet Paul Pines' Bowery jazz club, The Tin Palace. Apprised of Bronk's presence in the room, a lot of the young downtown poets came over to our table to introduce themselves and pay their respects, Bill purring like a big cat and then withdrawing into himself as though his most fearsome anticipations were being realized: he had readers, fans. He was afterward in no great hurry to depart. And when Cecil McBee arrived with the other members of his trio and commenced to make music, Bronk seemed to regard all that "braided water" we call "jazz" as the intrusion and relaxed and settled back and listened "to praise the music."

Bernard Malamud

The late Natalie Wood once expressed interest in making a movie out of my novel *Lilo's Diary*. My heroine was eighteen; Wood was then in her indeterminate thirties. When I told my colleague Bern Malamud that I had the eye of Natalie Wood, he advised me to sell the book but not to write the screenplay. He had done screenplays with *The Fixer* and one other property, I believe, and had been unsuccessful. "They'll tell you anything" he said, of Hollywood people. "Don't believe them unless they enclose a check."

Though nothing ever came of the Natalie Wood project, Bern and I got to be on friendly terms.

It wasn't always that way.

In the summer of 1966, in Bennington, Vermont, in a hallway between our two offices, Malamud introduced himself to me with a prophecy: "Your writing will do very well up here, but you'll probably drive yourself a little crazy and end up unhappy and divorced . . . and you won't be the first."

This small, frail person, with his jaunty little mustache, was about to go off on leave to teach at Harvard; I was his replacement. We'd been working most of the summer in the sauna heat of the old wooden College Barn, three offices apart, without either of us letting on that we knew the other was there. Two or three months previous to my being offered the job at Bennington, I'd been sent *The Fixer* for review, along with a very fine account of the Beilis case, on which Malamud's book is based, by the belletrist and translator Maurice Samuel. My review pointed out that *The Fixer* was overwrought and full of solipsism, not the highest quality Malamud, and it was very strange to compare his Yacov Bok, the prisoner character, to the actual Mendel Beilis in Samuel's account.

I wrote as I did, presuming Malamud and I would never meet. Even after the job as his replacement was offered to me, I assumed we would not run into each other, for he would surely be away while I was in residence.

I moved my family to Vermont and went about that summer revising a novel for publication. There was an office down the hall from which I occasionally heard the sounds of typing. I didn't immediately presume that the sign over the door listing office hours under the sobriquet "Bernard Malamud" meant it was he behind the door composing.

So it was that we worked that summer in an odd kind of tandem, trying as best we could to be unaware of each other, though once, after a furious barrage of typing down the hall, I got up from my machine and peered into the corridor and saw this thin, mustached face peering back at me. He must have been in his late forties at the time. As I ducked away, cursing my bad timing, I knew good form dictated that I use the next available opportunity to introduce myself formally to Mr. Malamud.

The next time I heard typing coming from behind that door, I knocked and Malamud appeared. We stood in the doorway and he issued his prophecy of sorts, in an affable enough manner, though he insisted on calling me "Elman."

"I hope you have a good time up here, Elman," he said. "I really do."

Then the prophecy. Then I wished him an equally productive year in Cambridge and we said goodbye.

By the time we met a year or so later, everything he'd prophesied had come more or less true.

How had he known? Guessed?

He said, "You reminded me a lot of Howard Nemerov, and things like that were always happening to Howard."

It was an attack of thinking I could read people's minds like an omniscient author that had me briefly committed to Bellevue the first time. I later wrote an article about my experience which made the cover of *New York Magazine* under the title, "All The Thorazine You Can Drink at Bellevue."

I was subsequently invited to appear on a number of television programs to discuss my ordeal. One of the panelists was identified as Natalie Wood's sister, and she kept telling the MC and the audience that I must be seriously disturbed. "You're not exactly the picture of mental health," I replied. Screen went to black, and then a commercial. When we came back on, Natalie Wood's overweight sister started in again on my problems. Did my family know?

"We haven't been on speaking terms for many years." Screen to black again.

I think Bern may have seen that show. He was not a soft man, and he became rather concerned about me. He sent me a letter recommending more distance from experience in my writing. As though to bestow a kindness with criticism, he recommended me for one of the very first NEA grants, and, later, was often generous and kind to me in small hospitable ways whenever I was in Bennington.

When I eventually remarried and he invited me and my second wife to dinner, he would often tease Alice about the number of girlfriends he believed I once had, whether she had used good judgement in marrying someone so much older than herself, like me.

Bern really liked Alice, I suppose. He tended to like to talk to women at parties. He was jocular, or courtly, or eminent, but always just a little serious. He confessed to both of us, once, that he'd always written in a very disciplined way. When he was younger he often had been envious of those who could take the time to consort with women. Bern said he felt a little deprived in that respect; I suppose we were all supposed to feel a little deprived in other aspects by such a confession of his own dedication, as though the pages of our lives had been dog-eared by devout concern with living. I often wondered what Bern's wife, Ann, who was usually present, made of such discussions.

We were colleagues off and on for nearly two decades at Bennington, and we got along OK. He told me once he was always pleased with my criticisms of his work, and they were usually right. He also told me he admired my tenacity, even though, apparently, he was of the opinion it would come to naught.

Bern had a habit of seeing some people as others. If you were a complete ne'er-do-well, you were like the art critic and poet Gene Baro. If you were depressed and problematic, you were "more like Howard" (Nemerov). I truly admired Bern's short fiction, his shorter novels, such as *The Assistant* and *A New Life*, and, later, *God's Grace*, which I reviewed with praise when it was panned by others. I committed few of my admirations to print, and usually kept my opinions to myself, unless he came up to me after a reading and asked. That happened after he wrote a story through the mind of Virginia Woolf. I told him I thought it vague, ersatz, and silly. Bern pretended he didn't really care, but he avoided me for a while. He later told me he had written reviews for his friend Ben Bellitt, when Bellitt was an editor of the *Nation*. The rare-book dealer Glenn Horowitz has also discovered in Bern's papers a pseudonominously published kid's book he wrote with a neighbor when he was living in Oregon, using his own photo on the dust jacket. Bern also told me he admired the

Russians but had learned more from Virginia Woolf.

We were never really close friends, and I never cared to be a protégé. We simply didn't admire each other in ways either of us cared to
recognize. Bern reminded me too much of some of my reproachful
Midwood High School teachers; he'd taught high school math at Eras-
mus in Brooklyn at one early point in his career, and the valedictorian
of my high school class at Midwood was his good friend. For his own
tastes, I was too manically wild, and socially inept.

Bern could be a very prudent man. At dinner parties he'd sometimes enjoy watching others make asses of themselves by attempting
to entertain the company while he hung back and flirted with the most
attractive woman at the table. His flirtations seemed much more innocent than those of his literary protagonist, the biographer William
Dubin. Mostly he seemed to wish to know things he felt excluded from
by virtue of gender or experience. How did it feel to be a married
woman having an affair with an impecunious and crazy poet? What
did falling in love feel like to a well-brought-up WASP from Tuxedo?
He despised some of his colleagues in the art department for taking
advantage of some of the Bennington girls, when that school was for
young women only, but he was not beyond importuning these young
women with very personal questions about their lives when they were
in tutorial (counseling) with him.

When he made money, Bern told me it would go into bank cer-
tificates of deposit and other safe bets. He bought a lovely house in
Old Bennington, but he kept the same wife, and a few of the same old
habits. Bern didn't like playing fliers. He and Saul Bellow were friends,
but Bern did not attempt to show off his intellectual powers with Bellow, or with anyone else. He was intense; not modest, just extremely
careful. He told me once that he'd figured out he needed an advance
of fairly large proportions every five years or so from his publisher to
complete his next project and supplement his teaching and other
income, and this he achieved sedulously until the end. I believe Bern
died fairly well-to-do.

His books went through numerous complete drafts. He tried to
research every fact and was meticulous with details about a piece of
sculpture, or an English department policy; he saved every draft he
made. After a while, he was publishing nearly everything he wrote
and finished. When something displeased him he filed it away. It must
have cost him a hurt or two to abandon his profiles of women: Virginia
Woolf, Alma Mahler; there were some others. They weren't what they
should have been because they couldn't be Malamud. He seemed to
know it.

One of my most embarrassing moments took place one summer at a Malamud reading during the Bennington workshops. My in-laws were visiting, and Malamud, my mother-in-law claimed, was the one writer she really wanted to hear.

Bern's talks and readings to the workshop students were often charming, and genial. He would appear the master they so much desired to encounter when they came to the workshops. Bern would answer questions about his work and career, or read from something he was working on or had recently finished. He paid the students the high compliment of reading his work in manuscript, unfinished work. He might begin, "I suppose you all want to know what I think of the movie of *The Natural*?"

The summer my in-laws visited he read a fine new story about an aging Jewish woman who buys herself a wig when her hair starts to thin. Malamud was able to offer us the woman from the inside out, with the wry care of the parable teller, who could abstract from that behavior of display a lesson about aging, eros, and love. It was a moving experience, first-rate short fiction, masterly in control. My mother-in-law, who had probably considered wigs, was made extremely nervous, anxious, embarrassed by Malamud's ironical empathies. In the middle of the reading she cried out, "Oh, no. . . ."

Malamud peered up from his text, startled, in the darkened hall, and then returned to it again. My mother-in-law's anxiety got the better of her again. *"What does he know about wigs?"* I heard her, sotto voce. *"How dare he?"*

This was altogether involuntary, an exclamation, a rudeness, at best. She was also expressing openly the same embarrassments and anxieties Malamud was trying to dramatize through his wig-buying woman.

To show I was not a party to any of this, I put my hands over my face as Malamud read on in that dark, hot hall.

I apologized afterwards to Bern, who seemed far less upset than I. "Everybody has relatives," he pointed out. "I guess my story touched a certain . . ."

"Wig," I pointed out.

He had open-heart surgery in California, and then a stroke, and when I next saw him he looked very small and unwell. He complained of loss of memory. He was still writing, he said, as much as he could.

The last thing I heard him read was from a work in progress about a Jewish peddler in nineteenth-century Arizona who gets kidnapped by Indians and is made a member of their tribe.

I was heading for the Southwest in a matter of weeks to teach at the University of Arizona. In Nogales I heard about a Jewish family that could trace many Indian connections through intermarriage from Malamud's period. I wrote to Bern suggesting he correspond with the family to document certain parts of his protagonist's Southwest existence, even as a comic figure. He wrote back to say he would surely look into the matter.

Some weeks after that, Bern dropped dead in the kitchen of his New York apartment while preparing a tuna fish sandwich for himself after a stint at writing. He was alone, as he had seemed in so many ways those last years of his illness. Bern did not lack for loving company, but he seemed to regard being ill and failing as a terrible embarrassment and isolation. How much he wanted to get better, to write again with his whole being. The stroke and recuperation were somehow an intimidation to him. He could recuperate, though taking good care of himself was like walking on eggs. He didn't always seem to know where to put his old weight and authority, with which foot.

I never knew Bern to be small or mean-spirited toward me, then, despite his sufferings. He usually managed to appear like a ghost of himself at parties, bestow certain blessings, entertain himself as much as he could, and leave early.

His wife, Ann, and I had this thing at parties. I was the fellow available for her to bum cigarettes from when she became anxious. I would see her watching him sometimes, supervising him, and I would appear with my cigarettes, or a drink. In those days Bern was often pleased to chat with men, as well as women, at Bennington gatherings.

He'd taken on the honorific of the presidency of the American PEN Writers' Organization, and he seemed to be working at it, after the first stroke, as a way of distracting himself from his writing problems.

I asked him once when he first thought of becoming a writer. He told me that when he was a teenager his mother died, and in his grief he began to express himself in various ways, and the thought must have occurred to him then. I heard him express other explanations to other people at other parties. Bern wasn't being deceitful. He was quite worried about himself, and when he started reflecting on his life many different things occurred to him, with rue, and he was just a little tired of being asked so many questions anyway. He only wished another chance to remember, to focus, and write.

II

NEW YORK, N.Y.

SY KRIM

The writer and editor Seymour Krim, who took his life after a debilitating illness late one summer, was not, at first meeting, a kindly seeming person. His published essays were my introduction to his personality, and they were pathbreaking, the original self-advertisements, but also raunchy and tender and aware. Sy was certainly one of the first writers of his generation to discuss his emotional problems and psychotic spells and hospitalization; his memoir of his friendship with the writer Milton Klonsky stays with me even now, thirty years after I read it the first time.

There's a posthumous manuscript called "Chaos," which others whose opinions I respect think is his masterpiece. Sy once read some of it to me in his tiny book-lined one-room flat near Second Avenue, and I can recall a powerful surge of language, the colloquial, the profane, and the elegantly poetic achieved through his invocations of an America far different from *Leaves of Grass*, though obviously inspired by Whitman.

He was a writer, and that is how it is most appropriate to remember him—a fine and often generous reviewer of other people's books, a writer of essays and imaginative prose—but Sy was also an editor and teacher, and there are so many younger writers here in New York and elsewhere whom he encouraged and helped that the entire list is hard to cite. For many years Sy held a regular weekly workshop class at St. Mark's Church and he was always available at other times to read and discuss a manuscript, if he wasn't traveling, as he did quite a lot in his later years.

The Sy Krim I first encountered in person was editor, perhaps thirty years ago, of a girly magazine, *Nugget*. The magazine was not a roaring success, and Sy's office uptown was small and cluttered. Sometime after reading *Nearsighted Cannoneer*, a friend showed me the magazine and said Sy was looking to publish young fiction writers in every issue, interspersed with the risqué photos and macho cartoons. I'd recently come back to New York from the coast, where my first novel had appeared to little public enthusiasm, and I had a grubby job in publishing and a bad case of stage fright, a kind of publication block that, after three unproductive years, was infecting my writing, too. I needed validation, and I needed a fan, and I sent a story off to Sy, hoping to please him.

It wasn't particularly well written or well dramatized; it was rude and a little vulgar, a story about a professor of Spenser who is seduced by a fairy queen student in the stacks of a university library. Sy called me a week after he received the story. "Why do young writers want to write about academics?" he asked me. "Who cares?" But he asked to see me in person, and a few days later I went to his office.

My surprise was how well set up and handsome he was, how youthful looking. I seemed haggard and old to myself by comparison. But I was also surprised by the pains he had taken with my story. He'd marked it up with editorial queries and changes and was prepared to go over it with me. "It isn't a particularly good story," he confessed, "but I'm willing to publish it because you look like you need to publish, and maybe this will help you a little. But don't write stories like this again. Write about experience," he said, expansively, which made me realize he thought I had some talent. Then we sat down and went over my imperfect story word by word.

When my story appeared I got a check in the mail for a hundred dollars and a copy of the magazine. It was the first money I had earned from my writing in three years. It also helped in other ways. When people I met asked if I had published anything recently, I could always interrupt my furrowing brow by saying, "Oh yes, Sy Krim just did one of my stories in *Nugget*." It made it possible for *me* to encounter the world with less shyness and shame.

I have always been grateful for such an act of kindness. I'm sure I'm not the only one to whom Sy extended himself as an editor (and sometimes as an agent) with publication and a lecture, and I know from our subsequent correspondence over the years that he always responded to manuscripts with notes and comments, never with printed forms. He put himself out for other writers and expected the same in return.

Once, about seven years ago, when I invited him to read at the Bennington summer workshops, he arrived at the reception and informed me that there were at least three women students on hand he would like to date while he was in Bennington and would I please arrange this for him right away?

I tried explaining to Sy that the women would probably not appreciate my being his agent, and he became flustered for a moment and cross with me. But when he read from his writings the next evening, it was immediately evident to me and others that Sy would have no need of intermediaries. He was swarmed.

I thought of him as a friend, but I saw very little of him over the years. We lived in different places and had different hungers. I always knew I could reach Sy and he would say something helpful and encouraging, and I knew about his problems getting published, and they were similar to mine, and after a while it seemed unfair to bother him any more. He wasn't well, I knew, and many wanted his help.

But now he is gone from his friends, and I know I shall miss him. He was a kind friend for a writer to have—young or old.

WALLY MARKFIELD AND OTHERS

Toward the end of my first marriage I had a girlfriend, Conny. She was older than I was, and well battered by life, savvy and very hip and sexy and kind to me with her body and her encouragement to my writing.

Conny had been married to a writer who committed suicide, an old friend of Isaac Rosenfeld and Saul Bellow, and she was raising a daughter by herself in a small brownstone flat on one of the nicer streets in Greenwich Village. Some days I'd come by and ring the bell and Conny would throw down her key in a silk hanky, if she was alone, and I'd run upstairs and we'd make frantic love.

Occasionally Conny also had parties, and I would be invited. The guests were all from high bohemia, writers, artists, and critics. Another of Conny's admirers was the art critic, Harold Rosenberg, with his limp and his hoarse voice, his florid features, and authoritative manner of a *Partisan Review* commissar; and Conny was also friends with Sy Krim and Wally Markfield.

Wally was just about to publish his classic New York scene comic novel, *To An Early Grave*, and he was always doing *shtick*, sending up the manners and the mode of speaking of everybody at the parties with the frantic mimeses of a stand-up comic. In some sentences he spoke, every other word was Yiddish. I enjoyed his performances, but his wife sometimes seemed impatient with Wally as the evening progressed. "Come on now," she'd insist, "its time we got back home to the kid." They were raising a child in a cramped flat somewhere on the Upper West Side and eventually moved to Port Washington in the suburbs.

Conny was related to the old Communist writer Joe Freeman, and he would sometimes be present along with his artist wife, Charmion Von Wiegand; and Harold Rosenberg and Wally, who were very anti-Communist Menshavik Trotskyites would rag Joe about his stalwart politics, and Joe would rag them back, and everybody ate Brie and drank red wine and got along just fine.

I was invited by Conny to these parties out of real generosity on her part. She was helping me stage my debut in intellectual-literary circles, promoting my short stories when they were occasionally published in magazines with her crowd, being my sponsor and friend. Various editors were always on hand, and I sometimes had the feeling Conny had been intimate with all of us, and now she was being my booster.

If so, this didn't really work out as well as she'd hoped, I'm sure. Love with Conny was great, but I really wasn't of her world nor shared the same political and social concerns. I hadn't been around in the thirties and early forties at the Bickford's Cafeteria, but I was grateful for the education I was receiving from the likes of Milton Klonsky, Manny Geltman, Dwight MacDonald, and other of Conny's visitors.

When my book *The Poorhouse State* was published, which was about welfare poverty on Manhattan's Lower East Side, Conny ran a reception for me, and Dwight MacDonald took me aside and told me he admired what I was trying to do and thought I'd written a good and tough-minded book, but "don't try to be Jim Agee, Richard. You lack the verbal talents." One way or the other I thought that was good advice and thanked MacDonald.

Later that night Conny said, "Dwight had a crush on Jim. Almost everybody in our crowd did. He was a terrible slob, but so attractive, especially to certain lady Communists."

When the *Transatlantic Review* published my story about a Young Communist League high school organizer with big bosoms I felt ten feet tall. A talented young poet named Leroi Jones was appearing in that same issue. Alice was my trope for female generosity, modeled in some ways on Conny, though nowhere near as hip. She successfully recruited my young Jewish protagonst with sex for ideological purposes in the language of Marx and W. E. B. DuBois.

Conny seemed to find my story quite amusing and duplicated copies for all her gang. It wasn't Gogol's *Overcoat*, but it had its moments. Wally was not amused. He seemed a little cross with me. "Don't ever sentimentalize Stalinists," he told me.

I said I liked my protagonist because she was full of ideological babble but she also had generosity and spirit.

"If that's what you think boychickle," said Harold Rosenberg, "it shows how little you really know."

MATTHEW JOSEPHSON

I sometimes used to walk in Riverside Park on fall days with Matthew Josephson.

Without notice he'd call on Sunday mornings and say he'd driven down from Sherman, Connecticut, or had stayed over at his pied-à-terre in the Village, and could we meet for a walk in a little while at the Boat Basin? He never asked me to meet him downtown, and I was never invited to visit him in town or in Connecticut, but we seemed to be friendly. Once Matty encouraged me to date his wife's attractive, recently divorced niece.

The calls were always brief and to the point: "This is Matthew Josephson calling," he'd announce into the mouthpiece loudly, "I'm in town, and I thought a walk would do us both some good. The usual place?"

Matthew would be leaning against a rail and peering out over the river when I arrived, and, as though gifted with some sixth sense, he'd turn just as I approached and smile at me through a mouthful of bridgework. He'd be wearing a trenchcoat with the collar pulled up, and he'd often have on a beret and be smoking. "Ah there you are," he'd say, his voice precise and witty, though inundated by saliva. It was almost a distraction to listen to Matty talking through so much spit. He seemed to suffer from a lazy tongue or an excess of humidity, an oral effluvium which sometimes made his nasal tenor difficult to follow, especially when he spoke French, and then sometimes he'd raise the volume, as he was hard of hearing, and that also seemed to increase the saliva flow and incoherency. One could attend him with patience, though, and then he'd be articulate, modulated, and acute, at once self-mocking and jestermocking, though never personally unkind to me.

Matthew had been one of the celebrated expatriates to go to live in Paris and there befriended Tristan Tzara and others of the original Dadaists. Hearing him recall parties at the home of Miss Natalie Barney, where he came to meet Miss Stein and Ford Madox Ford, or luncheons at the Closerie de Lilas with Kay Boyle, one anticipated a good deal of wetness, along with a certain sly salaciousness.

He'd been a stockbroker just before the crash and a surrealist poet and editor of *Broom* and must have been very lonely in Sherman, Connecticut at times; in looking me up on Sunday mornings Matty surely knew he had a fairly receptive audience. He was a good story-teller. He'd gone from the post–World War I avant garde to become one of the most successful popular historians of his time, the author of *The Robber Barons* and biographies of Edison, Sidney Hillman, and Stendhal, and somewhere in-between all that activity had found time to have romantic friendships with a lot of interesting women, includ-ing Katherine Anne Porter, about whom he would only say "she had the great talent as well in the looks department," though he usually was careful to avoid slangy vulgarisms.

When I knew him first he had been a target of some red baiters for his "agnostic and epicurean ideas" and had health problems, which he would never explain or specify, and was concerned about his son, though I never knew why, and was writing his memoir, *Life among the Surrealists*. I was introduced by Carey McWilliams of the *Nation*, and as I recall we spent a good deal of our initial time together talking about politics. Matty seemed to be anticipating another collision of the Great Powers. He didn't much like the Russians, but he liked the "superpa-triots," as he called them, even less. Matty also once confided to me that some of his contemporaries were not as they seemed. He said the Latin Americanist Carleton Beals was "probably a GPU agent." Matty seemed to think literature had culminated in the generation that fol-lowed Joyce and Proust. He didn't read many of the new writers. He was still a friend and neighbor of Malcolm Cowley but seemed sunk in nostalgia for a better time. A favorite curseword of Matty's was *Fos-ter Dulles*, which was usually accompanied by a fine spray.

He was raised in Harlem in a prosperous middle-class Jewish family, he told me once, but really did not regard himself as "a member of the tribe." He did not seem to admire the middle classes, and once when I mentioned a new novel by James Gould Cozzens, he sneered at "Connecticut writers." His son, Erik, was a business reporter for the *Washington Post* and his wife was employed by the American Academy in Washington Heights as its paid administrator. Matty always seemed startled by what television "was doing to writing."

It just didn't seem possible to him "to do that much anymore." He was getting ready to depart from a bad scene, which had honored him insufficiently, and in some ways he always seemed a little impa-tient for this to happen.

I had the feeling he felt deprived in his later years of a sexual libertinism that had once come rather easily to him and was curious about my own affairs with women. I had little to share with him then except a pervasive guiltiness which Matty was always kind enough to aid me in exculpating.

"Tender feelings," he would advise to excuse my faltering accounts of my adventures, "are often spoiled by being set down in detail."

Once, on a lovely early fall day, we spoke of Hemingway. Matty always pronounced the name as a series of light, rising syllables in a tone of astonished bemusement. When I asked how he regarded the author's accomplishments, his little moustache twitched on his expressive face, and he said, with a dryness to which I was unaccustomed from Matty, "You would really be surprised if you knew what a song of a bitch he could be . . . with women especially, but also with men."

The great writer had only just committed suicide, and I was not really prepared for so much bitterness. "We were all very silly at times back then," Matty said, "and Ernest could also be quite mean."

I never really understood why Matty chose me to interrupt some of his loneliness. He seemed at times in the grip of a nostalgia so pervasive it took him from the present moment; at other times he was lively and highspirited, then biting, remorseful, and cold, cutting conversation off whenever he felt like it, as though I owed him such deference. A week or two would go by, and then he would call me again, and again we'd meet and walk through frail, yellow leaf-falls in the park together. I came to anticipate these perambulations as interludes of surpassing melancholy but always agreed to meet him, as though expecting some eventual revelation which never really occurred: Matty never even suggested I read certain books and never volunteered to read any books I'd written.

His great admiration for Stendhal led me once to inquire why he was so taken with *The Red and the Black*, and he assured me then, "It's a young man's book. I was like Julian Sorel once. A lot of young men like us are."

I felt honored at that moment that he considered me to be like him in any respect and had to agree that, from my knowledge of the character in the novel, this was so. Recently, while thumbing through a translation of Stendhal's autobiography, *La vie de Henri Brulard*, I thought I could hear Matty's cadences in certain of Stendhal's words on a page: "The great drawback to being truly witty is you have to keep your eyes fixed on the semi-fools around you, and steep yourself in their commonplace ways of feeling."

Max Margulis

Max was always my best teacher, kind, and wise, astute. It wasn't always clear what subject we were studying together. Sometimes we talked about my writing; sometimes we talked about bel canto singing (a subject I knew little about), or acting, or painting. Mostly he talked and I listened, an epicurean discourse on the good life and its relation to making good art, not sham, or pretend art, not sell-out posturing. Max was always my guide to the authentic.

How he knew so much about so many aspects of the arts often was bewildering to me. I *only knew* that every recommendation he made of an artist in music, in poetry, in painting was a true penny. Max did not deal in false coin. His taste was impeccable and never arbitrary or put on, never farouche; there was inside him a universe of intense and focused experience.

He played excellent chamber music in a quartet with friends and had been a professional musician. He told me once during the Depression he played in dance bands on cruise ships and that once he learned how to keep time on the drums in a couple of days so he could get a gig on a Latin American trip.

Max wrote very little for print except in *New Masses* and some other leftist publications; what he wrote was often impressively percipient. I am continually referring others to his essay on bygone jazz in the *Massachusetts Review*, in which long before postmodernist jargon saturated critical vocabulary Max was writing about the way jazz artists consistently parodied themselves and the tunes and manners of their predecessors. He was a founder of Blue Note records, a roommate and friend of Bill De Kooning and some of the other leading-edge painters of our era, a man who taught me about breath and line breaks in poetry.

He was my neighbor on the Upper West Side, and we became friends so that I was invited to visit sometimes and always came away edified. Max and his wife, Helen, were civilized and intelligent and unpretentious and welcoming hosts, and Max was always instructing me and usually on the money in his recommendations.

In any sane society Max would have been honored as an innovative and inspirational sage, but he was hardly known in the great world. I feel myself one of the happy few, to echo Stendhal, for having known him at all and for his efforts to educate me and his humane and undeniable generosity. He told me once his interest in music came from his father, a singer, I believe, with the Chicago Opera in whose company at home Max met many of the great stars of the opera world.

Max could also recall individual performances he'd heard of Caruso and John McCormack and others with such distinction that he could convey how the artist had to breathe and comport himself without undue strain to achieve a magnificence of sound. He had an uncanny memory. He often did not approve of my flamboyance, and his own plain-spoken behavior was in sharp contrast. He kept his political views to himself, in the main. He'd been always on the Left, was exacting but never cruel in person, and never simply a vulgar Marxist, but sharply critical of liberal cant. When the Communist Party-dominated John Reed club founded *Partisan Review* at City College Max was on its editorial board.

Once he showed me a manuscript of some length he'd written on singing, and I read it and found it very elegant and informed. I was then well placed with a leading publisher, and they had a music list. I showed it to my editor. Sadly, he told me there was only one other book in print on bel canto, and they had published it and it sold so well they weren't going to change horses in midstream, but this music editor thought that Max's book was certainly, in his words, the "class of the field."

There were many gaps between the times we met, but whenever I dropped by to see Max, after giving him as much advance warning as I could, living out of town, he always seemed pleased to see me, and I fancied to myself that was because he enjoyed my company and took some sustenance from my presence. I'm not so sure of that now as I once may have been. I think in fact Max simply knew he was important to me, and to others like me, and for that reason he always made himself available. He worked with actors and singers on voice but was a lover of literature and introduced me to the writings of George Borrow and others I still treasure.

Thank you Max. It always was a pleasure.

John Hall Wheelock

John Wheelock was half a century older than me, so we were not close; that would have been, perhaps, inappropriate. But whenever we saw each other there was liking, and he would tell me things, important things, some of which were very personal, that influenced my life. Once he confided to a mutual friend, for example, that he could not understand how any young man, such as I then was, with a nice wife, and a healthy child, should wish to choose the uncertainties of the life of the free-lance writer. The comment pointed at him as well as me: he was wondering at the state of my *real* happiness, I suppose, which was fair enough, since I was not at all content with that woman, and he was also talking about his own past yearnings for children, which he had never been able to fulfill, though I believe he did raise a niece with the wife he married late in life.

It was typical of John to speak very personally and with immense restraint, from a very great distance, as though lurking somewhere beside himself at the luncheon table was his own caring and sensate double. He confided to me once that he had been practically sleepless for many, many years and was dependent on veronal, and when I seemed startled by such a confession issuing forth from so much dignified, almost soldierly restraint, he reached out his hand a little further onto the white table cloth as if to touch me, and by doing so assured me he meant me to know the confession was also a piece of advice. I was to do whatever was necessary to find a happy life for myself.

It was typical of my relationship with John that he discouraged me from writing poetry, after carefully going over an early manuscript, liking some poems mildly enough, not caring for others. But once I published a little book of poems some years later, he read all and wrote me a lovely letter of praise, carefully, in his trembling hand. John said he was getting very old, and feeble, and wanted me to know he admired my energy and curiosity.

We came to know each other when I was employed by WBAI as director of drama and literature. He taped several large hunks of his memoirs impromptu, I understand, for Eleanor Bruce, for whom he also recorded some poems and children's stories. After I became a Scribners author, I was reintroduced through my then editor, his successor, Burroughs Mitchell. For a while, about once every six months or so, he would invite me to have lunch with him at the old Midston House dining room on Madison Avenue.

Those luncheons meant much to me. John told me about his enduring friendships and passions. He insisted I must not grow impatient with myself; there was time, as his own career showed. He was generous and charming, always insisting that I drink a cocktail and wine with my meal, though he would not join me. He told me once he had to watch his intake of liquids very carefully because he carried an artificial bladder.

I came to know John's poems well by hearing him read them over WBAI and later reviewing them. His wonderful baritone voice was perfect for radio; the poems were full of ecstacy, and perception, at best, and glowed like embers. I admired what I thought he was doing, and for a while, imitated him, until I came to recognize that his persona was somehow not that appropriate to a tall, long-legged, manic Jewboy from New York such as myself, and started making my own very different poems, which he liked much better than the imitations.

I always felt John understood me, sometimes better than I cared to be understood. He was frightened by my big novel about a failed poet, *An Education in Blood*, when Scribners published it in 1970, but I think he recognized the character of the work, and did not entirely disagree, or disapprove: John knew too much about himself to do easy things like that. He was a man who had faced himself many times and could transcend pettiness of any sort.

He told me once his father had been the second best French hornist in the New York Philharmonic. A sad story. French hornists have chronic lip problems, so John's father waited in the wings to perform.

John was never second best. He had his own stature and a fierce truth he supposed about his ability to make poems from his experiences that others who cared as he did could enjoy. He was a craftsman, and a professional, and a poet. His career was so long and so varied, the enterprises so at odds with one another, seemingly, and the trials he had to endure so very real, it's probably hard not to think of him as trying all the time. That's why he impressed me so much; he did always try, and he was able, often, to be fair, if not just. He was the peer of all the fine writers he published and a friend to many. He was no snob; he had started his career as a bookstore clerk. He helped me to grow up—with his tolerance, his understanding, and his love.

WALKER EVANS

His voice was deep, resonant, from a region in his chest, a baritone. He smoked fancy cigarettes and dressed in elegant clothing,
waxed calf shoes from Peel Co., custom-tailored suits, fine white cloth
shirts. He sometimes wore what appeared to be gaiters on his arms to
keep his sleeves rolled back, and he was slight but thick-chested, with
a brisk walk, and a cane sometimes, or a furled black umbrella.

His face was dark from the sun and his features elfin, poised, regular. He looked directly at you as though you were posing for him and
kept his glasses stashed in a jacket pocket, almost like a lorgnette.
Glancing down at a script in a recording studio through his lenses, he
had the concentrated air of a watchmaker at work. His laugh was rich.
When he broadcast for me once he wore a green eyeshade.

I interviewed him for a sound documentary on James Agee, and
I suppose I was expecting someone as roughhewn as his friend Jim, so
I was not prepared for Walker's touches of elegance. His blue work-
shirts were of the finest chambray. (He told me once that Agee used to
extract his own abcessed teeth with his strong hands.)

Walker must have loved his friend Agee very much, for he said
when he went back many years later to visit the people in Alabama
they'd written about and photographed in *Let Us Now Praise Famous Men*,
he was very disappointed in how they'd all turned out. Now they were
just well-fed, middle-class rednecks living in trailer homes, in some
cases, with TVs and air conditioning. "I understand why they're like this
now," he said, "but it's still very depressing." I thought Walker must
have felt as a lover feels on returning to the sylvan place where he first
courted, only to find a honeymoon motel with waterbeds erected there.

Walker spoke of Agee loving nighttime best, when he could work
in great silence endlessly. As a photographer, he was, perforce, a day
person. The weather in his photographs is daytime weather, the light
unforced, natural. One knows the time of day, for flat early morning
light has invaded this side of a fading old barn.

He still had an office at *Fortune* when I knew him, and he seemed to have no feelings of discomfort about being a Luce editor. He told me I was to call and ask for him "around the shop" and they would know how to find him.

Walker lived in Old Lyme, had a central European wife much younger than he was, and seemed to have some doubts about that, though always expressed with subtle offhand rue. "If you call Old Lyme," he'd say, "you may not be able to reach anybody at all to leave messages, as she never seems to be around much during the day."

In the early sixties, personal answering machines were not commonly available. Once I called Old Lyme, and Walker was in his studio but responded with warm and persistent courtesies. This seemed habitual with him. "Yes, Richard, I'm pleased to hear from you. Tell me what can I do for you now?" he asked, for he had donated his time and writing to the Agee memorial and had given me personal introductions to Agee's drinking friend, Wilder Hobson, and to John Houston. I was truly grateful to Walker.

I said I had called to tell him the time and date of the broadcast.

"That's enormously considerate of you," he said.

I said his tape sounded wonderful and that his prose was wonderful to hear.

"I doubt if I'll be able to listen," he said, courtly. "It can be painful to remember. My wife doesn't like me indulging too much in the past tense. But I'll tell people, if you like. Mia, Jim's wife, friends of Jim."

I thanked him again.

Then Walker said, "I notice you're doing another broadcast about Hart Crane. I knew Hart in Brooklyn."

"Not so well as Jim?" I asked.

"I knew him a little," he insisted. "And it wasn't when he worked for a while at *Fortune*. I believe I met him elsewhere. We never were close. I don't think I liked him that well."

Since that time when I knew him briefly, I have always looked at one of his photos recalling Walker's baritone voice. I think of it as deeply southern, like the people he photographed in southern Alabama and cultivated, though I believe he was an Andover grad, a New Englander. His was the voice of a man larger than his size, a musical, sepia pronunciation, and sometimes a rich spitty sound like Art Pepper's or Lester Young's horns. It seemed to embrace words and fondle them with care and precision, complementing his brilliant steady hand and eye. I hear the dark registers of voice and light projected off his images as one: This is the barn, the weathered porch, a siding, a careworn man at rest.

To hear him reading passages from *Let Us Now Praise Famous Men* aloud, as I did a little while ago on archival tape, gives me thoughts about collaborations. The words Walker read were Agee's, but it seemed in Walker's voice they gained authority and fluency, were given grain and fiber and source.

If we were to meet in some future place, I don't think he would recognize me, but just a few words spoken, without catching sight of his face, and I would know I was in Walker Evans' company again.

RANDOLPH WICKER

A freshfaced young man presented his visiting card to me one day in the very early sixties at WBAI. He was dressed in a suit and tie and had his brown hair neatly combed back like a young salesman, and the card he produced from his attaché case was neatly embossed with black ink in a fine times roman:

> Randolph Wicker
> Director, Public Relations
> Homosexual League of America

Since I had never heard of such an organization I asked this person what he wanted.

"Call me Randy," he announced, puckishly, with a distinctly un–New York accent.

"Okay, Randy," I said. "What can I do for you?"

"I want to broadcast as a homosexual," he explained, straight-faced.

"About what?" I demanded.

"About being homosexual of course," he said.

Before I could say another word Wicker explained that though he was presently an organization of one he was hoping his league would grow exponentially if he got some attention from the press. But, I inquired, what did he have to tell our listeners?

Wicker directly replied that he'd recently heard a series of programs on WBAI from the BBC, the CBC, and other sources in which doctors, lawyers, and social workers discoursed on homosexuality, but there were no self-admitted homosexuals on any of these programs. Moreover, he pointed out, homosexuality was invariably treated in such programs as an offense, a disease, or a social problem, rather than as the way some perfectly healthy men and women related to each other and made love. What he wanted was to present homosexuality from the point of view of a more or less contented homosexual.

"Do you mean yourself?" I asked.

"Not necessarily," he pointed out, "but I have many friends who would be willing to talk about the way they live . . . and you could record them and broadcast the program unedited."

Believing that WBAI was created to broadcast alternative points of view I agreed without hesitation to Wicker's proposal, I think, to his great surprise; and within a few days I went with him one muggy summer evening to an apartment on the Upper West Side with my Nagra tape recorder and recorded a panel of four of his homosexual acquaintances.

The interview lasted one and a half hours, and was largely just what Wicker had hoped it would be: homosexuality from the point of view of the consumer. All of the four interviewees were articulate, educated professionals, one a political anarchist, and there was Randy, to boot; in those benighted days I agreed they could adapt pseudonyms to protect the little privacy they had allowed themselves to keep.

By today's standards of candor, I suspect, this program was a bit circumspect about discussing certain sexual acts, in order to appease the FCC. In other respects our conversation was really quite uninhibited. I served as interlocutor. We discussed whether homosexuality was a character disorder, a disease, a proclivity, talked about the various homosexual "lifestyles," though we didn't call them that, and about cruising, problems of fidelity, domestic role playing, sex roles, and other interpersonal situations relating to loving men. The participants were sometimes bitchy, sometimes crass, and sometimes funny, sad, winning, and sympathetic. As far as I know, "Live and Let Live," as we called this program, was the first uncensored and unmediated discussion of homosexuality to be broadcast by the mass media at prime time; and it called forth a variety of responses.

The *New York Times* critic Jack Gould called it an "important contribution to freedom of the airwaves," though he questioned the propriety of some of the remarks made by the participants. *Newsweek* devoted a feature article to the program as a breakthrough in broadcasting and understanding homosexuality. Jack O'Brien of the *Journal American* accused the station and me of obscene Communist invert propaganda.

It was used in an FBI investigation of the Pacifica Foundation's three FM radio stations, and eventually led—in conjunction with certain other programs broadcast by the station—to subpoenas of some of the personnel to appear before Senator Thomas Dodd's Senate Internal Security Subcommittee.

While the broadcast cost the station some problems such as the loss of a few subscribers and a lot of mail from hate groups saying we should be taken off the air, the public's response was favorable; it got Pacifica a large audience when it was eventually rebroadcast on all three stations. More important, I think, for people like Randolph Wicker it was the successful beginning of an effort, however naively articulated, to bring homosexuality out of the psychological closet and humanize those who happen to love men.

"Live and Let Live" was the first program of any length in which homosexuals were treated with the same respect when they talked about their lives as we commonly try to accord to other human beings. It helped create some of the dialogue that later made such talk possible in the mainstream media and television networks.

I believe Randolf Wicker also took part in some civil rights and peace demonstrations later in the sixties and seventies, but when I met him in the waiting room of WBAI with his little *carte de visite* he was still a very young man, probably still in his early twenties. I wonder what's become of his league? How he makes his living? Was that really his name? And how he survived the catastrophe of our era for men like himself—AIDS? He smiled a lot as I recall and never seemed bitter or meanspirited, but determined that people look at his little card and respond. A kind of optimistic huckster of self-respect.

Nowadays, I also think that he was a person of extraordinary courage and honesty for those days, and probably should be remembered among the minor cultural heroes of that interesting decade.

WILLARD TRASK

If he had not come to see me at WBAI one day and asked to read his translations of African poetry over the radio, I should not have known of Willard on my own. I was entirely in the dark that he had a reputation as a polymath and a translator and was even at that time, in the early sixties, engaged in translating the memoirs of Casanova, perhaps his greatest accomplishment, which won him a major literary prize.

There stood before me one day, chain smoking unfiltered cigarettes, in a handsome but frayed tweed sport coat, a man in his fifties with chiselled features in a weathered face and a leathery but melodious voice who said he would need at least an hour of our air time for his presentation, and possibly two or three, to do his radio anthology of the anonymous poetry of the various major language groups of the African continent.

"Are you a poet?" I asked.

"You could say. In a way. I work with literature," he replied.

He spoke like a discreet insurance investigator and kept himself well buttoned up emotionally. For all I knew, he could have been the CIA's disgraced former chief of station in Nairobi or Accra, or the Jamesian suitor of an American heiress of slightly insufficient means, but he was certainly well spoken in a careful and educated way, and when I asked if he did all the translating on his own, the man before me replied, "All except for the more exotic smaller West African language groups."

Trask's programs turned out to be very beautiful to the ear, amusing, and surprisingly witty and acerbic, occasionally ribald, but tastefully selected. In front of a microphone he sounded all the changes in his voice like a cellist performing an unaccompanied Bach suite.

We finally did, as I recall, three full-hour programs over a period of weeks, and the broadcasts were repeated many times. Trask had a voice of surpassing suppleness and range and baritone seductiveness, and he seemed to have a lot of time on his hands. He hung around the station chatting with the staff and flirting in an avuncular way with some of the younger women.

I was then producing a complete four-hour *Hamlet*, the entire text recorded early mornings before rush hour traffic above the boat basin around the turtle fountain in Riverside Park to simulate the sound of footsteps on the stone battlements of the castle at Elsinore, and my director, Arnold Tager, encouraged Trask to participate, which he seemed overjoyed to do. In that production in which Olympia Dukakis played the grave digger, Trask was the Player King, Fortinbras, Osric, Marcellus, and a few other cameos, and his line readings were elegant with striking intonation and moments of great oratorical power.

I was curious about Willard, but he didn't like to speak about his background or how he'd acquired so much erudition, and once when I dropped him off by cab at his flat above a store on one of the major East Side avenues, he seemed slightly embarrassed by the humbleness of his digs and raced from the cab, making no overture to offer me hospitality.

I've learned since his death more than a decade ago that Willard, like Casanova, had numerous inamoratas. There is, in fact, a certain class of Manhattan woman now in her late sixties, attractive, sophisticated, and on her own, who when I meet her at a party or some such, I am almost always certain to wonder if she was not one of Willard's lovers. I will simply ask, "Did you ever know a gentleman named Willard Trask?" and watch for the lingering grainy afterglow recede from their faces after all these years. Willard truly seemed to have made his way among the women of New York, and I have never heard any one of them speak bitterly about him.

But who he was and how he came to know so many African languages I was never able to discover. He had some small means and lived comfortably enough as a bachelor, I think. Once I asked him if he was related to the wealthy Trask family who had constructed Yaddo and later donated the mansion as an art colony in Saratoga Springs.

"I'm not related to anybody at all," he announced with that marvelous stentorian timbre. "I've never known what that's all about with certain people, but I've always been my own person."

Herbert Biberman

Herbert Biberman and Paul Jarrico were blacklisted Hollywood writers. Biberman was cited for contempt of Congress; Jarrico eventually went abroad to work in London and Paris. In the early fifties they produced the movie *Salt of the Earth*, a "socially conscious" product about the conflicts between Anglo and Mexican copper miners in a small southwestern town. It featured the proscribed actor Will Geer, with mostly supporting actors from the Mexican film industry, was funded in part by the "Communist dominated" Mine, Mill, and Smelter Workers Union, shot on location, processed and edited in Mexico and other places, and informally blacklisted throughout the United States when it was finally shown, except by certain theaters attended by the party faithful in New York, L.A., and Chicago. A couple of decades ago it had a revival and was shown by a lot of New Left groups on university campuses.

Salt of the Earth was not a successful work of cinema art, but its commercial failure had very little to do with its artistic shortcomings. It was, it seems, systematically victimized by nearly the entire motion picture industry, the major studios, the producers' associations, and the various craft unions. Biberman and Jarrico had a hard time getting technicians to work on the film and a harder time purchasing film stock. They could find no labs in the States who would develop their stock and synch up the sound, and no editing facilities were available for them to lease. A gentleman's agreement of the motion picture industry stipulated that people like Biberman and Jarrico were not to produce and distribute so-called "Communist-influenced" films. When they tried an end run around the monopolistic behavior of the Motion Picture Association by doing postproduction work in Mexico, they produced a scratchy, uneven negative.

Baseball players like Sal Maglie ran off south of the border to play ball and eventually got reinstated in the majors and played in the World Series. Not this pair: they couldn't even get work in semipro ball.

In the early sixties Biberman and Jarrico sued the motion picture industry, the major studios, and IATSE, the chief craft union, for restraint of trade in violation of the antitrust act in the federal courthouse before Judge Tyler. Sitting side by side in the courtroom like suitors overlooked by a marriage broker, they heard their pro bono lawyers outline the scope and detail of the so-called conspiracy, which they alleged flowed from a conference of certain industry types at the Waldorf Astoria Hotel. Chief counsel for the defendants was Irving Saypol, who, as U.S. Attorney, had tried and convicted the Rosenbergs for espionage. A hero of the cold war right wing, he red baited whenever possible.

I was one of the few members of the press in attendance throughout that long, rather dry, and boring process they'd brought about. The Lawyers Guild attorneys for Biberman and Jarrico were able to cite statements made by all the principals in their suit about blacklisting, but they were never able to show conspiracy in which all the principals had physically gathered in one room, or with documents, or on a conference phone and articulated for the record such a blacklisting policy. So Judge Tyler finally ruled, without a jury, that though he personally thought the plaintiffs certainly had every right to believe they and their film had been damaged, they were not able to prove conspiracy in restraint of trade.

When the verdict was delivered, I followed Biberman out onto the courthouse steps overlooking Foley Square and spoke to him. "Do I know you?" he challenged me. When I told him I'd been a spectator during the trial, he said he was "much obliged" that somebody had taken an interest in his grievance and invited me to chat with him awhile.

Biberman was a lean, dark man with a Barbara Streisand nose and a brooding Semitic face; he was as swarthy as Sal Maglie, with somewhat sharper features; in Hollywood he'd appeared in a number of Westerns as an Indian brave. He also wrote and directed a few wartime B pictures, for which he was very well paid at the time, including *The Master Race*, and *Nero Wolf*, and had married the tall, blonde actress Gail Sondergaard, who later became a camp idol because of her roles in some of the Frankenstein films.

Biberman was no longer an affluent person, but he still maintained a large rent-controlled apartment on West End Avenue quite near to where I lived, and he invited me up to that place for coffee or a drink.

It was the sort of place Hollywood might have used in a hamishe film noir about the murder of a J Edward Bromberg-type gangster or financier. The rooms were large, dark, dusty, ill-cared for, a decor of heavy satin drapes and oversized sofas and smoked mirrors. There was wall-to-wall carpeting of an indeterminate sorrel hue, like tschav, that seemed to have faded to beige, and, as I recall, a once fashionable stepdown living room. I imagined Ivy Litvinoff presiding over parties to raise funds for restoring a dam on the Dneiper River.

Biberman apologized for the state of his life in that place. He was presently batching it, as his wife was on the coast doing some sort of work, though she'd been blacklisted, too, for a while.

He assumed I must be a Party sympathizer, so he took for granted that I applauded his film, which I'd found under-produced, softcore neorealism for the most part. Initially we had little to say to each other. Mostly I sat like a big lamp finial with him in that cool, ill-lit decor and studied the dark, stolid features of this type who'd once played Sitting Bull and probably still patronized "the Sturgeon King," Big Chief Barney Greengrass.

After so many weeks of legalistic testimony and his own cross-examination on the stand, which had been articulate and dry but factual perforce, he looked as though he wished he could squeeze his brows together and cry a little; he seemed overwhelmed and in pain for having lost his case. He seemed in need of airing out, as musty and damp as the flat, while he insisted, truthfully enough, of course, that he'd always been a loyal progressive American, had violated no laws, and suffered immense penalties. The apartment seemed like the faded silver nitrate print of his former life as a Hollywood *maven*. Biberman made it plain he truly believed in seeking justice for himself and Jarrico through the courts and said he was hoping to convince his attorneys to appeal to a higher jurisdiction.

I had the feeling that Biberman would have liked to have had his case heard by a truly fair Hollywood jurist like Andrew Stone or Jean Hersholt, with pretty Marsha Hunt as his Portia, whereas having Judge Tyler was ordinary mediocre Wasp casting, unemotional, but correct.

I asked him what else he did nowadays aside from think about his case.

"That's just it," he told me. "There's very little I can do. I keep pretty much to myself but I have some old friends . . . and maybe there'll be some deals some day."

As we'd entered the building lobby I'd noticed the Joseph Weisman type in the raincoat who followed us in and sat down. Biberman said, "He only goes so far. He just sits in the lobby . . . the *shlub*."

"What does he want?" I asked when inside the dingy self-service elevator.

"Maybe he's seeing a dentist in my building." Biberman winked and shrugged. "An oral surgeon?"

Among those who were blacklisted but went on to make careers under front names or were eventually rehabilitated by the studios who were in need of their talents, Biberman would have seemed out of place. He had never been so talented that producers were willing to overlook his Party background. He'd been stubborn, a little self-absorbed, had never cooperated with his inquisitors, and never recanted. He still seemed to believe as he always had in the truisms of the CP Left, and seemed to have landed high and dry. No big new ideas flowed from his ordeal, and he was ineligible for redemption by this industry, ruled by completion bond companies and limited partnerships, which had destroyed the careers of people like him simply to head off congressional interventions.

That day in New York on West End Avenue, Biberman's subsequent enterprise as martyr of the domestic cold war, with Gwathmy-type paintings on the wall, was also coming to a close, simply ending with the drapes drawn, in a large rent-controlled flat with noisy, concealed radiators among smoked mirrors.

When I got up to leave him, he thanked me for all the time I'd put in on his trial and asked me to send him my piece when it appeared. I said I would. I glanced around this deconstruction of forties decorator prurience once more and asked what his life had been like when he was "really making it" in the film business.

"We had a good life," Biberman owned sadly, "but I never really made it. I was just a well-paid hireling, and then the witch-hunt came along, and they took away the work and the money, and, when we showed a little integrity, that's when they slapped Paul and me down hard . . . the liberals in particular, people like Mr. Dore Schary."

"And now?" I asked.

"I don't want to talk about now," he said.

I asked why he hadn't gone abroad to work as Jarrico had, and he indicated, like Sidney Carten, it was a far, far better thing he did by remaining in the States.

"Paul was from a more or less well-to-do background," he pointed out. "I was an American. What would I have done with myself in Paris?"

He shrugged again, as if by habit. Biberman had been a screenwriter for a while, so I asked if he intended to write something about his case or his career. "Why not?" he responded. Then, "Who really cares anymore?"

He just seemed so beaten, his last great hopes for legal vindication vanquished. A mediocre talent martyred to his politics and a less than brilliant film.

"I don't dream Hollywood no more," he told me.

With different politics and the same mediocre talents he could have ended up a wealthy studio executive, a producer like Ray Stark, who had the good sense to marry the daughter of Fanny Brice and then continued to share in the good life of Hollywood. Biberman was no dreamer, no idealist, and no genius. But that really never stopped anybody from getting rich in this country.

WILLIAM BUTLER

Bill Butler's fiction is hardly known in this country, or in England, where he was most often published by Peter Owens, though he wrote and published about a dozen novels and many stories here and abroad during the sixties and early seventies. Most of his adult years he lived as an expatriate in Japan, working as a teacher of English and a cartoonist and setting many of his novels in the Japanese landscape. "I have to be away from this place," he used to say, grimly.

The Japan Butler depicts in his fiction has little to do with tea ceremonies and other such exotica. *The House of Akiya* is about the dissolution of an Occidental marriage in a haunted cottage on a hillside above the sea where a lonely, equally obsessed American couple have come to rusticate for a while. *The Ring of the Meiji* is an ambitious historical fiction about the modernization of Japan. Though he grew up on the North American West Coast and lived in and around the radical community in Berkeley, California, was an early member of the staff of poet Lewis Hill's "listener-sponsored" Pacifica (Radio) Foundation (KPFA-FM), Bill Butler rarely wrote fiction about Americans living in the continental United States. He thought most of his countrymen were conformists, and hypocrites, middle-class sellouts, and American power a menace to the rest of the world, though shortly after the assassination of President Kennedy he published a moving dirge for the fallen leader in *Harper's*.

No matter where he hung his hat, I suspect, it was hard for Butler to forget a bitter childhood growing up in Portland, Oregon. If he never would talk about his family, his pained grimace when the subject came up was enough to divert the conversation. Though a sympathetic listener, he was also usually dismissive of other peoples' personal problems. He had a small reputation as a promising writer in England, and one of his novels was reprinted twenty-six times in paperback, but he was not a brand name. For a while he claimed he even managed to avoid paying income taxes. Very nearly invisible back home, he seemed to prefer it that way, owning very little and living with what he could hold inside an old suitcase during his often lengthy stateside visits.

He'd been in and out of the country so much over the years that I sometimes thought the America he imagined as his nemesis was almost entirely invented to block his recollection of stultifying banalities and stifling but ordinary lower-middle-class proprieties. But he never acted out like some bohemians; Bill's manners were curt, dismissive, but always *correct, as* though he knew the *punctilios of* the middle classes he despised and was subtly parodying them, so subtly his contempt wasn't always detected. In some of his most starkly-imagined fictions the settings are also deliberately abstract, or barely alluded to. An early story published in the *Paris Review* shows a figure climbing the glass facade of an office building which could just as easily be modern-day Tokyo as San Francisco, or New York, where he also was employed for a while by Pacifica at WBAI, the New York affiliate. *A Dialogue of Two Friends on a Sandy Beach* is a dramatization of an assassination conducted by one "friend" against another with the politeness and diffidence one associates with Asian codes of behavior. There's a scary allegory of childhood set in suburban America that is similar to *Lord of the Flies*, which Butler called *The Butterfly Revolution* and dedicated to a former president of the Pacifica Foundation, and there's an allegorical account of his days at Pacifica, *The Experiment*, which suggests the real life suicide of founder Lewis Hill after a staff revolt, though here again the external setting is of more significance than the unspecified interiors of the institute or foundation where the action occurs.

None of Butler's books had such great commercial success. No movie adaptations, no TV. In the main he was respectfully reviewed and dismissed. He would not deign to review other mens' books, never went to literary parties. Sometime in the seventies he appears to have stopped writing for publication; though some of his books, including *Akiya*, are still listed in print, his books are hard to find.

When he died of a heart attack in the fall of 1992, Butler had been living for some years in Allentown, Pennsylvania, with his dead sister's husband, Dale Miner, a former network news writer who was also an alumni of Pacifica. The grief I felt on learning of Bill's death in Pennsylvania was conflicted by a sense of weird dislocation, for I had long since consigned this wanderer to a category of old comrades who would never make their peace with this society. He seemed alienated from ties to people and places here, a lonely man who was too proud to compromise, make friendships, allies. He had powers of concentration way beyond my own or those of any person I'd ever known, could

work thirty hours straight on the air without a break, producing original live music segues and montages, mixing two and even three
recordings over and under each other at the same time, and then stop
and drink coffee and play the piano a while and seem refreshed.

I believed once Bill was almost certainly a genius and also truly
enlightened, with a sense of mission surpassing crass literary ambition. In fact, when I last saw him in the early eighties in New York,
over dinner, and he told me he was going to South Africa to teach at a
small black college in the Transkei, I felt diminished for my petty concerns with paying bills and trying to live with a woman. My friends
tell me Bill never left America after that visit, never went to South
Africa, and during his last years was calling himself by his dead sister's name, Elizabeth, and dressing in women's clothing.

I know of two Butler marriages. A woman of whom he spoke
with some anger was the mother of his son, Sigmund, whom he later
raised in New York, England, and Japan. Bill was still married to her
when we first met in New York, though he never cared to introduce us.
When I asked about her later on, she'd gone off elsewhere; he would
always be vague about what had happened and why she'd left him,
but occasionally he would hint that she was a deeply withdrawn and
disturbed person.

In the late 1960s I convinced Bennington College to hire Bill as a
teacher of literature. He was unhappy in rural Vermont and soon fell
in love with one of his students, a devout Anglo Catholic for whom he
underwent a religious conversion before they eloped to Europe. When
they later separated and divorced in Japan, this woman also had had
a child by Bill, I was told, but, insofar as I know, he had little contact
with his second-born beyond infancy.

In *The God Novel*, one of his last published books, Butler interrupted his italicized stream of consciousness narration, which was set
in and around the Croatian port of Rijecka, to interject a quote in bold-
face from Alfred North Whitehead:

> The worship of God is not a rule
> of safety—it is an adventure of
> the spirit, a flight after the
> unattainable. The death of religion
> comes with the repression of the
> high hope of adventure.

William Butler was also a jazz pianist and a classically trained
musician, a sound recording engineer and sound mixer of surpassing

skills, and one of the most engaging men I've ever known, though when I glance over what I have of his published writings, the scenes and monologues fail to sustain my interest for longer than a few pages at a time. They are written with a great deal of skill and intellectual rigor, are often projective of strange ways of being, like the best science fiction, and seem almost entirely devoid of the ordinary and of what James called "felt life." So well done they often seem synthetic, with no seams showing, no intentions misapplied, and just slightly invulnerable—as though defending themselves from a pain even more intense than they could deal with by the putting on of certain intensely alienated airs, just as in person Bill sometimes would squint and cast his voice upward toward a falsetto tone half mockingly, as though translating his thoughts into English from stage Japanese.

We met in New York in the early sixties after Butler was sent from California by the foundation to rescue its newest acquisition, WBAI-FM, from revisionists such as me who were employed at the station which had been donated to it by the CEO of Kimberly Clark, Louis Schweitzer. Management in New York had grown rigid and paranoid, and while some of the talent on staff who had been hired on were determined, with limited resources, to maintain a very high quality of intellectual standards and on-the-air performances, this was somewhat contradictory to the more ideologically motivated behavior of our parent station in Berkeley. We found many of their program offerings naive and pretentious agitprop, and they found ours as slick and superficial as on other good *music* stations of the period. After we'd rejected a slew of program offerings and Pacifica directives, the foundation sent along old Pacifica hand Bill from Japan to be program director and station manager, usurping a rigidly controlling management in order to inspire us to perform on behalf of what we all then called "the movement," that coalition of antiwar, civil rights, and other dissident groups just coming into prominence.

It was easy to like this newcomer, because he was no vegetarian peace-mongering holy roller, but a tough-minded and sardonic literary man who knew the history of the foundation from its inception and where all the family ghosts were hiding out. One of his first acts was to remove the internal monitoring system of bugs through which the previous manager had tried to eavesdrop on staff conversations. After a while, we started to collaborate on documentaries, my studio and fieldwork mixed by Bill's sophisticated musical imagination, and then for a while we were very close. I was one of the only staffers to whom Bill confided his requited passion for one of the station's producers, a married woman, and though Bill almost always remained a partisan of the official Pacifica line that the United States was the world's one great warmonger, he soon realized, as we had earlier, that for the sophisticated New York market it might be more efficacious to entertain than to lecture to the converted at the top of your voice.

He was relatively tall, thin, and wiry. His light brown hair had many strands of gray, and his face was lean and weathered by cares. He had an intense gray stare and a deep soft voice, a good clear radio sound. He had long, delicate fingers, and he dressed like an off-duty businessman, in white shirts and dark trousers. He was a heavy smoker. Bill was much influenced by the writings of Samuel Beckett, and there was also a physical resemblance of leanness and durability, a severity which he would only occasionally soften with a smile. He had bad teeth, and he ate and drank abstemiously.

During one of the first programs we worked on together, which was a montage of voices about the last days of boredom and excess before the suicide of the American poet Hart Crane, Bill made me very aware that his commitments were different from my own. "You know," he said, glancing up from his control board, "so much self-pity is typically American. I keep wishing one of these so-called friends of the poet would shake him and say, 'Stop all this nonsense.'"

He was a great admirer of the disciplined Japanese, and long before it was fashionable to mouth such things Bill was hailing Japan for its industrial and educational innovations. As a single father, he was also very appreciative of Japan's day care arrangements. Bill seemed to think his homeland was falling way behind Japan's infrastructure and technological adaptiveness; we were doomed to be wasteful, fat, and sluggish; the Japanese knew better how to organize social resources and economic priorities. After I resigned from WBAI and started publishing my novels with Burroughs Mitchell of Scribners, I talked Burroughs into reading some of Bill's work—which he admired—and publishing some. Burroughs did not have an easy time convincing Scribners to publish Bill's works, because the commercial possibilities seemed small, and those that were commercially most promising lacked copyright protection, due to the negligence of his British publisher, Peter Owen Ltd., which had never applied for U.S. copyright, as the law required, at the time of their publication in the United Kingdom. Eventually, though, a few of Butler's novels were published in small editions, and with a special brief preface by Butler in one instance that could be protected. Of *The House at Akiya* John Leonard—another old Pacifica hand who was then a daily reviewer for the Times—wrote, "Sentences written in smoke, of words falling down in mind like dark stones dropped into a pool of clear water. A sort of hypnosis results: the house itself becomes a novel; the reader, an occupant and prisoner." I also reviewed *Akiya*, which in those days I considered Bill's masterpiece, for *Commonweal*.

I think Bill was more than a little disappointed by his long-delayed debut for his American readers. It was better not to be known at all than to be given such a skimpy share of recognition. He confessed to me that Scribners had been no help at all, and though he thanked me for being concerned about his career, he said I failed to comprehend the advantages of his invisibility, that he did not regard himself as an American writer, but a world citizen, with affinities beyond our provincial literary logrolling scenes.

We never had a disagreeable falling out. When Bill ran away from Bennington with his new wife, I heard from him for a while, and then there were no more letters, and I rarely heard about him from old friends. But once, as I've mentioned, about seven years ago, he came back to New York, allegedly a stopover on his way to South Africa. I made a special trip in from Stony Brook to have dinner with Bill. It was a most unhappy encounter, though there was no open acrimony. The United States was engaged in counterrevolution throughout the world, we both now agreed, to defend an economy that could not compete otherwise. I had recently returned from Central America, having witnessed both the Nicaraguan revolution and the counterrevolution that followed it quickly, but Bill was quite dismissive of my experiences. He was convinced that Asia and Africa were going to be the places of confrontation between a retrograde America and the future of the rest of the world. When I tried to question him about his writing he avoided the subject. When I asked by whom he would be employed and how that had come about, he was openly hostile.

I was now the father of a second daughter, a four year old, and very involved with her childhood. Bill dismissed this as misguided sentimentality. Either I was lying to myself or hiding out from life in the suburbs with my new wife and child. I left the restaurant thinking my old friend was desperate, now that his son was an independent young adult, to find a cause to which he could attach himself.

I also think the shock I experienced when I learned of Bill's reclusion and death in Pennsylvania was that of déjà vu. Bill had always seemed genuinely, entirely American to me, as stoical as a parson from the "burnt over" regions of upper New York State. He had a powerful melancholy and considerable intolerance of mere playfulness. He also seemed able to exist for long periods of his life without female company. Though I thought I loved my friend, I was also wary of him, and fearful. He seemed driven and to have taken on all the chores of a literary career without any of the compensatory rewards. I'd like to know more about his return to the States, but I'm not convinced there's more to be known. Intent on hiding out, he first chose exile, and, after his son was grown and on his own, returned to bury himself in his own backyard, without ever, to my knowledge, reaching out to his old friends and colleagues.

His aloneness was always so reliable to him that we had all become—like the family about whom he would never speak—distasteful reminders of other possibilities, which he had always determinedly fled.

He was the loneliest man I'd ever known, and, through long, hallucinatory sessions at the typewriter, he'd once been able to assert his identity as a writer quite apart from that loneliness. It was the mark he would put on the world about him. When the world still refused to cooperate by honoring his mark with praise and money, his identity became more and more contingent, a conjecture between Butler and the void. In Allentown funeral services for Bill were held at a Protestant church; he'd never been a churchgoer. (I did not attend. What was there to see or say? To whom?) Most of Bill's novels and stories reeked of death. He seemed to be anticipating his own dissolution almost all the time I knew him. There is now no way anybody can reach out to him anymore.

MORRIS RENEK

In the late 1950s Morris Renek wrote and later published a comic novel about the divorce racket in New York, *The Big Hello*. In those days adultery was one of the only grounds for divorce in the state. Unhappily married men and women used to hire stand-ins to fake transgressions with them in hotel rooms. There'd be staged interruptions by witnesses briefed on what would transpire who could document all that was allegedly going down later in a court of law.

A copy of *The Big Hello* was sent to me at WBAI, and I enjoyed this New York comedy of inappropriate remedies, sleazy accommodations, and inept "adulterers" so much I arranged to have Morris read serialized installments from the novel over the radio.

He was very hard up at the time, with a wife and two young children to support. Just about the only income he had seemed to come from a German edition of *The Big Hello*. Though the novel was very New York Jewish, it was a hit in Deutchland.

When I finally met Morris he seemed small, strongly put together and round-faced; he could have been a hearty peasant supernumerary in a Pudovkin agricultural film saga. He smiled a lot as though taking pleasure in his own benevolence, and I will always recall the intense brightness of his eyes and that easy smile which was unabashed and fulsome, never just wry or ironic. He spoke with a somewhat hoarse voice, as though on the verge of tears, or some sort of joyful but harsh exclamation.

Morris was self-educated and tough-minded, a combat vet of World War II, who had been a shrimp fisherman in South Carolina and a part-time student at the University of Chicago. He wrote of hard-edged lives, people so real for being in life they had their own lingos. Like Saul Bellow's people, his characters were great knowers, but they were kept away from intellectual and academic pursuits. Morris wrote dramatic novels, not essays on Neitsche. He was in the middle of writing a second book, and occasional TV plays on spec, and I put him to work reviewing books for WBAI which led to his doing the same for the *Nation* and the *New Republic* and elsewhere for pay.

We became friends and would often meet for lunch. I had a small expense account and could occasionally treat Morris. Even on those occasions, he was very frugal. A thinly sliced lettuce and tomato sandwich on fresh rye bread and a glass of borscht was Morris' luncheon of choice, it seemed. He was getting by on what he could earn from writing, and when he made a sale sometimes the money had to last for weeks. His wife, Ethel, was also a frugal housekeeper, but she always managed to set an ample table when I was invited to their flat in public housing in the Dyckman section of Manhattan for lunch. Their household was always cheerful, no matter that they didn't have all the comforts and *chochkes* of affluence.

Morris had grown up in a tenement in Williamsburg, so he probably didn't find living in public housing a comedown. He and Ethel had friends in the projects who were people of color. Their politics were unpretentiously left wing, part genuinely radical and part CP-style "progressive." Morris knew some African American intellectuals, and sympathetic white journalists such as Oliver Pilot; he admired Izzy Stone, and, for a while, was taken up by the novelist Irwin Shaw whenever he came to town. His lifelong friend was an Italian photojournalist for *Look* magazine with whom he'd served as a GI during the war.

Morris and Ethel Renek seemed deeply mated and comfortable with each other. There was, I always sensed, genuine respect. They shared the same big, unabashed smiles. They were loving people. Morris was not a chaser, but he seemed to respond to the company of glamorous women. When they moved up to the more prosperous Riverdale section of the Bronx for a while to a duplex, the walls were so thin that their stuffy orthodox Jewish neighbors complained about the noise of their frequent and enthusiastic love-making, and they were so appalled they moved elsewhere.

Morris was the single most dedicated novelist I ever encountered. He would finish one novel and then start another. He was always at work for six and seven hours every day of the week and could not be disturbed, and when he was not writing, he was reading works of abstruse literature and history and doing research. He went to bed very early and was up by dawn. New York City was his scene; he wrote about it as a savvy insider. One of his later novels was about the corrupt nineteenth-century Tweed ring and so-called reformers like Samuel Tilden, and in another an executive in a big corporation led a murderous double life. He was respected but not easily published, admired but impoverished. For a while, he and I both wrote for extra scratch for *Cavalier*, a girly magazine edited by a toff named Fred Birmingham that gave over some of its pages to fiction and journalism by genuine writers for pay and paid us with review copies of books we could sell as well as fees.

Once Morris took employment, writing news for CBS. The money was astounding to somebody who was getting by on so very little, and he was greatly admired and promoted, but he quit after a while. He thought the work was idiotic and the news people all whores and sellouts.

Morris was very helpful to me; he read my poems and gave me honest feedback. He was encouraging without ever putting me on. Over the years we were mutually supportive friends. I trusted Morris. We spoke on the phone often when he wasn't working. I introduced him to people I knew, and he taught me a lot about writing close to the bone and got me to reread some of his favorite writers, such as Dickens and Conrad and Henry Miller. When Notre Dame invited me to teach Jewish studies for a semester, and gave me a budget to invite Jewish writers to talk and read, Morris was the first person on my list to get an invitation. He came to South Bend from New York by overnight railway coach.

Morris could put up with hardships like that for the sake of economy. That he probably harbored some contempt for me because I'd had such a pampered middle-class upbringing I only came to know after a while when I started to write about the scapegoating and cruelty in my family. Morris made it clear that he regarded this as being more than a little self-pitying. In some respects, I thought I was probably more disadvantaged than he had been. I'd been given an early education in self-loathing, whereas he'd been free to go out into the world on his own and take his chances. Morris was strong and not easily intimidated. He was pleased to have me as a fan and supporter, but his standards were so very high I never quite seemed to live up to his expectations, though he never quite explained why.

Like many strong men, Morris seemed to disapprove of what he construed as weakness in others. He told me once that in Williamsburgh where he grew up teachers held out so little hope for their students that they just handed out comic books for them to read in class and didn't bother to teach at all.

Once, some years later, out of the blue, he also asked me to return all his letters he'd written to me, which I did, though I never knew why he asked me to do so. When I insisted that he explain, he became very cross with me.

A year or so after that, the Guggenheim Foundation contacted me because Morris had put my name down as a recommender for a fellowship. I wrote a very positive letter on his behalf, but Morris was out of the running. He lacked truly influential friends and supporters.

It is not hard for me to praise Morris even now. His works are not sufficiently appreciated; he's a serious popular novelist who lacks a popular audience. One of his novels, *Siam Miami*, about a working woman in showbizz, could have made a great movie. Morris calls himself "a fighter," and I guess money people pick up on his hostility to the prevailing moneygrubbing bullshit and they don't want to promote it. In all the years I've known him he has never given up on himself. I wish he had such high opinions of others. Obviously, compared to his own, others' struggles pale.

Serious dedicated writers like Morris are, necessarily, self-centered. They live inside a saga they have created out of their efforts to reproduce and depict experience as vivid, gritty, and real, and they are often self-absorbed by their own myths. I continue to admire Morris for his determined stance and hard labor; I sometimes wonder if he feels the same way about me.

Literary friendships are easily diluted with contempt. Your friends are your peers, chums; even when they happen to be fans, too, they don't want to be public servants. I've come to that point in my life when I can't pretend to help Morris anymore, and he really can't help me. In the poignancy of that situation there is also some necessary hard-won candor at last.

ALFRED KREYMBORG

I met Alfred Kreymborg in the early sixties in New York when I was working on a sound portrait of Sherwood Anderson for Pacifica Radio.

I must confess I knew very little about the man who called me one day on the phone at WBAI and told me he was a poet and play-write, a former editor of the famous annual *American Caravan*, with Van Wyck Brooks, Lewis Mumford, and Paul Rosenfeld, and an old friend of Anderson from the twenties and thirties and had a lot of memories to share about him.

I didn't know Kreymborg's poems and plays, once highlights of the bohemian literary world in New York; and I didn't know of his connection to Hart Crane, William Carlos Williams, Edmund Wilson, Louise Bogan, Morley Callaghan, and so many others whose reputations have survived.

I was desperate to find people from that period with their memories intact and had placed a query in the *New York Times Book Review*, and when I met with Kreymborg at a Greenwich Village cafe a few days after his phone call I'd only done sufficient research to observe that his work was still in certain little-used anthologies, like that of Edna St. Vincent Millay, a has-been perhaps, but possibly with a great sense of recall. He told me that first and only encounter that he'd had drinks with Wallace Stevens at a cafe "on this very corner sometime in 1926 or 27."

It was a humid summer afternoon, and he was perspiring heavily, a man with glasses and a wilted brown mustache who presented himself to me as having been very much overlooked, like an old family ghost.

"I knew all of the greats at one time or another," he explained, "Pound and Hem and Red Warren and Marianne Moore. I knew them all, and Gen Taggard and Gene O'Neil, Fitzgerald and Nathan Asch, and Dreiser and Max Bodenheim."

Though slightly undifferentiated, his was a potential treasure trove to be sure; but he also seemed slightly ungenerous, grudging. He refused strong drink and looked unhealthy, precisely in the way some alcoholics appear to be when they are off the stuff. His clothing was decently rumpled and casual, but stained, as though he hadn't changed outfits in days, and was just coming off a bender. He wore a pale blue seersucker summer jacket, which he removed and hung over the back of his chair, a white dress shirt with short sleeves, an old glen plaid tie, and very baggy brown trousers, and he smelled of lack of sleep, that sour odor, and stale sweat, perhaps fecal matter.

"I suppose you've heard how Sherwood died," he said, "aboard the ocean liner?"

And indeed I had heard of the toothpick swallowed with a canape that punctured Anderson's intestines and led to peritonitis.

"He hadn't done anything good in years," Kreymborg added then. "*Tarr* was an abomination, boorish, over-written."

"I suppose so," I said. "Do you still write?"

"Of course," Kreymborg said, "but I must caution you. I'm very much passed over."

"I wouldn't be surprised," I said.

"No need to flatter me," he said. "I had a fine career and a full life as a poet, as an editor, and I had many wonderful love affairs."

He jutted out his jaw a little at me, and his weak chin trembled, and at that moment I was reminded of the movie actor Clifton Webb who could be so prissy and malevolent at the same time. There was a way in which their fine almost feline features were similar, only Kreymborg's were a good deal softer, less photogenic, a bank clerk's face, less affected than the movie actor's putting on of airs. He seemed to have no need to impress me as anything very much except a survivor of his own talents. He was old and had hit bottom, and it really wasn't so terrible, he seemed to be saying, just so long as you could get somebody to offer to pay for the drinks and you weren't thinking all the time about who you once were.

"I published Sherwood very early on," he said, "and others too. Hart Crane as I recall."

"How fantastic!" I exclaimed.

"You know I really wasn't very crazy about either of their writings," he said, "but I knew they were different, and I sort of felt an obligation to discover new and different writers."

"Very brave of you," I said.

"It gets to be a tic after a while," he said. "You just can't do it any other way. I wrote my fellow editors once that we were "digging the earth for enduring nutriment.""

"Where was that?" I said.

"It was a sort of dedicatory poem," he explained, "in an issue of *Caravan* dedicated to Steiglitz, the photographer."

"About your own work," I said.

"There's a lot if it," he said, "and you just can't gloss over it, as with some. The only way you can get my drift is to read a lot and slowly from my different periods in one or more long sittings."

He turned his pale face and stubborn jaw to face me then. "Would you care to try sometime?"

I knew he was testing me, and, if I failed to respond to his desperation, he would be less than generous about Anderson. But this really wasn't part of our deal, and I refused to be intimidated.

"Right now," I said, "I haven't really got that much time. I'm on deadline."

"Maybe later," he said.

"I hope so," I replied.

We were both being unnecessarily coy. Kreymborg didn't really have much time left for himself either, and he'd not failed to take in my message.

"It's really alright," he said and blinked. "Your loss." I could tell he was very hurt. "Nobody has much time for anything anymore," he added.

But he said nothing more than that and that afternoon recorded some recollections of Anderson and Horace Liveright, the publisher, in Virginia and in New York, for my documentary.

When we parted company, later that afternoon, he asked me if I was also a writer.

"I'd like to be," I said. "I'm still learning a lot."

"Yes, you still have a lot to learn," he said, bitterly, and left me standing in the studio, and some time later I learned he had died.

Ambition is almost always cruel. When I was young I could not imagine myself in Kreymborg's shoes someday. Now, past middle age, with so many books written I still care about and only a few still in print, I know the feeling of being overlooked.

So I just wish I had taken the time out of a life pointed only one way to try to read some of that poor sad man's poems. There might have been a few worth salvaging.

Kreymborg always seemed to have understood the wager he had made and lost on his own talent. "Superhuman vistas," he once wrote, "dwarf each dogged man . . . stranger and friend . . . striving to encompass the Brobdingnagian."

DOUG WARD: PEERS AND TEARS

The actor-playwright Douglas Turner Ward, founder of the Negro Ensemble Theater, and I once collaborated on a radio production of two short plays featuring that funny fat man Godfrey Cambridge. The entire production was under the superb technical direction of my good friend Gene McGarr, who is now one of the most successful voice-over men in the business; in those, days he was driving a cab in New York and learning the business with me, on a hands-on basis.

Gene and I always worked well together and with pleasure, as we did with Douglas, who was a very pleasant guy and easy to get along with. It was the sixties, when African American professionals like Godfrey Cambridge and Doug were looking for exposure. We held nightly rehearsals and two or three runthroughs before we finally got around to making a recording.

One play, *Day of Absence*, was a farce about a small southern town which wakes up one day with all its blacks having vanished. Naturally, there's nobody else who can do the *shlep* work, and the result is chaos.

One evening during rehearsal three young girls were murdered in Birmingham, Alabama, and the atmosphere in the studio was tense and morose. Doug Ward, who was very large and very handsome, was angry, upset, but after a while couldn't see much sense in long-distance grieving. When we took a coffeebreak, he abruptly declared he wished it was a weekend night. "Why?" I asked. "Because," he declared, "me and all these other dudes could hop the A train to West Fourth Street, as there's bound to be lots of guilt pussy all over Greenwich Village after an incident like this."

In those days Godfrey Cambridge was just on the cusp of making it very big in Hollywood. He was great fun to work with, a very sensitive and easy fellow. Our studio equipment kept breaking down, but Godfrey never complained. Once he had serious indigestion and couldn't stop hiccuping. Every time we tried to do a take, Godfrey hiccuped. For a while I thought maybe he was putting me on, so I went in the studio and asked what was the problem. Godfrey said he really couldn't control himself from hiccuping. I went and got a paper cup and told him to drink from the far rim only. Godfrey had really funny body language, and trying to slurp from a little cup out of the rim furthest from his mouth was a whole number for him. Pretty soon he was spritzing water all over the studio, but, when he took five to get himself together, there were no more hiccups.

If he had lived, I believe Godfrey would have been right up there with people like Bill Cosby. He was divinely touched, a real fool, silly and gentle and funny and smart, and he loved to work. Godfrey was always learning new things. He used to entertain me between takes with Shakespearian soliloquies in falsetto.

"I watch you," he told me once, "and I think you're just as funny. Always stepping on your johnson. I mean no offense, but you're not meant for little rooms."

He was right, of course: fat Godfrey had far more grace than a tall, lean fellow such as I was in those days. I'd sit down at the Collins board and all the lights would short out. That's why Gene McGarr was such a help.

He'd just returned from a couple of years in Spain, was broke, goodlooking, quickwitted, ruthless to get ahead. Gene spent some weeks with a bunch of junkies on the Lower East Side and recorded what's probably the best radio documentary ever made on the addict's experience, predating some of Burroughs' writings. He was a quick learn and pretty soon sounded like an experienced radio man and knew how to mix and cut tape with the best union engineers. Gene introduced me to Bill Kennedy and Hunter Thomson. He had a big Irish setter, and he named him Hunter, too. He has been my friend now twenty years, and I don't know, drunk or sober, if I ever had a better one. The son of a New York City cop who was so gentle he refused to carry a gun and therefore was given the wilds of Staten Island to patrol on foot, Gene once told me "going to Delahanty" was the lower-middle-class Irish Catholic aspiration foremost in his neighborhood in Queens: "You were set for life," he pointed out. "The police . . . the civil service . . . anything was possible then."

Gene went to Cornell on a football scholarship, and nowadays, though we are parted by a continent, I can turn on the radio and there he is, the voice on the searing edge of some shlock sales pitch, honeying, mellifluous, resonant but accurate.

When the *New York Review of Books* was founded during a newspaper strike, Elizabeth Hardwick and Jack Thompson came on the air over WBAI to plug their new project. In the next studio a perennial left deviationist commentator named Irwin Edelman was thundering on about the true meaning of Marx's philosophical papers of the 1840s.

Our studios were fabricated with Swiss cheese soundproofing. Every time Elizabeth Hardwick spoke about the intellectual sophistications *NYRB* hoped to bring to book reviewing in the United States, Edelman would bellow forth some Marxian argot as though in counterpoint. Irwin didn't really seem to believe microphones could pick up his voice, but he was earlier in his career very courageous and original in trying to save the Rosenbergs from execution. He used to shout into the box like Maurice Schwartz playing Hamlet. I used to call his tapes "the negation of the negation."

In a like manner, a number of the talks I produced during that period have occasional moments of feedback from Archie Shepp, who was playing scales on his alto, accompanied by Bill Davidson on piano, in the main studio.

One of the WBAI volunteers was a tall, thin Texan named Stoop, who claimed to be producing, in rather desultory fashion, a series on the art of country yodeling. He had all manner of Swiss bell ringers and longhorn recordings from the Pecos which he kept feeding into the Collins board, and he really hung around the place a lot. A nice-mannered man with gap teeth. One had no reason to doubt he was exactly who he said he was. Turned out he was, though he was also making his expenses as a paid informant for the Federal Bureau of Investigation. When I confronted him with this, Stoop was quick to admit he'd been "funning us," in his words, but he'd been "funning the Bureau too."

Stoop was paid on a piecework basis for spying on us, so he claimed he made up most of the stories he told the Bureau, and he claimed he always made them up pretty wide of the mark. Maybe that's why the FBI file I received from the Bureau, after applying under the Freedom of Information Act, was mostly blacked out.

Aside from the impudence of talking about myself constantly in these memoirs, I'm trying to set things down about others I've known as stories because it seems fairly obvious to me that my boldest observations may seem like mere platitudes in the decades after my death.

There was, for example, a Russian exchange student from Columbia University who used to hang around WBAI a lot. His name, as I recall, was Oleg. He was much older than most of us, wore his hair in a Joe College crewcut, dressed in sweaters and slacks and penny loafers. Very collegial, undidactic, friendly. Spoke English with a studied American accent and never seemed to push any line at us beyond peace and civil rights. Friendship among people. He had a wide range of supposed cultural interests: jazz, the blues, the Beats.

I never learned why he liked hanging out so much at our tiny station when he would have been welcome at the networks. He claimed to be studying our culture, which he knew better than most. Years later, after Gorbachev, it came out Oleg was the KGB resident in New York.

Some Pacifica alumni, such as Fred Haines, became accomplished writers for the screen and remain close to me thirty years later. Others stayed with the media and now staff NPR and Public Television news and public affairs programs. Few of those whom I admired were aware of my literary concerns and character. Perhaps they only saw in me a liberal, or, in Stendhal's words, "an exaggerated sentimentalist."

Crime writer Anthony Boucher produced a weekly program of antique operatic recordings from our Berkeley studios called "Golden Voices." Kenneth Rexroth recorded all of his autobiography on a home tape recorder in the Berkeley Hills. It sounded awful, but Rexroth complained bitterly when John Leonard edited out some of his burps and pauses. John also brought Pauline Kael on the air to review movies long before she got work with the *New Yorker*.

I first bumped into Nelson Algren, Jonathan Miller, and John Coltrane in the Pacifica studios. I got a second education there. So, in the words of one of Stoop's favorite country singers, Eddie Arnold, "Adios, pretty Ozark Fräulein."

ROBERT LOWELL: A LIFE STUDY

In 1961 I produced a sound montage for WBAI entitled "The Last Days of Hart Crane." Intercut from tape-recorded interviews and monologues of people who had been close to the poet during his last year of life, including the woman who had been on the boat with Crane on the day he committed suicide, this compact forty-five-minute "life study" expressed some of the pathos of Crane's increasing desperation, the weird unruliness of his last episodes, his boredom, his neediness, his lack of self-esteem, his growing dependence on unreliable friends and lovers. It was told, almost exclusively, in the voices of those to whom Crane had confided, or with whom he had been caught off guard—voices telling their story, almost as if they were struggling to the surface after being drowned with Crane, those silent gestures and clotted laughs, nearly thirty years after the poet's death.

"Hart Crane" was a success with our audience and gained some notoriety elsewhere, after being rebroadcast by our other stations in California, and later on CBC Canada. I received numerous letters from writers and artists, and a dub was requested by the Library of Congress; more than once over the next couple of years the program was rebroadcast.

It must have been after one such airing that I received a phone call from Robert Lowell. He'd heard the program the evening before and wondered if he might borrow the tape right away to listen to it again. I was very busy making another program at the time (and not permitted to lend out master tapes), so I suggested that Lowell drop by our offices that afternoon and I would allow him to listen to the Crane tape over earphones in my office on the Ampex machine that was not being used for editing.

About one in the afternoon Lowell showed up: tall, graceful, quietly deferential, almost timid, I thought, but very generous with his compliments about the program and, surprisingly, handsome. I had not presumed this from his photos, where he always looked so sqaure-jawed and Waspishly stern or "spacey," but the face he presented on that day seemed more youthful than I imagined it could have been, and, as I say, he appeared very fit and trim, and lean, almost studentish, I might have thought, and dressed in a casual manner: a corduroy jacket and slacks, I believe, and a neutral Shetland sweater.

It was a bright spring day, and the dust motes in my crammed little office, like specks of silver, seemed to spill through the only window on Lowell as he slouched against a bookcase while I was setting up the machine. He refused tea. He had some books in a sack. He smoked, as I recall, but his chin did not jut, as in some photos, nor was he thick and short of wind, as he seemed at a reading his final winter alive at St. Mark's Church with Allen Ginsberg. He was very bookish and quiet, at the moment, a very fine man at the peak or prime of life and oddly deferential, sweet-natured, with a strange lilting, almost vacant-sounding southern accent, and a lot of light in his eyes.

My office was a public thoroughfare to other desks in other offices (as well as an editing studio for the staff at large and a tape library); there was constant traffic. I ran Lowell through the operation of the large console Ampex, provided him with a set of earphones on a long pig's tail of lead wire, and told him to make himself as comfortable as he could while I got busy with other things. Very shortly, he was spread full out on our dusty grey wool carpet, alongside the machine, like some Virgilian shepherd in a bosky field. With his eyes closed, Robert Lowell commenced to listen.

Lowell spent all of that afternoon and some of the next on the floor of my office, as if he had dozed off there, or was zonked on the thorazine of Crane's last days. Over and over and over again, he played the tape. Sometimes I would forget he was around, and then look down, and there he was, his face perfectly placid, though attentive, as if drained of every sensation except for the sounds that were rushing against his ears muffled by those phones—he seemed to be administering to himself a very exotic variety of electric shock.

At the time I was no great fan of Robert Lowell's poetry, though I had respect for some of the things he did and had read mostly all of it, going back to my teenage years, when he was one of the preeminent "young" postwar poets to be found in all the anthologies of modern poetry. So for two days he was this polite self-effacing presence in my office, this figure somewhat larger than life, a reputation. We hardly spoke. I don't think he knew or would have cared that l was also a writer. I don't pretend to have any idea what he was thinking, or whether he was composing (for I saw no notebook or sketch pad), and I tried to go about my own business and not be disturbed or disturb him.

Lowell's concentrated listening was also very flattering to me, and with that studiously lackadaisical manner, and that easiness with his body, I found him a very gentle and unobtrusive companion those two days, but a presence, nevertheless, though not particularly odd, the establishment's most earnest representation to our struggling listener-supported radio station.

He left with as little disruption as he'd arrived. But shortly before he had listened to my program for the final time, he stopped the machine and spoke to me. His eyes were watery, and he looked tired and just a little grim. Lowell wanted to know if I had changed much of what the various people said about Crane. I explained that I had done very little except to edit out my questions and intercut the responses of the various speakers. Then Lowell shrugged at me and when he spoke his voice seemed oddly high, piping: "That must have been the way it was. . ."

He went toward the door. "I may want to listen again," he said. "Would that be possible?"

I assured him it would.

"Crane thought he could walk the streets on the other side of the moon," Lowell said then.

I saw Lowell again a few weeks later when I asked if he would contribute to a second such montage I was compiling on Ford Madox Ford's American years. Lowell had been Ford's "pupil" at Jolliet College, Minnesota, when Ford was writing "It Was the Nightingale," he explained; and he agreed to the interview, was genial, generous in his recorded remarks, verbally elegant. The words he used to metaphorize Ford's personality at the time were "pure sillabub," a refreshment made by whipping cream with wine.

That later memory of time spent conversing about a subject of current mutual interest to both of us is nowhere near as vivid to me as my first impression of Lowell. I noticed that his speech, like some of his least successful lines of poetry, had a tendency to strangle on latinate words, and he was disarmingly cooperative, a man, again, of such sweet good nature. But not so easygoing and stretched out as on those bright spring afternoons when he had said little but lay entirely muffled in earphones listening to the cracked weary voices of Crane's contemporaries depict what they knew of the last days and hours and minutes of the poet's life.

The poem on Crane Lowell eventually produced for *Life Studies* when I read it some time later I found rather disappointing. It was a truly dinky poem, end-stopped, turgid, flat, somewhat of a put-down, an Elizabethan wisecrack dressed up as modern: "Who asks for me, the Shelley of my age/*must lay* [emphasis mine] his heart out for his bed and board." It's also true that Lowell was much less ironical in his recorded comments to me about Ford than in his Ford poem in *Life Studies*. Then he was openly and simply grateful and adoring, and I found that charming, and I often wondered later, in the case of Crane, if so much attentive listening had been worth the effort of producing such a little pipsqueak-wrenched remark, or if, in fact, there was any connection whatsoever between his poem and my tape. Perhaps Lowell wasn't thinking that afternoon about writing of Crane, but of himself, or a third party. Perhaps I was just providing an atmosphere of suitable morbidity for his ruminations. Under earphones at times he looked even more youthful and worried, his brow furrowed, entirely self-absorbed.

I did not see Lowell again until the winter of his death, though I continued to read his poems, liking them much whenever he did not locate his persona in the grandiose architecture of ruin, and once I wrote him at Harvard to ask if he would read some of my work. It's hard for me not to admire a person who has been flattering to me, and tactful, and considerate, so I kept aware of him, and of the major events in his life; his divorce, his remarriage, the birth of a new child. He made *People* magazine, where he had a large, open, new smile. *I* was glad, and even somewhat envious. But I was not prepared for the physical and spiritual changes I and so many others encountered that crowded evening at St. Mark's Church when he read with Ginsberg.

He had gained weight and thickness. Separated from his wife and child, his loneliness showed in his slouch, his wide, staring eyes. His hair was thinner, all silvery white, his face now seemed very pink and fair. He looked so tired, so very very sad, and withdrawn. There were some hecklers in the audience, and he handled them with dignity and tact, and after reading the usual early poems about New England ancestors, and so on, he read a long, beautiful new poem about Ulysses' return to Ithaca and made some wise and generous remarks about being nice to "girls," as he called them. He was gracious and attentive while being tactically outclassed on Ginsberg's home turf. Allen read a mighty new poem about a confrontation between two bards that was full of verve and energy, though just a little hard to follow in places on first hearing, and afterwards he and Lowell were thronged by the usual St. Mark's crowd and, though I tried for a moment to get close enough to greet them both, I finally gave up and left the hall with my date, feeling very sad. I had the strongest of hunches that Lowell was dying.

He seemed to be saying that, not in words, but in the time and space he took to say words, in his thin voice, his wanness and exhaustion, the slightly flustered way he rebuked (and later apologized to) one heckler (Gregory Corso) and then seemed to plead at him with his eyes for patience and toleration. It was a difficult crowd in a packed hall, but hardly anybody seemed really hostile to Lowell; some people seemed concerned and upset by his mood and his appearance. He seemed truly broken hearted, and sad, shattered. His face could barely dissemble to grin without wincing. He had a sort of chest cough, an uneasy breath, and his unruly silver hair, like the frays of silk tasseling, loosely surrounded his large bare pink skull and brow, the aura of a bemused saint. Toward Ginsberg he was openly admiring, I thought, but timid as to how much admiration might be appropriate. Such a queer restraint. Lowell seemed very frightened. He seemed to know he was failing somehow to communicate beyond the strict circle he had drawn around himself. At times he seemed cross, then apologetic again, and winded and withdrawn, failing somehow, this dying middle-aged man writing poems about impotence and madness and failure had eliminated from his style the need to wrench it all askew with irony or erudition and seemed very vulnerable, to his weariness, his ailing powers, his own death: "To her suitors, he is Tom, Dick or Harry . . . ten years fro and ten years to."

There is much of that sort of writing, touching, but so sad, in Lowell's last collection, *Day by Day*, which, it seems, by just a few days, appeared posthumously. When I saw the title announced somewhere the next spring, after the St. Mark's reading, I thought of the advice I have myself received from doctors and well-meaning friends to try to live my life "one day at a time" whenever I was going through a heavy time. The title sequence to his estranged wife Caroline Blackwood reads very much like the record of a man in great pain holding his breath:

> Darling,
> terror in happiness may not cure the hungry future,
> the time when any illness is chronic
> and the years of discretion are spent on complaint—
> until the wristwatch is taken from my wrist.

This poetry is full of longing, to be a child again engulfed by loud music or laughing with the woman he loved, and one reason why the longing is so painful is that the poet keeps talking about his recent bouts with madness with the disarming candor of a man who has failed at love.

Again and again the poems are made to skate over that brittle ice.

There's very little sententious writing here; the lines move, and breathe, and hurt Lowell more than others; they are very humanly put, like Hardy at times when he was a much older man, but humble like that, and the pain of it all is terrible. A slow waiting for death and wishing for death: *"I wish I could die."* Lowell writes: "Less than ever I expect to be alive / six months from now."

And again:

> A man without a wife
> is like a turtle without a shell—
> this pending hour, this tapeworm
>   minute,
> this pending minute, I wait for you
>   to ring—
> two in unhealth.

The book is, in part, I think, the record of Lowell's last bout with his madness and his recovery and estrangement from his public self and return to childhood hurts and hurting:

> Is the one unpardonable sin
> our fear of not being wanted?
> For this, will mother go on cleaning
>   house
> for eternity, and making it unlivable?
> Is getting well ever an art,
> or art a way to get well?

There are moments when he touches very close to some truths I have experienced in my own life

> These days of only poems and depression—what can I do
>   with them?
> Will they help me to notice
> what I cannot bear to look at?

There are also those moments of simple verbal accuracy that are almost sublime:

> August flames in the rusty sorrel,
> a bantam hen hatches wild pheasant
>   chicks,

the dog licks ice cream from a cone,
but mostly the cropped, green,
    sold-off pastures.

Finally all the death here is a discouragement to poetry, wasteful, joyless, painful, lacking any positive value, I think, to reader as well as writer, as Lowell sounds his familiar unhappy note "Why is it so hard for them to accept / the very state of happiness is wrong?" And behind this is Lowell's most damaging confession: "I want to make / something imagined, not recalled."

So much bitterness and rage, it seems, even in these close-to-final poems, and so much about that old injury, his childhood, his parents, and the harms that were done, and the methods taken to cure and restore that have failed him. Or did he fail them? It's the pain of both at once. The "downlook" and that clinical language of despair:

I am a thorazined fixture
in the immovable square-cushioned chairs
we preoccupy for seconds like migrant birds.

I prefer to remember Lowell when he had confidence, and a seeming ease with himself, when he was this charming, slightly strung out guy hanging around for a couple of afternoons in my crummy office with his dreamy eyes and his light, easy manner. It may be he was a great poet. The evidence from this book suggests Lowell thought he was not and never could be: too much thorazine and not enough loving. But he was so intelligent and courageous and gifted and energetic it seems a shame he couldn't do any better the second time around with Hart Crane's suicide in Day by Day:

Where is Hart Crane,
the disinherited, the fly by night, who gave
the drunken Dionysius firmer feet?

I think all that literary musing wasn't very good for Robert Lowell.

HUNTER S. THOMPSON

This is the way Hunter's first book on the Hell's Angels came to be published. He was freelancing for the *Wall Street Journal's* Sunday paper on the West Coast. In the midsixties he arrived in New York and, just around twilight one early spring evening, called me because we had a friend in common. Would I like to take a spin with him in Central Park?

Hunter came by sometime later, in denims and leather on a big Harley motorcycle. Since he couldn't park on West Seventy-ninth Street, he insisted over the building intercom that I *come* down and join *him* on the street.

He was tall and thin and sandy in those days, as I recall, pleasant to look at and plain-faced, like one of the Walton boys on TV, but with eyes like Billy the Kid. After I shook hands with this stranger and we chatted a moment about our mutual friend, Hunter got aboard his big hog again and told me to get on right behind him. He offered me a couple of red uppers, from which I demurred virginally, then swallowed a few himself and told me to embrace him and—baroom!—we took off.

I don't recall a single instant of exhilaration; I was plainly much too scared even to experience my own fear. I just hung on as we bent around the Natural History Museum on one wheel and sort of flew across Central Park West and entered the park, and then he let out the throttle and we went roaring downtown and around the pond and headed uptown again toward Harlem.

Somewhere in our trip the night came on, and I began to plead with my family dentist for more novocaine through the glow of big yellow fog lights. *Alavei!* In those days I used to tell myself if something wasn't scary it probably wasn't worth doing. But I know I blacked out for a moment behind the Metropolitan Museum of Art because when I was conscious again I heard Hunter saying something about "rites of passage," and I inquired if that was one of the first fourteen amendments.

"You've got just barely enough courage," he told me then, "to compensate for your lack of balance."

I was still recumbent on the back fender as we puttputted back along Seventy-ninth Street looking for parking spaces.

After this moving introduction to the future Gonzo journalist, I felt obliged to invite Hunter up to my flat for a drink. In those days he was not much of a boozer, as I recall, and took a beer, but I swigged Early Times. Then he told me the purpose of his mission to the Upper West Side from the outer spaces. My friend had told him I was very well connected with editors and agents, and he'd been writing something which the *Journal* probably wouldn't touch and probably ought to be his first book. Could I put him in touch with people?

Hunter had what my mother used to call "poise," which would have served him equally well selling mutual funds or shingles and siding. It wasn't a question of my not wanting to be helpful. He had me feeling uncharitable for not getting on the phone right away. But I asked if he could show me what he had written or tell me about it, and he reached inside his outer garments and pulled out a sheaf of pages. This was the opening of Hunter's book on the Hell's Angels, and, as I now recall, it described him being roughed up and urinated upon by a gang of unruly brutes in leather and why he'd been curious enough to hang out with them, and penetrate their mysteries, as it were. Something about fascism.

I have always assumed from my own experience starting out that helping other writers would not diminish my own prospects in any way. This writing was also vivid and vernacular, and I told Hunter so, and said I would try to think of someone who could publish what he was writing, because I'd never seen the subject treated so devoutly before.

I really wasn't as well connected as Hunter thought, though I was a contributor to Carey McWilliams' *Nation* magazine and, a few days later, with Hunter's permission, I sent on a xerox of the pages to him. Carey was quick to respond, as he was always very interested in California fads going nationwide, and he published a version of Hunter's work within weeks.

I was then writing nonfiction books on upsetting social conditions for Sara Blackburn at Pantheon Books. Sara was the wife of the poet Paul Blackburn, a generous person and an enthusiastic editor. When we next had lunch and I brought along Hunter's manuscript, she got very excited about a book on the Hell's Angels and said she would personally get in touch with Hunter as soon as possible. (Eventually Sara left her husband, so she and Hunter could be together for a while.) In fact, Sara never got to publish any of Hunter's work. When the Hell's Angels book was discussed at the Random House sales conference, Jason Epstein got so worked up he took the project away from Pantheon, offered Hunter a better contract, and published it as a Random House book.

The sixties was a period when even straight types in publishing and the media went fissionable over bearers of frisson such as the Black Panthers, the Hell's Angels, Don Juan the Shaman, the Diggers, or the followers of Wavy Gravy. Since the miseries of ordinary people were considered boring, writers and editors were more entranced by menace, mystery, and sleeze which comported itself in drag.

When it appeared, I reviewed Hunter's book as first-rate participant-observer journalism with a thumb in the eye of the reader in the *New Republic*. As my association with him expanded into a correspondence, he kept insisting he wanted to write fiction. I thought most of what he was writing was make-believe that he would validate through direct experience sooner or later, if he hadn't already done so. Certainly, he was vivid, for a time, his stories were mostly about himself; he really wasn't interested in other people except as self-projected imagery. But for all I knew about him after his first great success, he might have also been the "ghost" for Carlos Castenada's psychotropic *Don Juan* or written additional dialogue for *Trout Fishing in America*. Hunter had sufficient talent and moxie.

The more I knew the man, the less I enjoyed him. All I ever learned from his depictions of Las Vegas and political conventions I knew in kindergarten. Hunter had a lot of energy and an impressive gift for verbal cartooning. I don't believe he was ever in fear and trembling of anything except friendship. He was always pointing out that I was a snobby, uptight Jewish intellectual who couldn't find his way out of a back alley without tears. I suppose if I'd been black he would have told me a lot of race jokes.

Once I stopped off while in Aspen where I was visiting a beautiful woman friend whose name I had given to the title of one of my novels. I got in touch with Hunter in Woody Creek and suggested we take a meal together. Hunter suggested another motorcycle ride. We never got together.

I sometimes wished I hadn't assisted this old Hell's Angel on his road to stardom. He'd have gotten there anyway without me. I've always much preferred the plain style of George Orwell, but now I suspect some of St. George's adventures in Paris or Wigan Pier were also concocted, in part.

Speaking of Pantheon Books in the old days, I once inquired of the publisher why he would not consider printing my fiction, as I had to publish all my novels elsewhere than with Pantheon, my publishers for nonfiction, and people thought that Richard Elman, the novelist, and I were not the same author. The man explained that if he published my novels "people would surely think you made up your journalism." A bigger soul might have wondered if they wouldn't suppose my novels to be true.

SAUL NEWTON: NEWTON'S LAWS

The last time I spoke with Saul Newton, the notorious chief therapist of the Sullivanian cult, he said I had a heart the size of a pea. I'd never really considered myself a big-hearted man, but I took exception to Saul's insult and, consequently, had to find new living quarters.

It was 1972. I was a wash-out from a string of New Left affairs, bunking between marriages with four Sullivanian shrinks in a brownstone on the Upper West Side of Manhattan. They believed in the politics of fucking a lot; within the group they did it also willy-nilly. When you had sex with a Sullivanian, first came pleasure, then came your summary. All your faults were enumerated. It didn't help to answer back tit for tat. You were guilty of "romantic focus" or a "distancing maneuver." They actually made celibacy feel good.

Blanchette, one of Saul's lay analysts, was my regular Saturday night date. We met when I was looking for an apartment and she was trying to get her cat spayed. It wasn't a relationship made in heaven, but we were both less lonely than we'd been. Being a shrink herself, she found digs for me in the house of her friend who was once her shrink, and a former lover, Blanche said. Oddly, I wasn't even jealous when they sometimes slept together.

I really didn't love much of Blanche. I didn't even love myself. But Saul, who was now her therapist, said she was thirty-five and should be having children. He said he wanted me to be the father. I said I really wasn't that crazy for Blanche, nor she for me, and therefore, didn't think we ought to be having any children together.

"I understand," Blanche said. "But Saul won't like it."

"He's a coward," Saul shouted to his number two girlfriend, who said I was just being a royal pain in the ass. "I'm sorry," I said. "But I do like to be somewhat infatuated. With Blanche, as things stand . . ."

"Don't be," she said. "I understand. You're shy, not used to me. We need more time." She asked would I, at least, consider being a standup guy and remain a part of her "sperm pool?"

I pointed out I really couldn't be in the swim. My sperm, in the past, had needed a booster of clomid, which I wasn't about to take to fertilize her womb because there could be any number of side effects, such as baldness, spells, floaters, night blindness, strokes, tumors, impotence, abnormal weight gain, swollen breasts, irregular periods, dropsy, and prostate cancer.

"It's a matter of playing out all the probabilities," Blanche pointed out calmly, "We'll surely increase the likelihood of conception by increasing my sperm pool input," she added.

I said I already had a child I loved and was having a hard enough time providing for her. Saul butted in again. My relationship with my eight-year-old daughter, he averred, was possibly destructive at best. If I had any cullions at all, they should be at the service of Project Blanche. "But," I pointed out, "she never wanted to have this child. You want her to."

"Goddamn psychopath," he shouted. The veins were popping in his forehead like coaxial cable, his little grey goat beard oscillating against his chin. "You have a heart the size of a pea!"

"Saul please," Blanche said, "don't! Please I really . . ."

"Shut up, you cow!" he shouted. "Why must you always be so needy?"

That's the day I left Sullivania. It was cold. I had no place to go. I bunked with a friend, another exile from the Swamp of Despond, as we used to call Saul's therapeutic community of over two hundred prelapsarians, until such time as I could extricate my various possessions from my quarters.

One of these, of course, was an eight-year-old daughter, whose mother was still a part of the group, and when I tried to see her it was just as I had always feared: my kid was, I was told, presently unavailable to me. They had her stashed somewhere with bodyguards. A Sullivanian baby sitter told me I wasn't feeling well enough and it was best for my daughter if we had no contact at present.

One of Saul's vixens also had me informed that if I ever bothered him or his people about their treatment of my child, he would put a "contract" out on me, and besides l would die anyway, on my own, probably a suicide, out there in the world on my own. But if not, he'd just have to see to it himself, as he'd had to do in Spain during the civil war when, an International Brigadier, he regularly dealt with deserters and cowards.

I thought my reluctance to father another child was a sign of prudence, not cowardice, and I spent some time helping myself to feel better, under the circumstances; then I consulted a lawyer, after discovering that Saul had one of his epigones spread the slander at my daughter's school, when I came for a visit, that I was trying to murder her and should be barred.

I sued for custody in hopes of normalizing my visitations.

The matter dragged on many months because the other side was represented by a lefty attorney who had previously represented Julius and Ethel Rosenberg. Domestic cases paid his rent, but he thrived on martyrdom and was fairly adept at all the strategies for getting stays and postponements. He hoped I would grow discouraged, walk away, or find some other interest, like bridge or bowling for dollars.

I loved my daughter, as I had never loved any other human being, and I knew she needed to see me regularly, and so my lawyer got the judge to rule, in the interim, that I should be allowed limited visiting privileges, even occasional overnights, if l would agree to an interview with a court-appointed psychiatrist. I also had to take a Rorschach test.

Worried I might "fail" the Rorschach and lose my child forever, I consulted with a graduate student in psychology at Columbia. My expert suggested that if I would just identify every ink blot I was shown as a vagina, I would probably be considered the picture of mental health.

The day of my examination was hot, overcast. My examiner was a motherly, gray, German or Austrian Jewish psychiatrist with an accent like the late Walter Slezak.

We met in a bare little room with a long table and windows overlooking the steps of Foley Square courthouse. She flipped page after page of ink blots on me and to every one I responded with that one word—*vagina*.

"Ja?" she asked, more than once. "That too . . . ?"

"I think so. It looks like that to me at any rate."

"Ja," she replied. "So . . ."

And flipped still another oak tag on her pad to another ink blot. Blue, red, green—they were all very pretty vaginas to me, some sideways, some even upside down.

My examiner remained unflappable, though concerned. When we were finished she asked if I would like to rest a minute, and she offered me a glass of milk.

Within another week the decision came down that I was to be allowed normal visitation and time with my child over the holidays and during summer vacations. I felt reprieved from Saul's vendetta against me and my child, but I also remained angry at the *soi-disant* Harry Stack Sullivan Institute for putting me to such trouble and expense just to prove I was not a "murderer."

I was also quite broke. Then I heard through the grapevine of ex-

Sullivanians exiled to adjacent blocks on the Upper West Side that Blanche had indeed gotten pregnant through her "collective" and birthed a little girl but she had not really enjoyed motherhood, nor had the baby, and the gang of four who ran the institute had given the child over to the custody of a third party, an alcoholic.

My prophetic soul . . . I was now truly angry: Blanche had been pretty foolish to allow herself to be bullied and manipulated by this popinjay, Saul, and now she and her child would bear the scars.

I tried to contact her, to console her if I could, but of course I was an outcast from the group and she was not allowed to have anything to do with me. Once we met on Broadway, and her eyes were so glazed over from valium that she looked like a Judy Collins record jacket or one of the showcase windows at Charivari.

Once I passed Saul with one of his girls in front of the Red Apple Supermarket, and he was pushing a baby carriage. We didn't speak. I was afraid of what I might say or do, and he had a hostage with him, a baby in a pram. But, some time later, a friend who knew my history told me I could actually see the old trickster cavorting any time I cared to on the stage of the Truck and Warehouse Theatre down on East Fourth Street on the Lower East Side in the cast of a Suilivanian review performed by the Fourth Wall Company, a Sullivanian offshoot.

I took a date, and we bought two tickets and sat in the rear of the house. I'd grown a beard, so the ticket taker, another one of Saul's elite guard, didn't recognize me. The house was hardly filled, and we were probably the only consenting adults in attendance. All the rest were kids dragooned from various settlement house programs by various Sullivanian agents of influence in the field; they were black and Puerto Rican, and it seemed pretty obvious to me, when the house lights dimmed, that the much admired "alienations" sought after by this company of white Brechtian amateurs had already taken effect in the stalls, for they were restless and rowdy and probably would have preferred a cloud buster demonstration or a kung fu flick.

What I saw was an untalented version of the San Francisco Mime Troop. As I recall, the theme of the evening's entertainment was, though virtuous, not overly fastidious: The United States with its nuclear hardware was no friend to humanity. A startling revelation. A woman with a skunk streak down the center of her lustrous black hair recited a sort of prologue. You couldn't argue with stuff like that unless you were Dr. Mengele's PR man.

Somebody banged drums, tweak of an electric guitar. I can't really remember the plot; the drummer looked like the overweight slob who used to knock skins for Sha na na.

I remember Saul, or someone imitating him, dressed as a camp Uncle Sam, doing a buck and wing. Blanche appeared as a Nicaraguan *campesina*, and a couple of Sullvanian toddlers were also in the cast, or perhaps they'd just wandered away from their baby-sitters onto the stage.

Watching the man who had caused me so much pain and trouble perform so lamely, limping and loping about before a bunch of bored and aimless kids who could never afford his cash-and-carry therapy sessions any more than they might understand why children should be kept from their parents when many of them were feeling so father-less and deprived, I thought about my time in Sullivania and my last encounter with Saul, and then I remembered our very first encounter.

It was at a group banquet in Amagansett, Long Island on Water's Edge Road. I was the only nonshrink at table, a new recruit. Blanche told me Saul really liked writers, but he seemed chary of me, and I later learned he thought I was out to do a job on his group in the press. The meal was bluefish baked to a turn. Saul's Corsican chef, an anar-chist, doing penance to the Stalinist Sullivanians, prepared a special ice cream bombe for dessert. People seemed to be unusually mellow; some were holding hands. The man opposite me had just finished explaining why he'd given up his career as a painter to become one of Saul's therapists. "I really love Saul," he said.

"You mean you had no talent?"

"I love Saul," he said. "What else matters?"

"Talent, sometimes," I replied.

"I didn't love myself that much," the man said, sheepishly.

Then Blanche asked me to follow her around the table to meet the great man, whom I had only glimpsed through a wine glass darkly until that moment.

"Elman?" He glanced up from his brown study. He'd been pre-occupied changing water into wine. Unmitred, his head was as large as Bukharin's recantation, his lips coarse as chicken gizzards, a mean, petulant, interesting face. He had no wand or staff but said, "I know your wife."

"We're getting separated."

"I just said l knew her." Saul added, "Did you think I meant country matters?"

I said he could have meant it in the biblical sense.

"Know-it-alls and wise guys," he muttered.

I swallowed very hard. "I understand you were in Spain with the Lincoln Brigade."

"Though I speak with the tongues of angels," he said, glancing away and then back again.

He bared his leg. I thought I saw a scar. "Is that from a wound?"

"He that believeth in me shall live."

I wondered if I truly had enough life insurance.

"Who are your heroes, Elman?" he asked, suddenly.

I shrugged. The writer Isaac Babel was certainly one of my biggest heroes, but I wasn't sure Saul wanted to talk about Benya Krik, an Odessa small fry compared to his feats of derring-do with depressed Upper West Side women.

"I defy auguries," I announced. "I'm not even sure I have any heroes."

"To be weak is miserable," he sneered. "Personally, my two heroes are Chairman Mao and Harry Stack Sullivan."

All I knew about Harry Stack Sullivan was he would eat no fowl larger than a chicken and he wrote about his cases in a language estranged from English. I asked Saul if he also fancied Saul of Tarsus? Nostradamus? Gramsci?

"Know ye not this parable?" He seemed to wish to lay his burden down. "I've always hated Jewish intellectuals like you, Elman. Though maybe you're different. I will say unto you," he conceded. "We'll find out if you really want friends."

"I guess he didn't want to talk to me after all," I told Blanche later, as we started back toward our seats.

"Saul really was taken with you," she said, and then somebody dropped a plate.

That same weekend one of the faithful, pretending we were friends, tried to rape me. When I refused, he suggested I was a difficult case. He'd gone through millions of dollars and many women since entering therapy as a falling-down alcoholic, but now that he knew who he really was, he was healed, more or less and could help me. We would be friends in rape.

"You don't really like women," he assured me.

"Not these women," I replied. "You're right about that."

But I slept out on the beach of Gardener's Bay alone.

That same weekend one of the patients from another group house died in a car accident going to or coming from the shore. I can't remember all, but I do recall her surname happened to be Putz.

When news reached the beach at Amagansett, Saul and a girl-friend retreated to their quarters and stayed there all day and night. Everybody was just very gloomy as though a promise of eternal life had been withdrawn.

The mullahs were now on the lookout for the psychopath who had smoked marijuana with the deceased shortly before her accident. Smoking marijuana was strictly forbidden in or about the institute, so many people had long faces from expiating the common guilt. People said, "Saul thinks we have a narc among us."

I glanced down the beach. Nobody seemed to have enough savvy to be a police person. They were all sucking pacifiers, crying on each other's shoulders.

"Maybe Saul's the narc," I said. "He could even be Beliel, or one of the other fallen angels."

"You don't know what you're saying," came the reply. "Don't let people hear you."

Downtown, on stage at the Truck and Warehouse Theatre, it was helizapoppin time. Kicking away in thespian drag like Julian Eltinge, or some other old trooper from the Orpheum Circuit playing Monckton, New Brunswick, the chairman was going through changes. Saul's so-called presence meant he couldn't sing and couldn't dance. So what? He had been called. To do what?

As he hobbled about and lifted his leg like a dog above a hydrant, I realized his message was plainly and simply Saul, in his seventh decade, with his incredible *chutzpah*. He charged indecent sums of money for his professional reproaches, and he was barely even educated, messed with people's lives and hopes and dreams, intimidating them to bear children they did not wish to have, to mate, to divorce, to be estranged from their kids, and to squander their loves and their lives. And he could do all this because he'd learned all their secrets voluntarily from them in therapy and was not ashamed to blackmail them with all the things he knew.

I can remember watching a celebrated modern painter with a big six-figure income and galleries showing his work around the world cower before a withering summary of his character structure and then try to appease the old devil with a gift of a painting allegedly worth thousands of dollars. Saul couldn't be bought except with money.

"*You're all a bunch of desperate fakers, liars, and scam artists,*" he would tell the artists, "*and you know it, which is why we talk.*"

Saul had his own act, himself—he played God. He had always been on stage, since our very first encounter, chosen by himself to be himself, the chosen one, the biggest bully in his gang, a lout, a *bulvan*, though now he was merely speaking in tongues to these bored neighborhood kids, whereas, on his own turf, his heartless work had been a sort of ventriloquism in which he claimed to speak for the needs of others, resulting in loss and pain and heartbreak and tears, for Blanche and possibly her child and for my child and myself.

I whispered to my date that I could endure no more of this graybeard playing Orpheus and had to leave.

"Absent thee from felicity a while." As we went out through the rear of the theatre into the harsh Lower East Side evening, Hamlet was dying and Horatio held his breath in pain.

"Anything wrong?" asked one of the saved at the door.

"Newton's a million dollar talent," I said, "a combination of Walter Brennan and Gallagher and Sheen. Old Mulcible."

"You think so?"

"The real article. Anti Christ! I know it. I'm in the business. The only thing is, he just isn't funny. Maybe you ought to lock the doors like they do at EST and have him piss on the audience. The old burning lake bit."

"Hey, hey," the guy said, catching on.

"He could also appear as a serpent with Ralph Royster Doyster," I said, "or turn wine back into water like Blackstone."

"That really isn't funny," the pointy-eared guy said, whom I recognized now as one of Saul's spawn of children.

"Well, have him call my office," I said, "and I'll book him into Darkness Visible."

I handed over the card of the gray-haired woman who did my Rorschach and turned and ran down the block and kept on running, with my date trying to catch up to me.

And though I never went back to see Newton do Lear or Timon of Athens, sometimes I'm awakened by the throb of my pea-shaped heart against my chest, and I'm just so thankful I didn't give at Blanche's orifice and got Saul angry at me.

Manhattan Island is full of spirits, and very soon we all must bow and scrape and bend down low to kiss such heaps of dust that also will be trembled into dust. I wish that bastard Saul blanched cullions for all eternity in his passionate pilgrimage from tragedy to farce. Selah!

Richard Price

I read one of Richard Price's manuscripts when he applied to the graduate program at Columbia, and I had no doubts he should be admitted. It was from a novel in progress he was calling "Walking Johnson." *As* I remember, his protagonist was very sweet natured but a little dumb, did nothing except walk about and think to himself, but the prose was fresh, alive with vernacular and the rhythms of a lonely man's lopings and stridings, and the writer seemed intelligent, with a good ear. I was pleased to recommend him for a scholarship.

We met in class maybe four months later, and he was equally quick-witted and charming, with an eye for all the pretty women, but in those days also very shy, with a lame arm and self-conscious about his disability, which appeared to be a birth injury. Through a brilliant piece of his own miscasting, Richard's wise cherub face was playing a dead end kid.

He told me his family was working-class Jewish from "the projects." He'd been in the Labor Relations School at Cornell, as I recall, when the urge to write got the better of him and he took some writing courses. "Walking Johnson" had been his learning bike, he said; he had other projects in mind about the Bronx and gangs.

I never had any doubts that Richard was authentically the man he said he was, ambitious and savvy, but I could never quite follow why it was so essential that he appear only so, when he was also, quite apart from all that, very well read, even cultivated about the arts, and quick. He always insisted he was just another Allen Fried hard rocker from the Bronx, but, unlike a lot of his late sixties generation, he was strung out on words in books as well as music and fame and films. Richard was also very much like many young people then and now, having some problems with his family and with making female friends. He was still spending too much time, he wrote me once "with Mary Fist," meaning his lack of a girlfriend had him resorting to the habits of adolescence. Much older than he was and recently divorced, I thought I was having a few of the same problems of loneliness and middle-aged horniness. When he asked me if I knew whom he might see for help with some of his problems, I recommended my doctor, whom I thought of then as a friendly man, a psychologist.

Richard and I saw quite a bit of each other for a little while as we now seemed to have friends in common. The gang we were in was open to very free sexual experimentation, if you were willing to put up with a lack of privacy or romance and lots of hard-earned reproaches from your various partners. They were all for experimentation and opposed to the hard-bitten habits and mores of the nuclear family.

I was involved in order to keep an eye on my child who was in the custody of my ex-wife, then a very flaky member of this group. To help pay my way, I taught private creative writing classes to psychiatrists who were very suspicious of writers and never wrote anything but enjoyed hearing literary gossip of which I knew very little.

Richard even took a private class with me along with some other patient friends, both good and lousy writers, for hardly any money in tuition. The shrinks all thought he was a genius and told him so. Probably they wanted to fuck him. I didn't want to fuck Richard, but I thought he had lots of literary gifts, and when I endorsed him for a Stanford writing fellowship which he received, some people in the gang were angry at me for sending him so far away. Used to easy sex on the Upper West Side, he found Stanford a little stuffy. He wrote back a lot that he was homesick in California, which he likened to Hieronymous Bosch's *Garden of Earthly Delights*, and wanted to show me his new manuscripts over Christmas vacation.

He was always very tuned in to my life and work and also the works of others, such as the fine Irish-American novelist Michael Stephens; Richard was truly a keen-witted man of intelligence and talent, and he would become easily enthusiastic about the writing of his peers, including that of friends he met in the group, whom he recommended to the program at Columbia, which was usually a mistake. I can also recall him recommending to me a four-hundred-page manuscript of Gothic horror by a Stanford classmate from Darien, Connecticut.

He must have written the first part of his novel *The Warriors* in Columbia and at Stanford and then back in my private class. I thought it was very promising work, influenced by Selby, Mailer, even my own "Fredi and Shirl and the Kids" to a degree. In fact, in one Stanford letter to me, Richard even described his own family as "Milton and Harriet and the Kids." *So* I was not surprised when he told me he'd been circulating the incomplete manuscript and that a major publisher had offered him approximately fifty thousand dollars advance for this first novel, but he must hurry to finish it within six months. I told him he should take his time. If it was worth so much to one publisher it might be worth just as much or even more to another. They were really not to hurry him.

Richard also consulted his therapist, to whom he was paying good money for his sessions, and he or she convinced him he should be very angry with me. She and he, I guess, thought he needed to sign the contract.

"Why not finish the book?" I pointed out. "It's your first."

Now he was indeed quite angry with my advice, and we hardly ever spoke again as friends. His book came out and made a good-sized splash, though there was a certain amount of sagging and repetition in the second half of the novel.

Through my recommending him to speak to my psychiatrist friend, Richard had become involved with a notorious cult, the Upper West Side Sullivanians. Having found out through bitter experience how ruthlessly these so-called friends were controlling other people's lives, I left the group some time after the suicide of the writer Joel Leiber, but despite my fearful warnings, Richard stayed in a while longer; he seemed to be having a pretty good time with some of the women there, and he liked the parties, I suspect, everybody dancing away to rock 'n' roll. His novel *Blood Brothers*, though set near Richard's home turf, the Bronx public housing projects, unlike its predecessor, The *Wanderers*, was rich with Sullivanian psychobabble. The *Times* asked me to review it, and I pointed this out in print, hoping to get Richard to see that his new friends might eventually be even more harmful to him than a cocaine habit. He was now extremely angry with me, called me on the phone, and accused me of trying to damage the success of his new book out of envy. I can't remember any of the names he called me then, but it was pretty vile stuff, and the brunt of his accusation was that I had enviously tried to sabotage his success. I pointed out that he had much more to fear from his friends than from enemies like me, because he was beginning to sound like the morning-after "summary" one got from certain Upper West Side women.

"It's only my opinion," I said.

"Well, it's none of your business," Richard said.

Sometime later he also left the group, married, and eventually had a family.

This is a story with a happy ending. Richard is a million-dollar movie writer, and he writes serious books about drugs and street kids and the police. I admire his talents more than ever, and when I see him on television, or hear him on the radio, he usually has decent, funny, intelligent things to say.

We've seen each other only once since then. I was doing my weekly commentary at NPR's studios in New York when Richard dropped by to be interviewed about his work in films. I was sure he was still furious with me, so I tried to stay out of his way, but he very graciously made it a point to announce to the assembled NPR staff in the main room that I had been his teacher and very helpful to him when he needed a friend. Then we shook hands, and I've never set eyes on Richard again.

FRED BUSCH

We both went to the same high school in Brooklyn, many years apart. I am possibly a decade older than Fred. But, I suspect, until fairly recently, I flattered myself that he looked older, a somewhat paunchy patriarchal figure, as I recall. Representations of such a figure often appear in Fred's novels, and they are usually men with a lacerating sense of self and a conscience, sensate, sensual, seeking ethical solutions to small, dramatic, almost unresolvable dilemmas.

About twenty-five years ago I read one of Fred's early novels published by New Directions, and I was impressed by the rawness of his domestic scenes, by the household accidents he dramatized. In one of those early novels a character loses his toes to a lawnmower while taking care of domestic chores. This was John Hawkes' ferocity hiding behind a Jewish *ponim*.

Fred was living upstate in a lonely village far from literary people and teaching at Colgate. When we corresponded I was aware he felt underappreciated; I reviewed his early fiction very favorably for *The Nation* and arranged for him to be invited to the summer Bennington workshops as a faculty member with his family. We were friends, I thought. Fred seemed to think I was possibly a little wacky. The basis for this was that I had suffered a severe anxiety attack en route to a reading he'd arranged for me at Goddard College and had failed to make much sense to the assembled audience or his faculty friends.

Even after this unfortunate incident occurred, we remained collegial, more or less. At Bennington over a couple of summers we saw a lot of each other, but I always had the feeling that even my good-natured high spirits were disconcerting to Fred: not only did he sometimes regard me as manic, but he seemed secretly convinced I was a maniac.

Fred had very little basis for such a judgement. I'd been summarily fired by Columbia for publishing an intemperate letter in the *Times* critical of the political views and affiliations of the director of our program, who had supported the murderous coup in Chile, and I was trying to piece some kind of living together out of adjunct jobs, personal appearances, free-lance writing, and other hack work, and I was pretty desperate. I'd recently remarried, and my new wife and I both wanted a child. I recalled reading that Fred was on the NEA panel, and I dropped him a note and told him he should be aware that I'd applied and could really use assistance.

I don't think he ever communicated with me as a friend again. Probably I should not have leaned on him that way, but Fred had always claimed to admire some of my work, and I was faced with a lot of difficult choices. Like so many humane and otherwise liberal-minded people, Fred found emotional disorganization almost as threatening as a lawnmower running over one's toes.

I still read Fred's fiction when I come across it in books and quarterlies. It's beautifully done, I think. I wouldn't say humor was his strongest point, but there are well-organized comic moments. Usually there's an awkward, overweight, owl-eyed man of conscience at the center who, in the midst of life, must choose to act in a responsible way among often some pretty irresponsible people. Sometimes these heavyweight souls are doctors or sheriff's dispatchers or hard-pressed husbands, and they are usually matched up with difficult women and sometimes in love. Their competencies are tested, and they are shown to be earnest even when inept. Fred knows a lot about middle-class despair and such domestic hazards and pleasures. He certainly has a lot of compassion for big-hearted men like himself. He's a good writer and always stretching and reaching for greatness. That must be very frustrating. He's spent a lot of time in England and greatly admires Dickens.

Joel Leiber

Joel Leiber sold one of his novels to the movies. It starred Richard Benjamin and Paula Prentice and was about a young man who walks other people's dogs on the Upper West Side. It was one of those cloyingly contemporary sixties stories, embarrassing enough because it was full of a modish abject cynicism. Obviously this had to be treated as cute comedy.

I believe Joel worked on some other movie properties during the last year of his life. He was a middlingly successful free-lance writer for the *Saturday Review* and other publications. You probably saw his byline a few times without being impressed by what he wrote; I did.

I am telling his story because he was the victim of "cruel advice," not from me, but from others to whom I inadvertently introduced him.

Joel sometimes reviewed books. Whenever he reviewed my work, he always gave me very high praise. And always afterward I would receive one of his novels in the mail. I found his writing silly, usually cold and thin; I was indifferent to it. Sometimes I now wish I hadn't been.

I never told Joel my feelings about his work, never said anything about the books I received. Nor did I ever ask him to review my books. Expecting to be noticed for my work, I sometimes felt the special quality of attention I received from Joel to be intimidating. The last time we saw each other he said, "Just because I admired you doesn't mean I'm dishonest and we can't be friends."

That was the night before he killed himself. Joel didn't seem angry when he spoke, but purged and deeply exhausted. But when we met the first time in person, after so many encounters in print, he did seem in a rage.

One day Joel called me, a perfect stranger, to invite me to a party at the apartment of his agent to celebrate the release of a new novel. I went because I was lonely and curious. He was just back from a stint in Hollywood. A number of extras from the publishing scene were on hand, as well as his wife's family and his own. Joel was ferret-faced, angular, thin. He told me his children were playing in another room of the flat, and then he said he needed to speak to me right away on a confidential matter and took me into the hall with him.

There we had a good view of all the company but were nevertheless private and secluded. I saw Joel's wife, a pretty, blonde, somewhat fey-looking woman, and I saw the relatives sitting like gloomy bookends at either corner of the couch. When I asked what I could do for him, Joel told me with a singular lack of embarrassment, in a flattened out monotone voice, that his wife was having an affair. She also used LSD, he claimed, and she was very irresponsible with the children, he alleged. The families, he said, hers and his, were planning together to have her committed.

The means this man was proposing to deal with his own pain, jealousy, and rage over his wife were extremely odious to me and drastic. I felt compelled to argue with him. None of what he alleged, even if it were all true, seemed grounds for locking a woman up. I suggested he consider something less drastic, such as marriage counseling. "Think of the children," he said. "You think of them," I reminded him, warming as I spoke until I felt I'd gone beyond my usual indifference to the plight of married couples. But sometimes the giving of even good advice carries with it a responsibility. I was now a bystander of some intimacy in the public spectacle Joel was depicting as his domestic life. Somehow I'd been implicated.

He thanked me for the advice I'd given him and some days later he called, seeming contrite. He was very desperate, really needed "to see" someone for his own well-being, as I had already surmised. Could I recommend a shrink to him?

I had some faith at that moment in the person I was seeing, so I made the referral, feeling very virtuous for coming to the aid of a hard-pressed woman and her kids, if not also Joel, for my own psychiatrist informed me he truly wondered if he could be of genuine help to a "hard case like Joel," since he was not awfully fond of the man he'd encountered through their consultation. "Do you like him?" he asked me, as though for guidance. "I hardly know him," I replied. "Well," he said, "for the children's sakes." He referred Joel to another of his colleagues. After that we rarely saw each other again except at certain parties our shrinks' "group" ran for the recently divorced and separated. Joel seemed to be doing better than almost anybody else I saw at these parties. He always had a woman in tow; he seemed in good spirits, thanked me for my help, told me he was getting an ordinary straight up and down divorce, and no more threats of incarceration.

In the months that followed I heard of him dating one artist friend of mine, then a writer I knew, then a student of Ayahuasca rituals of the Peruvian jungle. He dated a record industry exec and a woman with five nipples, he told me.

Joel later went back to Hollywood, made some more money, found himself a nice young girl-woman, bought a spread in Vermont. He thanked me once for my help. I did not think he should. But there was no more talk of his estranged wife and what she was up to. Whenever we met I became his best friend in the world for as long as he focused on me, though he was easily distracted by women and meeting famous people, and he was clearly the one who was doing well, better and better. He dated a debutante with a fortune and then a very successful folk singer, a poet friend of mine. He had his children living with him and his girlfriend some of the time.

"How are you feeling Richard?" he asked me one day in front of Zabar's, as though I were his patient.

A year or so went by. I was living in a flat with two dogs who barked at my goldfish and a girlfriend with whom I was breaking up. It was the end of summer. We were at a Chinese restaurant. I peered across the aisle, and there was Joel, alone in a booth, spooning hot and sour soup: sallow, yellow-eyed, really down in the dumps until he saw me looking at him. Then he smiled. He seemed very glad to see me, signaled with his eyes for me to come over. I sat down with him for a few minutes, and he told me things were better than ever. He'd just purchased a penthouse apartment on West End Avenue.

"I heard you were making it," I said.

"Yeah I am"—laminated, flat as a narc's ID photo. In fact he'd always seemed strangely inappropriate to me ever since he told me what he wished to do to his wife so that I couldn't now tell if he was being more bleak than usual.

"Don't be a stranger anymore," he said.

"We should chat some time," I owned.

Perhaps he sensed I was not being terribly enthusiastic, but it was mostly my own life that seemed problematical to me at that moment. I wanted to be rid of my unhappiness with my girlfriend, so I could live my own life once more. I wanted to buy myself an alto saxophone and a parrot.

Joel said he was glad to hear I was doing okay.

"Yeah sure," I told him, even though I wasn't. Hard to say what I was thinking or what he felt.

The next morning around eleven I was at my writing desk when the phone rang. A mutual friend had just heard over the news how Joel had jumped from his penthouse apartment, killing himself instantly.

As his friends now tell it, his girlfriend and her mother were having coffee out on the terrace when Joel, without saying a word, walked past them into the air and the sidewalk below.

When I told this story to the writer Judith Rossner, with whom I spent some time in those days, she said suicides made her grieve as other deaths did not. I'd just scrapped a novel about a West Side murder I'd put a decade into after reading Judy's *Mister Goodbar* and realizing I was writing her book much less well. I was grieving then more for my book than for Joel, but I did feel badly for having seen him the night before and not having been able to guess he was that close to murdering himself.

I still wonder, if we could have spoken frankly, might I have saved him? Joel was as hard on himself as on others. Though I did not dislike him, I really did not love him enough to reach beyond my self at such a time. His act reminded me of how wrong we often are about people's abilities to cope. So much seeming outward hardness and cynicism, and inside the man was wired to short circuit. His last novel is about a paranoid episode among some sadistic psychiatrists on Fire Island, and it's almost as frightening and crazy as his real life was becoming, due to my unwitting interventions—the numerous girlfriends and the inability to be loving, then the making of a commitment to this one young girlfriend and heartbreak, impotence, rage. The shrink to whom my psychiatrist referred Joel took a real dislike to what she thought was his misogyny and threatened him, shortly before he went out to dinner the evening I saw him, as I later learned, that if he didn't agree to what she proposed for him—a period of more or less celibate group living with his male peers—she would have nothing more to do with him and he might just as well go out and take his own life.

He told me once he admired me, but I was in and out of hospitals and just barely hanging on. There were days I wished my life were already over, but I never once thought of suicide. Death would happen soon enough, I figured, unless I could find a way to survive. Maybe Joel's flattering me was the flip side of his desperation. I was the rope the drowning man imagined he could grasp and use to pull himself to safety. Maybe he had already made up his mind to do himself in or his doctor prophesied the way she did because she thought she could not reach her patient by the usual means.

Are there really other means?

JULES OLITSKI

After my first wife and I broke up, I was camping out in a studio not very far from her apartment on the Upper West Side. Because I had limited storage space there, most of my clothing and books were still in the apartment. I had a key and was allowed to come and go to get things during the day when she was working.

One Monday I had a business appointment downtown and went up to the flat around ten in the morning to get my only summer suit. All the shades were still drawn, and the place was still in darkness. When I entered the bedroom to go to the closet a naked figure cried out in alarm and, cowering after he sprang from the bed, started apologizing for being there, explaining that he and she had been out late and he'd slept over after she went off to work.

The man seemed a little afraid that I was about to do some violence to him, but all I really wanted was my summer suit. At last I was able to calm him down with assurances that I meant him no harm, and he retreated to the bathroom. When he emerged again wrapped inside a towel I suggested he shower and shave and, meanwhile, I'd make coffee and an omelet for the both of us. That's how I came to know the noted postmodern abstract color field painter Jules Olitski.

I think he was angry a lot of the time I knew him. I know I was. I didn't mind his dating my ex-wife half so much as his later dating of my girlfriend. But how could I blame him? Janey was gorgeous, and she'd made herself available to him. I blamed her, not him.

For a while, we hung out together and sometimes shared meals. Jules was breaking up with his longtime girlfriend, the painter Susan Crile, and looking to meet "new people," as we might have said back then. He also said he was very interested in writing fiction and was so successful as a painter that he seemed to have the leisure to carry it off. But he was reluctant to show his work to me or to anybody then, it seemed, though, eventually, he published parts of an experimental novel in *Partisan Review*.

Once we both applied to Yaddo at the same time to keep each

other company. Jules said he was going to write. I had a book to finish. We became interested in the same woman, the widow of a famous editor, and when she seemed to favor me, Jules abruptly left Yaddo after sending me a brief note about "seeing gray birds everywhere."

He was not an easy man to know well. He worked late into the evenings and slept through large portions of the day, whereas I was teaching at the time and had other responsibilities that kept me on a daytime schedule. Some evenings he would invite me to his spacious studio on East Broadway and I'd watch him don his surgical-type mask and spray paint. The studio was spacious enough to contain a grand piano and floor-to-ceiling pillars. Jules might sometimes interrupt his intense concentration on an area of paint to go over to the piano and practice scales. He was determined, like Michelangelo, to experience himself in all the arts, and he drank more than I did. But, when he wasn't trying to play parts of the classical repertoire, the radio often blared pop and rhythm and blues. As I recall, his all time favorite "golden oldie" was Rosemary Clooney singing "Come on a My House."

I always thought his paintings were rich and suggestive of flux and stasis but, since they deliberately avoided any paraphrasable subject matter, found it hard to talk about them with him. One was presented with vast opalescent pools of a tinted seminal hue, large areas of subtly modulated color which he would sometimes later crop and trim at the suggestion of others or through his own perceiving and then edge with magic markers. Jules's paintings sometimes bore portentous titles, Russian place names and proper names, but they were easy to take in; one simply had to permit oneself the pleasure. The paintings were the experience of pleasure, as intense as certain moments of release. He told me once he was still dependent on the judgments of the critic Clem Greenberg because Clem was unique in having a glance unmediated by pre-existing ideas. He looked at only what the painter was painting and experienced only that.

Jules was born in Russia and came here when he was very young. He and I were raised in the same neighborhood of Flatbush in Brooklyn. He'd gone off to study in Paris after the war with Ossip Zadkine. He told me once his father had been a Soviet commissar in the early days after the revolution and had perished in mysterious circumstances.

He seemed to be very bitter about his early career in New York when he'd gone through very hard times. He told me once that he'd lived in unheated lofts, with only bread and soup to sustain him and had such a hard time getting shows that once he invented a pseudonym for himself as a Russian refugee recently escaped from the Soviet Union and brought his slides in such disguise to a leading Madison Avenue dealer, who was impressed with the work but still refused to give him a show.

Jules said many years later when he was famous he met the same dealer again and confessed to having deliberately misled him, and the man said he remembered the incident and had suspected the ruse.

"Why didn't you say it was your work?" the man told him. "I would have probably been more interested."

I had fallen for one of my students after she graduated Bennington, so I could hardly blame Jules for dating very young women. His work habits then encouraged loneliness. He could seem very delicate and, at other times, robust and well fed and highly sexed. Stocky and wide-faced, with high cheekbones and strong hands and narrow shoulders and thinning wavy hair, with the face of a *muzhik*, I always thought; there was always a note of complaint in his voice, a sort of nasal crabbiness.

Sometime after we met I was invited to spend a weekend with Jules and some other men in Amagansett. We would be telling each other our histories, which was fashionable for men as well as women to do in those days. Jules was reluctant to speak about himself, but when he did he was articulate and very moving. He was very clear that he was from an early age aware of his own genius, though he was often miscast by others as a misfit. He became an abstract painter, I recall him saying, after throwing a dish of sour cream against the wall in his mother's flat and noticing the wall afterwards. Later he was very shy and distant again and excused himself from the company early. He seemed to miss the presence of a sympathetic female audience.

Jules did not like wearing the mask when he sprayed because he found it hard to breathe. There was one time when I watched him work that his ecstasy seemed overwhelming and other times when he would stare blankly for many minutes, almost as though not blinking his eyes. It wasn't remotely like what one sees at the mix and swirl concessions at carnival midways. Jules used to spend as much time or more looking as spritzing. He seemed to be discovering his paintings through the way the colors fell and mixed together on the canvas, or held themselves separate and subtly apart. Then he'd stop and pull himself back, perhaps take a drink, and start again, his eye exact, censorious, sometimes chain smoking, which he could not do wearing the mask. It was clear to me that one aspect of his genius was being able to be such a good student of his own paintings.

If he usually was very competitive about the painting scene, he was also about writing, which I found hard to understand. He'd read and admired *Ulysses*, and every novel he asked me to recommend had to measure up to that high standard. But with painting he could seem exceedingly tolerant. He told me once he regularly took advantage of accidents.

He was a man of moody and uneven temperament and had serious depressions when he would keep from human company. Even though his work was being purchased by museums for five-figure sums, he sometimes seemed to feel apprehensive about his success, that his acceptance by the art world was, at best, still tentative and grudging. He complained to me once that there was a deliberate policy at the *Times* not to review any of his shows. When the sculptor David Smith died in a car accident in Vermont, Jules and his colleague and competitor Kenneth Noland bought up large quantities of Smith's unused steel and began to fabricate sculptures. Some of Jules's low squat constructions were shown at the Metropolitan Museum, but to my knowledge a lot was never utilized and, for many years, lay in a big pile on a side road off the Bennington College campus.

He knew many painters but, except for Larry Poons, did not in those days regularly seek out their company. His income was large, and he had many professionals managing his affairs. He claimed to be greatly envied and sometimes abused by less talented contemporaries. At various times he tried to convince me to try my hand at painting and to walk away from my daughter's life as, he inferred, he had had to do at one point with his own daughter, Eve. I did buy paints and materials and made a lot of big messes on my living room floor with dry pigments and various gels, but I never took his advice about child rearing. He taught at Bennington and owned a large property that had once been the home of a colonial governor of that state. From his second wife, Andy, he'd acquired property on an island in a lake in New Hampshire, and it was to this place that he'd go to hide out when he was feeling at odds with himself or others. Jules suggested to me he learned a lot from looking at lake water while fishing. He also pointed out that, though he was now prosperous enough to have many studios and residences, he considered them all luxuries and had done some of his best work in the living room of a small Upper West Side flat.

The art world in those days was certainly different from publishing as I knew it. My publishers kept thinking of big numbers and, in my case, were usually disappointed. Once in Vermont, when I had occasion to drop by Kenneth Noland's studio, his dealers from London and Paris were on hand and Ken and his brother were laying out rolls of closely hued, striped canvas like rug merchants at a Turkish souk.

The dealers seemed to be buying up his merchandise by the yard.

This was harder to do in Jules's case, I think, because the fields of color were dependent on scale and could not easily be chopped and divided up. The drops of paint contributed to an uninterrupted surface.

A painter of Jules's prominence, moreover, really was solely interested in attracting the attention of a limited number of connoisseurs and dealers. Nevertheless, like Noland and others who were also prominent then, Jules seemed to have a whole support system of scholars and curators and groupies, some of whom I met. It seemed to me that success in that world depended on the accumulation of prestige. In order to be purchased by the great collections, it was useful to socialize with the Rubens brothers and encourage essays written by Harvard art historians, even though the paintings were intended to be autonomous and mute. The common way his groupies put it was that Olitski and these others were already installed in art history. I must confess this sometimes seemed to me to be a very fancy form of sales promotion.

When I knew Jules, he sprayed and squeegeed paint on the canvas without much impasto; his surfaces were dense and deep and shimmering. He had been through an earlier period of figurative works in thick black and white relief. Some new works I've seen are much more built up, though he more or less remains devoted to abstraction. I once asked Jules why he painted as he did, and, after assuring me that no genuine alternatives for an artist at the cutting edge existed, he showed me some of the paintings of the masters in the art books, and we looked at areas and details together, and it was clear to me that he saw himself as very much in the tradition of such greats as Velasquez (and also the mosaic artists of Ravenna), except that he had managed to eliminate illustration so as to make painting itself all the more eloquent.

A lot of the most recent art seems to be about parody, or else—to use an art history term—is "text laden." Much seems cheapened by a vulgar expressionism. Jules's work is increasingly remote from the artistic center, lonely, elegant, austere, at times, beautiful to me. And his new monoprints of imaginary landscapes are elegantly serene, and sometimes quite dramatic.

I can remember telling him once that I thought painters had *a* definite advantage over writers as artists because who they were and what they were thinking and feeling were never quite so directly linked to concepts and articulated, as words *seemed to* demand; they could remain more or less mute, hidden, and much less vulnerable.

Not surprisingly, Olitski agreed.

LUCINDA CHILDS

Her silences were eloquent, and frequent, large elipses plopped between a gesture of her hand, the tossing of her sleek, graceful head. They seemed to suck the air out of a room.

Tall and slim and small-breasted, with wonderful eyes, she moved inside the body of a youth painted on a Grecian vase, with a squared, indignant posture that could quickly turn light and playful. She rarely spoke except in closely argued, thought-out sentences, beautifully arranged pieces of syntax through which she seemed to be perceiving things abstractly new, and her writing conveyed mind and feeling, though she was loathe to do it very often.

When I knew Lucinda she seemed to be taking respite from her career as a dancer and choreographer. She lived alone in a large, clean, well-furnished flat that was cool with available light, and she gave lessons in the Alexander technique, in effect reteaching people how to walk and breathe. I am very tall and long-legged, and I slump over quite a little, so I was advised to take such lessons, which I did for quite some time. It was not an entirely successful foray, for I was much too interested in bringing my instructor to a conversation or in seeking to engage her glance, and she was strict and devout about demanding my obedience and attention.

As I recall, the technique involved certain perambulations about a large bare space accompanied by the constant injunctions of the instructor:

"Let the neck grow!"

"Let the shoulders rest!"

"Let the lungs breath in!"

Words to that effect! I found these commands hard to follow because they insisted I must relearn how to breathe, though they were enunciated clearly enough and often repeated, like breathing. I simply lacked the immediacy of connection between mind and body Cindy had to make concentration possible and inevitable. When she demonstrated for me I was credulous. When it came my time to perform the same steps I was awkward and stiff, splayed out, frightened, insensate.

Cindy reproached me for my lack of self-discipline. Our lessons ended, but for a while we remained friends and used to see each other socially. A physical connectedness to this person abstracted from her flesh and bone as vivid sinew seemed tantamount to challenging Bjorn Borg to a set of singles, though I was attracted to her beautifully epicene marine features and clear eyes, her intelligence and gentleness, her face framed by boyish short hair, and her quick wit sporadically expressed, so that we passed some time together and kept each other company.

It was, as one might imagine, not so easy to engage such a person in light conversation. She could rouse all her person into her shoulders and eyes and seem highly censorious and yet remain mute. I found myself staring at her a lot of the time in search of clues. She claimed to love men as well as women. What could she possibly find to love in me?

The times we spoke, I always found Cindy sensible and unpretentious and clear in her advice, though fraught with caveats; and though we shared few interests I always took pleasure from our encounters and felt less alone, as if I'd gained an older, wiser sister, although I was in years the senior person. I did not always understand her anger. It seemed to flare up behind her lips against her set mouth, imploding suddenly in her person before she was calm again and compassionate.

Her anger never really was directed against me. It seemed to be directed against a whole realm of prior experiences, humiliations, and learned distrusts. All I knew of her previous life was that she was well born and carefully educated. She had worked at Judson with Merce Cunningham and others, been involved with a painter and with a garrulous, over-confiding critic, and had suffered some sort of loss of trust in herself, a lack of confidence, and depression.

Then she seemed better and started dancing again with her own company, but just as she rarely spoke in conversation so she seemed barely to move in performance. On the stage she posted herself with great dignity and strength in various places, and other dancers seemed to be drawn toward her minimalist stance and away again, or she momentarily to them. There was no music. Her dancing, like her person, seemed to be about silence and scrupulousness and thoughtfulness, and I was left with the feeling one has after watching certain mammals perform repeated unintelligent acts. If what I saw could not be interpreted by my conscious mind, that didn't mean it wasn't eloquent and mindful and moving.

Sometimes her reproaches actually seemed loving as well as stern. "You are not taking good enough care of yourself. You can't expect that of me," she told me once. "I worry about you and I shouldn't."

I came away at one point from time spent with Cindy feeling myself fortunate for having access through her to quite another realm of being, a different, quieter zone of life. She was, for a sentence or two, or even a paragraph, the most impressive writer of prose I'd ever encountered, so close to thought her words reminded me of the Levantine French poet Jabes, though her sentences, never rounded off, always came without closure, as though each led directly toward a little death. Her stories were usually only a couple of paragraphs long. Was anything lacking?

We were walking together on a busy New York street, and I noticed how our steps didn't match, though her stride was almost equal to my own. We'd been talking about poetry, and she related it to the sense of bodies in movement and arrested motion. For a moment I heard her words, and then I heard her stillness, and that changed me somehow, so that I could no longer chatter on and fell in step with her, moving to her motions as though automatically and seemingly mindless.

When bodies speak to others, little is misunderstood. Cindy and I, of course, would remain separate. The consolation of that afternoon lasted only as long as our walk together on that sunlit street one fine spring day, and then our circumstances changed; I left the city and have never been in touch with Cindy again.

ALLEN GINSBERG AND OTHERS

In one of his final interviews, Ezra Pound, in Merano, Italy, after being released from St. Elizabeth's, confessed to an attentive and admiring Allen Ginsberg that his failure as a poet had much to do with his long-standing "suburban anti-Semitism." This must have come as a surprise to Allen, who arrived as a fan and was trying to offer Pound comfort. Pound was, for once, extremely tough on himself. He seemed to know he was speaking for the record, and he said his faults as an artist had been a literary provincialism every bit as blinding as what he, as literary cosmopolitan, had attacked and burlesqued for so long in his narrow American contemporaries. "Suburban anti-Semitism" was certainly much less grand than the flamboyance of fascism.

"Poets though divine are men," Ben Jonson, in middle age, wrote to a young woman in Scotland after leaving behind his picture, the gesture of the lover he had once been conflated by a pot belly, flatulence perhaps, and jowls. But Jonson claimed he was no less fervent for there being so much more of him.

In general, I agree with Jonson that human failings are not necessarily diminishment. And I think Allen in his life was quite often as human as he would have liked us to believe he was. He consoled Pound, the anti-Semite, as he later was able to converse with a CIA spook like James Angleton, without being himself diminished in the process, and even imagined a shipboard dialogue with the ghost of T. S. Eliot, his diametric opposite. James Angleton really wasn't that hard to talk to after he retired from the agency. You'd call him, and there'd be this voice recorded in the depths of a sauerkraut barrel.

I doubt if Angleton regarded Allen as his friend, though Allen could seem very sweet natured, a real good guy, just a little sad, at times, and the only times I've seen him act in a hurtful way was by inadvertence. Once, I gave a reading with him downtown at Brentano's. Allen asked to read first before a huge audience. He was going off afterward to perform with the Clash. When Allen finished reading, he left and the house almost entirely emptied. Following such

an evacuation, I felt like John Jay Chapman making an act of conscience in that empty hall in Coatstown, Pennsylvania.

Moreover, Allen's reading that night was pretty awful. A few
songs on the concertina and some of the usual doggerel about "cock-
sucking." I say that without malice. I think he continued to write truly
interesting and beautiful poems right up to the time of his death, at
least some of the time. Trouble was he didn't always do so, and sometimes he presented the same old tiresome blah-blah-blah.

Whenever I was asked by the PEN, I put in my nomination for
Allen to get the Nobel Prize for Literature. Since the fifties I knew of
nobody more influential worldwide, nor more humane. He was imitated everywhere, the manner, if not the incredible ear for language
and openness of feeling.

I first bumped into Ginsberg around 1956 in Berkeley when he
was reading from *Howl* to huge new audiences, with Kenneth Rexroth
and other Bay Area literats in attendance. He seemed boyish in those
days, though he must have been in his late twenties or a little older;
and I was a curious Wintersian, repelled every bit as much as I was
attracted. We rarely, if ever, spoke.

I used to see Allen at WBAI, too, and during the late seventies,
when I became interested in writing about the literary networks of the
CIA, I found myself consulting with Ginsberg, who was engaged in
similar research for the PEN Freedom to Write Committee. Allen, of
course, was especially interested in the CIA and the drug trade. He
didn't wish to know about all the literats who'd toured Eastern Europe
for the Congress for Cultural Freedom, perhaps doing a little recruit-
ing on the side, and about the young writers from abroad recruited by
the agency to return home as "agents in place."

We met in his apartment on the Lower East Side, a large shabby
flat near Avenue D in a building he seemed to own cooperatively with
a great many young followers: poets, artists, musicians, hangers-on. It
was a sunny day, and we sat together in the kitchen next to an open
window abutting on a fire escape. The sill was clotted with paint and
the sun so hot the sill seemed to bubble and ooze. I thought of Allen's
mom telling him: The key is in the window. The key is in the sunlight
in the window Allen. Don't take drugs.

We were drinking strong black tea out of, as I recall, jelly glasses.

He was just beginning to teach young poets at Naropa in Boulder
and, later, as John Ashberry's replacement at Brooklyn College; and he
was very sincere, and conscientious, and friendly. He also liked the
health insurance and the regular wages, a friend from Brooklyn College informed me, as he'd never really held a straight job until then.

Allen told me that day he thought not everybody who collaborated with the CIA was in the same leaky boat. Some were honorable men. He personally seemed able to talk to anybody, as he'd talked with Pound, without compromising himself. His recent death deprives all of us of that candor.

Once, at a John Weiners reading, I asked both Allen and Weiners if they could recall the San Francisco days of my dear friend, the painter Keith Sanzenbach, who'd committed suicide in 1964. They'd all lived together in the Filmore and North Beach, and hung around the Co-existence Bagel Shop, and so on. Allen said he thought he could remember Keith; he said he thought he'd lived above Keith once on Gough Street. That made sense to me, because I used to go to Allen's readings with Keith and his wife, Nicki. Allen said he thought he remembered Nicki; she was tall and pretty. Weiners seemed to regard that whole time as a blank. Allen spoke with great kindness and sadness. Suicides were no novelty to him. He'd known of a lot. Keith's whole generation of West Coast painters had died untimely deaths from drugs, other forms of suicide, and there had been so many dead writers. Allen reminded me that Keith was not the first or the last of his generation to die by his own hand; he spoke softly and raised his voice to take leave of me, his voice of the same timbre and nasality as that of Lenny Bruce, I thought.

Certain other memories, though, persist, from that time as images: the tall, balding (Hungarian, I thought, though he was actually Puerto Rican) man of rather stiff military bearing who always used to accompany Anais Nin to parties as her husband, friend, silent courtier, all three, I never could be sure with Hugo. He always seemed so stolid and to be on duty, never seemed to utter a word, a deep saturnine frown and imperial shoulders. Anais, on the other hand, wore so much makeup into her seventies I never could be sure if I was actually seeing her or an effigy of the way she looked at thirty-five as confected by some wax museum. Anais's voice: odd, a pressed tin artificial sound, more like the noise made by a Crackerjacks premium than a human sound.

Once she handed me a canape at a literary party and insisted that what looked like paté was really catfood. I was to taste it and see.

She once told me I had eyes for all the women at a particular party aside from her.

I said there was a considerable difference in our ages and outlooks.

"And," she said, "*I'm* an artist and you like floozies."

"I'm really not interested in any of the women at this gathering," I said.

"You really ought to be ashamed of yourself," was all Anais said.

LORE SEGAL

I once told Lore Segal she could make a career out of telling fortunes with cards or tea leaves.

She replied she thought that was pretty much what Elie Wiesel was up to with scripture in his public lectures at the Y on Hassidism.

Lore is a skeptical person. I suppose she is usually rational. Too aware of charlatans, she never makes much of a display of her feelings, is cool and witty, rarely prophetic, and not usually unkind. I've never heard her use profanity, and rarely does she resort to superlatives. High praise from her can be to "show good sense." I think she still translates a lot from German inside her head.

In the sixties I used to go to her flat on Riverside Drive at her invitation, sometimes to chat and sip tea or sherry. Her mother, a Viennese, would always be on hand as chaperone. It seemed as though, having been separated from her daughter for so long by the war that propelled Lore to sanctuary in England and eventually the States, her mother was being extra careful in her parenting of this by-now-grown woman, and Lore still permitted herself to act like a daughter in her presence, though she'd long since been an independent woman.

It would be late afternoon; her children would be off at play somewhere. Lore's husband was David Segal, a leading editor at *Harper's*, but they seemed to be living apart. He was rarely about the flat. Lore or her mother would prompt me with topics for conversation. I'd begin to talk, and the ladies would compliment me with mysterious glances. Lore's mother called me "Mr. Elman." I think I was being considered as a replacement for David by her, if not by her daughter. I was very lonely and confused at the time and took advantage of Lore's hospitality, paying little back. Though I liked chatting with her, I preferred to chase many available and unattached younger women in those days. I never told Lore that, though I think she guessed I dropped by usually when my expectations had been let down by one of these "heartless creatures." If she'd ever been disappointed by David's bothersome taking care of his own needs, she never made me feel guilty or intrusive. I found being around her and her mother as soothing as a cup of chamomile tea, but this was not always soothing to Lore, who grew impatient with her mother's observations, though she never suggested we meet elsewhere.

I first encountered her at WBAl when we serialized all of her reading of her first book, *Other People's Houses*. She was very fine to look at in those days, a Mozartian profile and a fulsome figure, a clear, sharp, elegant voice. She was, as I recall, a great admirer of the Bloomsbury crowd, especially the novels of Virginia Woolf. Much later we were colleagues at Columbia. She taught one graduate class, and I taught another. It wasn't long before I was invited to her house in the late afternoons.

I sometimes thought Lore and her mother were vying for my attention to distract themselves from worrying about David, who would die of a heart attack off on his own. Being at her place wasn't like my encounters with other younger New York women, where the hospitality was minimal and the quarters were cramped. Lore's apartment was commodious and well furnished. We seemed to be somewhere other than in New York and in a different time. Among these two refugees I had foundered on a reef of brief sanctuary in their continuing diaspora from Europe.

We definitely liked different books. Lore's husband was successfully publishing John Gardner, and she admired him, too. I thought he was pompous, a little padded out. Another friend was the author of that academic classic *Hermaphrodeity*, an elegant but long-winded comic novel about the ambiguities of gender which owed a lot to Virginia Woolf.

Lore owed a lot to Virginia Woolf also. She admired the writing and always seemed to be disappointed that the Upper West Side wasn't really Bloomsbury. She could also be rather snobby, though she also had the "good sense" never to be confrontational about her opinions. I'd been brought to Columbia to replace Edward Dahlberg who had offended his writing seminar by declaring that none of the students knew how to write prose and then tried to make them emulate the classical models. It seemed I would have to take a less confrontational approach if the students were to do anything other than complain that they were being put down, and I tried whenever possible to validate their writings when I could. So Lore and I often quarreled in a friendly way about what students to admit to the program and who was worthy of encouragement. Lore was interested in all the women writers, of course, but she could be generous to men as well. Her attitude toward teaching creative writing was fatalistic. It almost seemed foretold who would achieve first rate work and who would falter, and she did not believe in encouraging those she considered second rate.

The problem was that her skeptical attitude toward talent was supported by an imperfect ear for the vernacular, and she wasn't always able to judge what was a fresh performance and what was not. If her standards seemed to be very high and unbending, she was also quite a reasonable person and, with some grumbling, showed "the good sense" to work as best she could with whomever she was assigned to help.

I admired her first book about her adolescence as a refugee from Europe in the houses of strangers, but found the persona she later adopted for herself in some *New Yorker* stories very coy and a little silly, a European shrinking violet. Nevertheless, I continued to have respect for her skepticism and high standards. She was no fanatic of Jewishness, like her friend Cynthia Ozick. Although she traveled to Israel with Cynthia, Lore continued to be critical and acute.

Our friendship faltered over time mostly because I was so unavailable to friendship. Once in Bennington we talked about this. I reminded her how we'd once been friends. Lore was more accurate. "Once tried to be friends," she corrected me.

The coup d'état in Chile resulted in the execution of thousands of ordinary citizens, many of the left. Shortly afterwards, a Columbia colleague visited Chile and reported back to the *Times* that the "nightmare" of Chile under Allende had ended.

I had been troubled by the Columbia program's connection to CIA conduits like the Farfield Foundation and wrote a letter to the *Times* which was published, pointing out that calling Allende's rule a "nightmare" was truly symptomatic of the geopolitics of Langley in the aftermath of the Chilean military's murders and repressions. I was then a senior member of the staff and had a higher rank than Lore and was employed with more regularity. It's probably no accident that she and other women also used the occasion to complain about their unequal treatment from Columbia and benefitted from my seeming kamikaze behavior.

Shortly afterward I was invited to lunch and told I would not be invited back to teach at Columbia the following year.

I truly think Lore thought separating me from my job would be good for both of us. In those days it wasn't always possible to make common cause with women. They had their own personal agendas to carry out. In recent years she has treated me with cordiality and respect. There's a certain class of New York literary woman who always compliments me on my lovely wife and children when we meet. I take it they are not that crazy about much else that I've done. Lore is one such.

We were once on a panel together about Holocaust literature. I was there because of the novels I had written twenty years earlier. Lore's early childhood in Vienna marked her as a Holocaust survivor. I had recently returned from Central America where I'd witnessed massacres of the left and the right and was possibly distracted. Lore was jittery. She'd never before been on the Holocaust circuit. With delicate remorse, she tried to recall the lost father of her childhood in Vienna at the time of Anschlüss.

Aaron Appelfeld kept urging me to visit Israel. Lore had recently been, and kept, silent. I thought she was more aware than most of those in the symposium of how parochial were our concerns in a murderous time, and if she chose to bear witness she would not historicize it unduly beyond her own memory of loss. I respected her for that and told her so. But she felt her performance was inadequate compared to the "genius" of her friend Cynthia Ozick, for whom the Holocaust is always imminent, ongoing, though she herself was spared, as I was in Brooklyn, from ever knowing of it at firsthand in the Pelham Bay section of the Bronx.

The dislocations and disruptions Lore suffered in childhood must have been hurtful and scary, but she has always remained more outgoing and on better terms with the world than the people she befriends. When she was a young woman she was close to the African American writer Horace Cayton, co-author of *Black Metropolis, a* difficult man and a drinker, whom she wrote about fictionally in the sequel to *Other People's Houses* with compassion and humor.

She may have allowed decorum to overcome her disappointments from time to time in dealing with authentic literary bureaucrats such as Frank McShane or Clark Blaise, but I've never experienced her that way. Lore has never for one moment failed to reproach me when I've misbehaved in her presence, which means, I suppose, that she has noticed me, just as I am always noticing her, not without reservations.

ELIE WIESEL

I have very positive memories of my encounters with this survivor, though we disagree about almost everything of note. When *The Twenty-eighth Day of Elul* was published, my editor asked me to whom galleys should be sent for comments. The novel was set in Transylvania during World War II. With some qualms I suggested Wiesel, who was from a small Transylvanian city not too far removed from my invented city of Clig. I suggested him, but I assumed Elie would be, at best, a little critical of what I, an American with no direct experience of the *Kurvan* (massacre), had tried to invent.

Some weeks later I began to receive telephone messages from my wife that Wiesel had been trying to reach me by phone. In the interim I had grown fearful of Wiesel's disapproval, and I was much too scared that I was going to get a scolding to return his call. She finally reasoned with me that he probably wouldn't be calling to do any such thing.

When I reached Wiesel he said he was very moved by my book and wanted to review it. He could write something for either *Commentary* or the *New York Times*. The choice was mine. I said would he please write something for the *Times*? Wiesel's endorsement gained the novel legitimacy with other reviewers and an eventual audience.

He asked to meet me some time later, and I visited him in his sunny studio in a tower of the Master's Institute above Riverside Park. He told me that though I was not at Auschwitz I bore witness through my imagination along with him and so many other children who had perished. He suggested there was another novel to be written about the young woman in the *Twenty-eighth Day*, and that's how I came, eventually, to write *Lilo's Diary*, which I hadn't planned to do until then.

That first meeting was in a small and square room with windows on all sides, and Wiesel in his shirtsleeves seemed very vulnerable in the center of that room as he came from behind his desk to grasp my hand. His face was all narrow angles, it seemed, but his smile was broad and genuine, a slight man of intensity and strength.

We've kept in touch over the years. When my daughter Lila was born he sent a telegram, welcoming her to this world. When I was writing about the sanctuary trial in Tucson he wrote me a statement in support of the right of political asylum and the sanctuary movement.

I greatly admired his novel *The Gates of the Forest* as a work of fiction and reviewed it, and I admired his speaking out directly to Reagan when that clown went to Bitburg to commemorate the SS dead.

Much of Wiesel's early writings were in French. He was a friend of Andre Schwartz-Bart, whose novel *Le Dernier Juste* I consider one of the few masterpieces of what colleges today classify as "Holocaust literature."

When Wiesel's review of my novel appeared I received many letters from survivors saying they also had testimony to give, stories to tell. Some sent along manuscripts. These were so grim and awful to contemplate I turned them back. The truth is I did not think I could tell other people's stories. My Hungarian novels were motivated initially by a desire to disguise my own shabby experiences of childhood in dealing with intractable institutions and people; and it was only because I came into contact with many who had survived *Kurvan*, and had also gotten to know Isaac Singer so well that I could mimic him, that I came to imagine my experiences within that cruel world of strangers and terror during such a brutal time.

Except for *Gates of the Forest*, I think Wiesel's novels tend to be somewhat polemical and schematic, and I am not in sympathy with those who regard him as a prophet rather than a mere writer and an activist, and many of his causes are not my own.

I also think some aspects of his public life after Auschwitz have elements of a major work of imagination. Wiesel continues to live his life *as if*—in terms of an essential central fiction. So much in his past was turned into ashes by the *Kurvan* that he has reinvented himself as a celebrator of human life rather than simply grieving endlessly. He's really remarkable for his energy on behalf of victims. If they tend to be, on the whole, European, he's capable of considering other alternatives. He spoke out against the "genocide" in Moslem, Bosnia. When I suggested he also consider the quotidian massacres of Mayans in Guatemala, he listened.

" What shall we do?" he wrote, pleading with me for guidance. "What?"

I pointed out it would simply help if people knew that genocide was taking place in Guatemala.

In *Night* Wiesel tells us God perished for him when he, as a young boy at Auschwitz, was forced to witness the murder of his entire family. Living in Paris and New York, he seemed to find his contingency unbearable. *The Accident* is a novel about a suicidal victim. How fortunate for so many that Wiesel reinvented a God-sanctified world for himself, conflating Sartre and Merleau-Ponty with the Baal Shem Tov, founder of Hassidism, so that he could still bear witness to the ordeals of so many voiceless others.

CHARLIE'S BIRD

There I
go there I go there I
go . . .

　　　—"Moody's Mood
　　　　for Love," by
　　　　King Pleasure

Drummer Charlie Watts of the Rolling Stones and I got pretty thick during a tour of the south and the southwest the summer of 1972. We were, it turned out, both great Charlie Parker fans. Watts said the Stones were basically "just shit, though just about the best shit" there was around on the rock scene, whereas Parker was "a great artist, a genuine artist, Richard."

He was a little older than Mick and Keith, a little more reserved. He'd been a jazz drummer once and an art student at the Slade. He inscribed to me a small picturebook he'd made and published for children, a kind of child's life of Charlie Parker, "the Yardbird," written and drawn by Charlie Watts in browns and yellows.

Yardbird was depicted in Watts' book as a little different, odder, than all the other chicks in the nest. He started as a little brown cheeper and fell out of the nest, or was jostled, and grew into a large-sized honker and a wailer, the original big bopper. Watts signed his book to me with love, and I was very grateful for the gift.

He was talking then about leaving rock 'n roll for 'something else' and once did record some jazz sessions with his own group which were commercially unsuccessful, but he's never left the Stones. Hard to turn your back on so much money.

"Richard," he said to me, most earnestly, "we are the best of the shit, but you mustn't make too much of that, because compared to Parker and Dolphy and those cats, well, we're just shit . . . tit arse . . . if you know what I mean . . . shit."

I got to know the jazz singer Eddie Jefferson just a little bit before the time he was shot coming out of a club date in Detroit by a former dancing partner. Eddie hadn't seen the man in twenty-five years. His nemesis sprang at him as though they were just coming off the band stand together.

Eddie was such a friendly guy it was a shock to all of us to believe that somebody had been holding a grudge against him for so long; he was always affable and cute, generous to younger musicians, easy with most people, a slim man with a dancer's body and a spry look that could be molded to fit his moods.

We met when he sang at my friend Paul Pines' club, the Tin Palace. He was very pleased to sing "Moody's Mood for Love" again at my request. Eddie was supporting two households somewhere in suburban Queens or Long Island, and he had never made the big bucks, but, though he was aware of the general public's ignorance of his reputation and style, he did not seem to brood much about his feelings of neglect. "I had some really good times," he would say. "I worked with all the giants . . . including Mr. Charlie Parker," and then he would do Parker riffs with his lips, and a fast shuffling of the feet.

The jazz drummer Roy Haynes also suffered from feelings of neglect after playing Birdland with Parker and the greats. When I used to bump into him at the Hobbit Hole in Selden, Long Island, during his irregular series of one-night stands, Haynes wasn't easily solaced when I told him how much I still admired his crisp, strong, precise drumming. Haynes tried to get me to help him remedy this neglect.

Roy decided to bestow on me the honor of ghostwriting his memoirs. He was confident we would eventually make some bread, he told me, through an intermediary. Meantime I was to scribble, write the book for nothing, on the come, as it were. I really was not quite so confident and demurred.

Eddie Jefferson was also working on his memoirs. I believe, with Paul Pines because they were close friends. He was sometimes very businesslike and brusque, except with Pauly. After his gig at the Palace Eddie would sit and drink in the club and talk about his days with King Pleasure, Parker, Miles, and others, but he never seemed to be holding many grudge cards. He wanted to sustain the illusion that he was still up-and-coming, chipper, capable of getting happy and making an audience happy, too. In those days, his most constant sidekick was a very talented young, white alto player named Richie Scott.

News of Eddie's murder hurt everybody in our crowd. Like waking up sick after a party. Paul Pines, not a soft man, broke down and cried. We all got sicker and sicker thinking about that ancient grudge enacted against this basically grudgeless man, and then the sadness came. Some of that mood, I think, is conveyed by transformation in Paul Pines' novel *The Tin Angel*.

On West Seventy-seventh Street in the early seventies I lived two doors down from Miles Davis. The local pharmacist's delivery boy was always dropping off his prescriptions in little white bags at my place when he couldn't find anybody home at Davis's. Then I'd have to wander over as soon as I saw life about the place and give the man or one of his flunkies the stuff.

Davis had been strung out, at times, and I didn't know if he was scoring legally, or what, but I was loathe to put him uptight. I'd wander over to his place with that little white bag, with an air of entirely *faux naïveté*, as though I'd never even heard of Miles Davis. "Is, er, Mr. David here . . . Somebody left a package for him at my place" (holding that bag in front of my nose like a dead mouse).

He had his place done up with a facade of carved wood, like some kind of South Sea islands tribal hut. Every once in a while I'd know he was at home because I could hear him blowing sweet clinkers and dissonances. Whenever I saw him on the street I tried to pretend I was a Brahms enthusiast.

Underneath all those African or South Sea islands facings and carvings, it sometimes gave me pleasure to see Davis' friend, the actress Cecily Tyson, so tall and fine, waiting to be admitted.

Miles was often out of town. All sorts of deliveries would pile up. I'd be holding all sorts of items in my vestibule until such time as I saw activity about the tribal hut. Once, coming from a bitter and frosty interview with my former wife, who claimed she neither had the time nor the interest to mother our child but would not allow me to have custody, I came upon Miles with his horn in a little velvet bag that looked like it could have held a Jewish *siddur* and other things on the high holidays; he was with the very fine Ms. Tyson. They embraced, and then he found her a cab, helped her inside. Afterwards, he looked up and saw me looking at him as the cab drove off, and the man just grinned.

At thirteen I read Mezz Mezzrow's *Really the Blues*. Such a vicarious experience I got from the adventures of this first of the "white Negro" hipsters that when I finally heard Mezz play at Condon's I was disappointed to discover how much better he was as a storyteller. Mezz made his clarinet sound like it was clogged with chicken soup.

The back alley outside Condon's stank of muggles and mezzes (his patented name for maryjane); and when I tried to get close to this stoned old Jew from Chicago, he told me, "Don't watch me. Watch the spinning duck." And he was gone down the alley with two ladies of the night and a dealer before I got a second look.

In New Orleans I met Clarence "Frogrow" Henry and Doctor Longhair. They spoke more jive than the UN General Assembly. The Bullfrog had hands with a two-octave spread.

I saw the Pres, Lester Young, when he was just old and tired, a last minute fill-in, at a "supper club" adjacent to a Jewish cemetery on Ocean Parkway, Brooklyn. He was all soft, spitty melody and sad reed whinings, with not a honk of protest. No leaping Lester then. Wouldn't take off his porkpie hat. Said, "I'm not dying. I just sound as though I am." Then he was gone.

I used to like to hear Jimmy Rushing when he sang at the Five Spot in New York. He always seemed to be having such a good time up there above the bar with the band, shimmying and shaking and sweet as Fox's U-bet syrup in a glass of seltzer.

Once I went with Al Goldman, and he called over Mr. Five-by-Five to have a drink. Jimmy had other plans, so Al brought over Zoot Sims, who was playing backup with Al Cohen. Zoot sat with us a good hour, and he did nothing but talk about books he'd been reading as though he'd just discovered reading. He rattled off names like Faulkner and Joyce and Dostoevsky with so much enthusiasm and avidity that I was actually envious of him for having an experience so new to him, so fresh.

At Al Goldman's place once I also met Elvin Jones, the drummer with fullback shoulders, and his tiny Japanese wife. Elvin has hands like butterflied legs of lamb. His wife was small and pretty. Coltrane's former sideman was spending a lot of his time in Japan, not only because the Japanese like to listen to jazz, but because he was some sort of folk hero there and regularly appeared on TV commercials exploiting his size and the size of his hands. In one tomato juice commercial, a small Japanese was metamorphized as big, bad Elvin Jones because he drank the juice, or so Al Goldman once insisted. Al also said that this great jazz drummer was earning a large part of his living from gigs such as that.

At least the big man wasn't starving and going to pieces, like so many in the jazz life, Al said. I learned a lot about all that from Al Goldman, and I also worked for him for pay, as his ghost, fill-in writer and lecturer, and sounding board. Al researched more extensively than any writer I ever knew. He was plugged into the pop world, but he had this other aspect—of the serious Ph.D. academic, with a thesis on De Quincey, and a highly regarded text on Wagnerian music drama. Nevertheless, some people are always asking why he was so mean to the reputations of great pop figures like Elvis Presley and John Lennon.

Al's so-called meanness usually consisted of telling the truth about a figure, instead of joining in the chorus of hypes. He didn't invent any of his characters' rages, chronic depressions, skagged-up habits, or fucked up bodies. Al was always trying to solve the problems of why talented "successes" often died strung out at an early age. His 1970s collection of essays on Rock 'n' Roll, *Freak Show*, is brilliant magazine journalism, candid camera impressions of a scene with as lasting impact as the scene itself.

Until his untimely death, Albert was one of the few truly funny standup comics who didn't do it for a living. Al was never able to work a public room; he'd freeze. He used to perform for friends at parties— Phil Roth, Jack Kroll, certain women friends. He almost got chased out of Charleston, South Carolina, where he was living the gentile life and investigating the drug trade for a book, because nobody who was anybody in town could take a kidding from Al about the town elite's alcoholism and avarice. Al let it be known in *Esquire* magazine that Charlestonians spent all their time getting drunk and waiting for their rich relatives to die and leave them money.

When we were working together on his Lenny Bruce biography, Al's research mania got a little out of control. He seemed to have a take on every waking minute of Lenny's life after he left the navy, and he kept it all in big metal file cabinets. What he still lacked was direct testimony from one of Lenny's numerous women about what sort of lover Lenny was. Not from Annie Ross, his girlfriend, nor from Honey, his former wife. I volunteered to ask Faye Dunaway. She'd been Lenny's girlfriend, briefly, in New York when she was playing the Marilyn Monroe figure in Arthur Miller's *After the Fall* in Lincoln Center.

I found Faye's private number in my files and called her up and put the question to her as bluntly as possible. How was Lenny in bed? Faye didn't seem to mind remembering, and what she told me was said in a very ladylike and loving way, but it was also a whole lot sadder than anything Al ever wrote about Lenny Bruce.

"Richard," she said, with a voice exhausted of feelings, "though I really liked him, not that much ever went on . . . most of the time he was too strung out, distracted. . . . When I knew him," she added, "even then, back in the early sixties, he'd already lost all his pleasure."

Once, at Goldman's, I met a Southerner who alleged himself to be Margaret Trudeau's lover, and the dealer for just about everybody else in New York. Al was writing a book about the Columbian marijuana trade, and this "Tommy" was his informant. He had numerous scandalous things to say about the prime minister of Canada and how the Royal Mounties guarded them, Margaret and Tommy, when they were shacking up in New York.

"They're probably all true," Al insisted.

Albert Goldman wrote books that made a hypocritical world look at itself. Some people got angry and blamed him, when their best friends died, for writing so negatively about certain scenes. With a body full of uppers and downers, and a snake in his arm, what man can really say to posterity he has been misunderstood?

I think Al believed dying before your time wasn't much fun, for anybody.

Among other things, I shall always be grateful to Al for the review he wrote in *Life* magazine for Davey Scherman of my *Fredi and Shirl and the Kids*. Goldman pegged my style perfectly. He called what I was doing in that book "a comic strip."

III

RELAXING AT THE TOURO

ELMAN: THE MAN AND THE MASKS— A NIGHT IN EVANSTON

Once, on an interview program in Cleveland, where I'd been sent to plug my latest novel, I was reminded by mein host of my great previous writings on Yeats and Oscar Wilde, "not to mention your magnificent Joyce biography."

Radio interviewers don't always have time to read the books their guests have actually written. They use researchers and grab for convenient tags and labels. When this happened to me in Cleveland that time I copped to the false ID of Richard Ellmann as a matter of convenience and let the interview proceed. He asked me what I was now working on and I said a monograph on the *Yiddishe sprecht* of Leopold Bloom.

"I'm sorry I haven't read much beyond the title of your novel," the interviewer said, with my book staring directly at us.

"You know old chap," I said, "in Oxford we have a saying that the other Joyce was a traitor. Haw! Haw!"

Not that I didn't respect the other Richard Ellmann just as much as any other of his admirers. I even had to admit I once considered changing my name because when I first started writing I often received reproachful letters from important editors pointing out that my latest "creative work" was not of the "same qualities of mind" as my writings on the Irish masters, and, of course, sadly, I always agreed.

For a brief while Richard Ellmann and I even conducted a correspondence in the form of derogatory limericks on the confusions some may have had regarding our names and manuscripts. We did not meet, however, until I was sent to Chicago to promote another book, and he being the only person I knew at all in the Second City (and having a lot of time on my hands between recording sessions for TV and radio) I called Richard Ellmann at his home in Evanston.

"Hello Richard Ellmann. This is Richard Elman."

"Well hello . . . where are you?"

I explained I was even then at the Drake Hotel on an expense account.

"How lucky," he said. "You must come out . . . tonight. We're having a party."

He gave me an address in Evanston and said I should go by cab. It wasn't awfully dear. I'd be expected around eight.

My cabby took me to an ordinary two-story frame house on a residential street. The house was owned by an artist named Cohen. I rang the bell and was admitted by the host who joked when I introduced myself, "Come off it! Dick's already here."

In the living room was a whole collection of animated David Levine caricature faces, drinking, standing about, sitting on over-stuffed sofas, and smearing chopped liver onto crackers for themselves. I recognized each by its distorted caricature aspects. The bluish haired lady with the imperial glance and the handsome long chin was, of course, Hannah Arendt. Stephen Spender was tall and straight-backed, with lots of wavy, gray hair, a Shellyan profile. Dwight Mac-Donald appeared to resemble a hasty india ink drawing of a salon wit. Daniel Bell was bulbous, bespectacled. There was no face in that room that did not seem to recall a page out of the *New York Review of Books*. I searched for Richard Ellmann and, in the process, was relieved to observe that I was hardly being noticed, so animated was the drinking and the conversation (in more than one language). I accepted a high-ball from the hostess and tried to remember if I had ever seen the professor caricatured, or in a photo.

Presently a pleasant, cherubic-looking chap heaved to starboard and greeted me, "Richard Elman, I presume."

Professor Ellmann handed me a smear of chopped liver and asked what I was doing in Chicago. When I explained, he linked arms with me as I chewed and took me around the room to introduce me tête-à-tête to Hannah Arendt and the rest of the company, including Saul Bellow. There was the critic Tony Tanner, my old acquaintance Harold Rosenberg, a woman who'd had an affair with Dylan Thomas, and the widow of a renowned Hungarian sociologist. In all cases, with our arms still linked, Richard Ellmann introduced us by saying, "We're Richard Elmans."

A bit intimidated by such high-powered company and so much easy hospitality, I went from person to person, and even had a long conversation with Ellmann about my old shipmate on an Atlantic crossing, the Irish playwrite Denis Johnston.

So it was I struggled to be part of the evening, and I must have succeeded in fair measure because, when it came time to be seated at table, my dinner partner was selected by my hostess to be Hannah Arendt.

"So," she commenced, with the pouring of wine, her voice textured like gravel in a mess of honey, "You are Elman of *The Poorhouse State*."

"In a manner of speaking," I replied. "My friends call me Richard."

"We'll see," Hannah Arendt said. She turned away from me then to discourse on intellectual freedom and the CIA (because right about then it had been revealed in print that *Encounter* magazine had been subvented by the agency in Langley, and it seems some people in the room were feeling very bitter about such revelations).

Hannah Arendt did not seem at all surprised by what the CIA might have done nor by what some of her dinner companions were now saying by way of plausible denial. She called all their remarks "Kwatch!"

I found I had almost as little to contribute to the conversation as I had eyes for more spaghetti, but she turned back to me then and fed me more with two forks and poured us both more wine and smiled at me kindly, agreeably. Between frozen smiles I searched for other subjects of possibly mutual interest. All the people around the table save for Arendt were still pretending some measure of indignation at the CIA. My dinner partner asked me to call her "Hannah," and we spoke about where I lived and how I supported myself. Then she commented on my height and good looks and troweled up another helping of spaghetti for my plate.

It was sometime over the coffee and fruit that I recalled my former doctor in New York was, like Hannah Arendt, originally from Koenigsberg, East Prussia. Dr. Rael Landau was a man of fading and lonely pretensions about his life as an unconventional healer in Washington Heights and a former social lion in Weimer Germany, and he was always curious about my own career as a writer in New York. Who did I know well? See? Once he had even asked me if I had ever run into his old schoolmate, Hannah Arendt. Having assured my doctor I kept more modest intellectual company, I now wondered if I should mention Rael's name to my dinner companion. Richard Ellmann was telling the others about the bawdry in our correspondence and getting very few laughs.

My doctor had informed me once, "If you ever do meet Hannah send her the regards of Rael Landau. She'll remember."

I thought he must have been putting himself on with injections of fetal tissue.

Hannah Arendt said, "For another glass of wine I could tell your fortune with the spaghettis."

"Later," I winked as I poured for her. Then I said, "I have regards for you from an old schoolmate."

"Really? Who would that be?" Her brow seemed marmoreal.

"Can you recall a certain Rael Landau from Koenigsberg?"

To my wonder she broke into the sweetest of smiles, as though surrendering to memories utterly incomprehensible to me.

"I must be dreaming," Hannah Arendt said. "Do I remember Rael?" She spoke to me, to the vacant air, to all assembled around the table in a heavy metal Prussian accent that seemed to bend and flex around the corners of her memories. "I was thirteen . . . maybe fourteen. He was my first boyfriend. It so happens we used to meet behind a jewelry store clock in Koenigsberg. It was his father's shop. How could I ever forget Rael."

Hannah Arendt was very silent for most of the rest of the evening, as though lost in old memories. But, after a while, Professor Ellmann cleared his throat and asked Stephen Spender if he truly knew nothing as a former *Encounter* editor of the CIA's involvement with the magazine. "Come off it Stephen," Harold Rosenberg barked. "I knew. We all knew. What was the problem?"

"Kwatch," Hannah Arendt again said. Then she said to me, "You must visit me in New York sometime. I make a wonderful hazelnut . . . ," swallowing the last word.

"Everything Hannah bakes," Rosenberg assured me.

Richard Ellmann asked then if I'd like to tell everybody about my new book. I thought not. Hannah Arendt left the party early, alone. When I got ready to go, Richard Ellmann was again gracious about shaking my hand warmly and telling me to please keep in touch.

Pearl Kazin and her husband, Daniel Bell, offered me a ride to my hotel. They were anxious new parents, concerned about their baby sitter. I spent the trip back with Pearl berating Danny Bell for a review his old friend Irving Kristol had written of my book on the welfare system in which he'd alleged I was some kind of subversive Comsymp.

"Irving wouldn't do that," Bell protested.

"O yes he would . . . and did," said Pearl.

I called Ellmann the next day and thanked him for the entertaining evening with his friends and told him what had transpired once in Cleveland. He said that sometimes happened to him too, and he hadn't handled it quite so well.

"What did you say?" I asked.

"I'm afraid you are mistaken," honest Richard Elimann said.

For accepting Ellmann's invitation of hospitality one cold lonely Saturday evening I have never been sorry. It was the least I could do, I now realize, in making amends to this great scholar for the confusions and even indignities he may have had to endure for sharing a name with me.

Spooks

When he retired from the CTA in disgrace I sometimes called James Jesus Angleton on the phone in Alexandria and we chatted amiably enough. The former chief of Counter Intelligence told me the agency had subsidized *Encounter* magazine in London in the late fifties to influence snobbish Indian intellectuals on the subcontinent who were in danger of turning Stalinist and preferred their ideas to originate with the likes of T. S. Eliot in London. His voice always sounded deep and weary, as though broadcast from the bottom of a well. He told me the agency only supported its friends in the arts community and could always tell who its friends were. How? I inquired. They were friendly, Angelton said.

A former chief of station in Beirut, Lebanon, who was Buckminister Fuller's brother-in-law, told me during an interview as we were being monitored by a silent agency spook in attendance that the agency kept its prized intellectuals on "very long leashes," but they were "leashes nevertheless," and could be brought readily into line.

In Nicaragua in 1978 the U.S. ambassador was a Spanish-speaking college professor from the Midwest. When he gave press conferences about the excesses of the Somoza regime he was always accompanied by a certain Mr. Martin of the embassy. Mr. Martin sometimes spoke for the ambassador, but we were never allowed to take his picture or record his voice.

I once wrote to Allen Tate to inquire if he had agency connections during the time he was lobbying for Ezra Pound to be awarded the Bollingen Prize. He sent me back a most intemperate postcard threatening a lawsuit.

When I wrote to Kenneth Burke in Berkeley to inquire about the same matter, he replied, "It wouldn't surprise me."

The American Congress for Cultural Freedom which was chaired by Professor Sidney Hook paid a lot of attention to Pacifica Radio in the early sixties. Hook wrote a number of letters to the FCC that they should consider revoking our licenses for allowing Communist sympathizers to broadcast over our airwaves. Another prominent person who directed his ire against our broadcasting policies was William F. Buckley of the *National Review*, even though we permitted his publisher, William Rusher, to broadcast his views on a regular basis.

John Leonard once told me that he was hired by Buckley when he was a student at Berkeley and, fairly soon, was a regular writer for the *National Review*. Buckley even sent him to Cuba in the aftermath of the Cuban Revolution and published his not entirely antagonistic reportage. They had a falling out when he was assigned to review a book on McCarthy by New Yorker writer Richard Rovere. John was handed a dossier on Rovere's past Communist affiliations and told to incorporate some of the material in his review, and, I believe, it was then that he resigned.

I spent some time in the late seventies having various State Department documents from the cold war "declassified" for an essay I was writing on "The Aesthetics of the CIA." Most led nowhere, but a few were very revealing. One from Assistant Secretary of State Adolf Berle said American cold warriors were to regard their Communist opposites with the 'hauteur' of a maître d' in the first-class restaurant of a giant ocean liner. It was also proposed that T. S. Eliot's *Four Quartets* be translated into Russian and dropped by airplane all over the Soviet Union.

STUDS TERKEL

Studs had me on his Chicago radio program a couple of times to talk about my books, and his copy was always well marked. In his shirt sleeves, collar open, tie knotted halfway down in front, he looked formidably squat, a race track tout, a businessman—florid face, a loud voice. He reminded me a lot of my Uncle Joe, the electrical "contractor" and former six-day bike racer, a kind of side-of-the mouth immediate intimacy, though no slouch about doing his homework, a man who liked to gab a lot and be gabbed at.

He asked many more good questions than I knew the answers for and didn't always wait for answers anyway. Sometimes he seemed disappointed I wasn't saying what he hoped I would say, about politics, in particular. It felt like he was trying to prompt me to be as colorful as he. And he was always prefacing his questions with brief speeches showing his thoughtfulness and erudition, which was not always apparent from his rather brash tone when speaking.

I guess I was unprepared to have a "conversation" with a man who was so on all the time and had expected just to be interviewed. I can't say I really enjoyed the experience, though I was grateful for his interest in my books and the exposure. But sometimes it felt as though he was urging me to be full of verbal gesture and theatrical enthusiasm, and I really preferred to have the words I had written speak for themselves. Maybe I was a little intimidated? From the way he spoke of Nelson and Norman and Saul, I gathered Algren and Mailer and Bellow were all his close buddies.

He was older than I was and in those days was not yet an author but a popular radio personality, a Chicago sage. I distrusted myself talking about my books and only agreed to be grilled at the insistence of my publishers.

"You really are a very serious person," he seemed to insist once live on WFMT, and all I could do was mumble in reply that "trying to write" was important to me.

That was, I believe, when I published *An Education in Blood*. The

Chicago *Daily News* book critic, Joe Haas, published a lengthy rave-up, ranking me among the modern immortals such as Beckett. A couple of days later Haas dropped dead of a heart attack. I ended up feeling guilty that all the violence and blood in the book had led to his demise. Studs had also read the review, and he continued to make reference to it during the interview. Afterward, I felt as pummeled as Meyer Lansky's adding machine. Maybe we could do a retake?

Studs said it all went well enough and generously took me to lunch at a nearby coffee shop where he sometimes hung out. He was holding a huge cigar like a prop, but I don't recall him smoking it, and wherever he walked on that pleasant afternoon people greeted him and stopped him and touched him on the arm, and Studs seemed to know everybody in the neighborhood from the bookies to the executives. As we walked he presented me with concise tumultuous biographies out of the side of his mouth of the people we were encountering. This one was connected; that one in the baggy sharkskin suit could buy and sell half of the Loop. The women all had histories, too, even the cop on the beat, and Studs seemed to hold the book on all of them in a concise nonjudgmental fashion such as Longy Zwillman must have shown whenever he peered into that locket he owned, which held some of his girlfriend Jean Harlow's pubic hairs.

Studs' show of street smarts was the work of an accomplished actor-raconteur. I had the feeling he could tell me which of the ladies was estrous and randy that day and who was not and find me dates and also counsel me and them on our love lives and also hip me to the inside story of Hank Greenberg's swinging at low, inside fast balls and how Leopold and Loeb had made love together.

We stopped at a bookstore, and, when the owner confessed he hadn't yet ordered my book, Studs seemed even more disappointed than I was. "What's wrong with your publisher?" he asked me, crossly.

I was beginning to feel like the biggest loss leader in Marshall Field's window. Studs gave off so much energy that I wasn't always certain if he was aware that Richard Elman was a nom de plume for Phil Cavaretta and my real name was Anonymous. To our waitress he declared, "This is Dick Elman, and he's just written a truly compelling novel about a man murdering his wife in the bathtub."

After such an introduction the accused settled for lean corn beef and headed for the men's room.

When I was a young man Saul Bellow had been kind enough to recommend me to the MacDowell Colony after reading a manuscript I sent him. Over lunch I told Studs about how sorry I was that at a recent literary party I had been too shy to go up to Bellow and thank him again personally, after so many years. "You never can tell with Saul," he told me. "It's probably just as well." Studs patted the waitress when we were leaving, a gesture more affectionate than licentious. "Don't be a stranger," she smirked, as though we were all now old friends.

Studs lived on a dead-end street of two-story brick houses not far from Old Town in the near north side, and on another visit to Chicago he once invited me to drop over and even stay overnight, if I needed to.

It was different seeing Studs at home than in his milieu on the streets or in the radio studio. His wife, Ida, was short and faded and sweet, and she seemed to preside, and Studs spoke much less brashly around the house about everything. He seemed subdued, deferential to Ida, as if atoning for something or other. His grown son was driving a taxi in between classes at a local college. Money seemed to be a problem in those days, and I got the feeling that Ida and Studs could necessarily be frugal. They served a meal of cold beet soup and other Jewish fare with good rye bread. But there also seemed to be a tension about the place as though Studs hadn't really been around that much lately and everybody was just getting used to each other again, so nobody really had the time to get to know a stranger.

Come to think of it, I'm not sure who I was when I went on tour to Chicago. When I mentioned I'd visited with Richard Ellmann and a whole lot of other literary people in Evanston, Studs called him "Dick" also. He wasn't in the least bit confused about our identities. Sounding me out, Studs played good cop, bad cop unaccompanied. What did I think of Abby Hoffman? Jane Fonda? Mark Rudd? Germaine Greer?

Studs claimed to want to talk about the New Left; despite the fact that we were both against the war in Viet Nam, I found I had very little to say to him about people I didn't know, and he to me. Studs seemed to be lecturing to me more often than talking. He referred to me a lot as "kid" and "Dick," and I really wasn't crazy about either nickname. I said he should hereafter refer to me as "Clancy," as in Clancy Sigal.

"Not a chance," Studs said.

The last time I saw him was in his publisher's penthouse flat when his first book was published. I believe this was the same flat in which Norman Mailer had once had an altercation with his wife Adele when he had stabbed her.

I can remember feeling mournful about lost time and then having an argument with a writer named Davis about Proust and Mailer. I said *Guermantes Way* was right around the comer in Pomander Court. He said Charlus would have felt right at home in *The Deer Park*. I said this must be the Faubourg West End Avenue. He said if you're not part of the solution you're the problem. Then I said this was the same place where the stabbing had occurred, and he said it was, of course, in the building next door. I said it had to be this building because there was a Chinese restaurant on the ground floor. We began to exchange insults and almost came to blows about the fire bombing of Dresden during World War II.

I went into the other room because I certainly didn't want to disrupt Studs' party. Everybody from Kurt Vonnegut to Bella Abzug was in that room, though I didn't see any of the types Studs had interviewed for his book on working stiffs. I had a fleeting thought that there really weren't any working stiffs left in New York, so, after so many years, Studs had figured out how to make fictive oral history out of his relentlessly gabby style of talking, and I can recall feeling very pleased for his success, though just a little out of it. I was being denied visitation with my daughter by my ex-wife's doctor, lawyer, CPA, the cleaning woman, and a spin-off from the William Alanson White Institute.

Studs was really so high that day that I certainly didn't want to confide in him about what was going down. It was clear he was about to have a major literary success, and he was glad to receive as much flattery as he'd once bestowed so generously on other authors.

I was standing with a drink, talking to an ordinary nondescript fellow who turned out to be George Gershwin's natural son. I'm sure Studs recognized me more or less in such a press of beautiful women and hot hors d'oeuvres, for he kept calling out to me, "Dick, come on over here," and when I protested more than once that I detested such a nickname and never used it, he looked a little surprised that somebody could take offense at something he repeatedly said as a mark of affection.

"Don't be such a jerk," he told the room finally with a huge grin. I left the party early with the novelist Carol Hill, an old friend, and confessed to her on the street before going back to my place alone that the world looked very different when you had your head up your ass.

A day or so later at another Farrar Straus cocktail party I did another jerky number—introduced myself to George Gershwin's natural son as Susan Sontag and to Susan Sontag as Gardner Mulloy, the doubles champ.

NURUDDIN FARRAR

Somewhere on the top shelf of the cedar closet in our house above the Sound, folded double so that it will fit, is the thick U.S. Navy pea jacket Nuruddin Farrar wore as part of his mufti all the time he was at Stony Brook University a few years back. He asked us to keep it for him should he ever return in the wintertime to this part of the country. He asked as though also bestowing a privilege, as was sometimes the case with Nuruddin. "Wear it if you like," he told me, whimsically, "but I think it will be much too snug for you."

He was here most of the time in the fall or winter, replacing Amiri Baraka, who was on leave from the Africana Studies Department. Nuruddin was not terribly happy about being here, found the weather a bit too raw and humid, the students he had to teach illiterate, and the place boring, and refused to lower his literary standards. He used to tell me with some pride that when his students complained about the rigors of his class on black literature, he would chastise them that he was from Africa and everybody there was black, so being black was no basis for special consideration.

He was from Somalia, from a middle-echelon family, I gathered, accustomed to the hauteur of the elite, but had been in exile in Europe for many years, in Germany, England, Italy (many Somalis speak Italian as part of their legacy of colonial subjugation) and France, with occasional forays to the States for visiting professorships and much-needed cash. He seemed to have many friends in all parts of Europe and North America, but no truly close attachments at that point in his life, aside from his family in Mogadishu, about whose welfare he seemed very concerned. Nuruddin told me once he found it difficult to write when in situations of intimacy, so, when he felt the desire to write a novel, he chose a city where he knew no one, in a strange country, where he sometimes didn't even know the language, and wrote there until the work was finished.

He was thin and slight, of medium height, with fuzzy black hair and brown skin and fine, handsome features, and when I knew him he seemed to enjoy encountering strangers so long as he was able to maintain his implicit dignity in their presence. When we first got on speaking terms and I invited him to dinner, he quickly returned the invitation, and we were required to visit him in his bare semifurnished apartment in Port Jeff Station, where he prepared an excellent and savory couscous.

Nuruddin's presence on the Stony Brook campus was typically overlooked by insensitive university officials who did not seem to have any idea that they had a celebrated international author on hand. When this came to my attention, I was trying to run a not-yet-funded institute for the promotion of creative writing under university auspices and immediately invited Nuruddin to give a reading, which I said I would do my best to publicize. I could not offer him an honorarium, however, I explained, as he was already a university employee. He then pro-ceeded to complain to me about all the money problems he was having with the university which, as I recall, still owed him for a flight to Amer-ica from Tanzania, which the Africana Studies Program had promised to reimburse; there also seemed to be certain other irregularities about the amount of salary he was being paid. (This took many months and the intervention of many colleagues to get squared away.) But Nuruddin, who was not given to putting on self-important airs, was also genuinely pleased to be asked to give a reading and readily consented.

He soon began to spend almost as much time in our social circle as with his racially separated colleagues in the Africana Studies Department and developed a particular fondness for Tom and Jean Flanagan, who were also very pleased to entertain him. It was my pleasure to see him as often as I could and to visit with him sometimes in his bare flat and just chat.

Nuruddin is very brilliant and can be quite severe, a critical per-son, but exceptionally kindhearted under that. His skepticism could also be self-lacerating: "You question, you challenge, every thought which crosses your mind," one of his characters perorates. Though grateful to Baraka for getting him temporary work in the States, he remained critical of most of Amiri's recent performances as a writer. Nuruddin seemed to feel that Baraka was simply much too easy on himself and motivated much too strongly by vanity and ideology.

When he left us in Stony Brook he was going to Uganda, he told me. I was then doing the finishing touches on my novel *Tar Beach*, which I originally had called "Uganda," and when I told this to Nuruddin and he asked what it was about, for lack of any better way of explaining short of handing him the manuscript, which he had little time to read, I said it was a novel about a Jewish family in the forties, in which the main conceit was derived from the British Colonial Office offering the Zionists Uganda in place of Palestine. Nuruddin told me he could not respect a person who would make fun of his own origins. He seemed disappointed in me.

He was from a Muslim background and politically an enemy of Israel. In fact he often said that though he had been invited to teach in the Jewish state he would never go there. But he was equally critical of Islamic fundamentalism, from which he was definitely lapsed for a long time. In London he'd been friends with Salmon Rushdie and had been given *The Satanic Verses* to read in manuscript. It was the year Rushdie's novel appeared and he was driven into the custody of the British Secret Service to shelter him from the ayatollah's worldwide threats of assassination. Nuruddin confessed that when he'd read the Rushdie manuscript his friend had seemed concerned and asked if he thought it might cause offense, "and I told him I honestly didn't think so." He then added that some of his own novels were equally offensive to Muslim authorities and had been castigated by Islamic censors, but he'd never been threatened with death.

As I mentioned earlier, he had a large number of friends in places of sanctuary all over the world. From London and Minneapolis and Germany, women would come to visit with him for a few days at a time while he was here; he'd been close with the late Angela Carter in London and with many of her contemporaries. In Albany, where he went to give a reading at my recommendation, I introduced him to my friend Bill Kennedy, and he returned the favor by introducing me to Chinua Achebe, who was pleased to give a reading for my fledgling institute.

Nuruddin received a warm and appreciative reception wherever he went. His reading voice was thin and reedy. His novels were written with sustaining intensity about male adolescence or young womanhood. They were freighted with the transformative gestures love brings to a harsh world where women and men endured and suffered from ancient impositions of subjugation: male supremacy, religious superstition. They were clearly written by an enlightened soul for his Somali audience to invoke the experience of growing up in a primitive clan-ridden society (which practiced female mutilation, for example), but they also found little that was exemplary in the old colonialist mentality and were read, perforce, chiefly by exiles in London, New York, and Rome, or by academics and left wingers here and in the other African states. Continuing to write must have been very difficult for him at times. "You doubt at times if you exist, outside your own thoughts, outside your own head," he told me.

Nuruddin was distrustful of his own ordinariness, his qualities of common humanity that made his mind palpable. He sometimes seemed to feel that his publishers and agents showed no real connectedness to his fictions, and I think that could make him quite unhappy. I would come across this black-garbed figure on the campus, and we'd go off to have tea or coffee together. He'd be fairly bleak at first and carping, as though cautioning me to keep my distance, but then he would soften and ask about my daughter, with whom he could be affectionate and gentle, or my wife, Alice. He seemed very much to need looking after, though he would not have said so and was pleased to have me taking notice of him.

For example, before his reading took place, he demanded I print a souvenir broadside of a passage from one of his novels to be distributed among his audience. It was customary, he insisted, meaning it had been done before for him in Minneapolis when he gave a reading there, and there was no way he would consider reading if I did not agree to do this.

A large crowd came to the reading, including his agent, whom he did not know very well but had traveled out all the way from city by train, and all received broadsides, and afterwards I had a small party for Nuruddin in my home. He seemed happy to be among well-wishing strangers, but unclear if his largely white-faced audience were truly perceiving his fiction, and in need of familiars.

Then spring came, and soon it was time for him to leave Stony Brook, as the semester was ending, and he came by the house and asked if we could store his jacket for him. I had the hunch there were people in various localities around the world storing various possessions for Nuruddin pending his return someday, and I was pleased he had included us among his custodians. Could it be, I wondered, that such deposits left with certain people rather than others meant he felt he had unfinished business with them to transact at some future date?

One recent Christmas a card arrived from Nigeria in Nuruddin's hand. He wanted us to know that all his family had survived the atrocities in Somalia and that he was now married and living in Nigeria. A few months later I heard him interviewed on the radio in Washington. There had been rumors circulating that he might be considering a political career in his country, and I was pleased to hear him reaffirm his calling as a writer of fiction.

It also pleases me to know that, even after his marriage, he continues to move about the world making friends and being critical and detached but kind. That means maybe he'll be back in Stony Brook someday and will be wanting his old pea jacket to shield him from the damp Long Island cold.

W. H. Auden

The first time I met W. H. Auden, he was drunk in Syracuse, New York, at the home of Professor Sanford Meech, chairman of the Syracuse English Department, and I was one of his student escorts.

A faculty party was going on below in Auden's honor. Auden was shy; he preferred to be in the upstairs bedroom of Meech's adolescent daughter, drinking blackberry brandy from a bottle and listening to Kay Star records on the girl's low-fi leatherette portable phonograph.

I told Auden I'd been reading his poems in a new Random House "collected" edition, and I had particularly enjoyed "Casino," which begins, as I recall,

> Only the hands are moving
> to the wheel attracted,
> are moving as deer trek
> through a wilderness.

"What did you say about deer *drech*?" the poet demanded.

I said I was puzzled as to the meaning of this very portentous and suggestive poem set around a roulette table at a gambling casino sometime before the end of the world.

"I think," Auden said, "I was drunk when I wrote that stupid thing," and swallowing air, commenced to sing along with Kay Star.

He was well set up, and somewhat fair and smooth skinned and comely in those days when I met him that first time. A man in his forties, his prime. Looked a little plump but spruce, and not at all epicene.

Some twenty-five years later at Columbia University I was shocked by the face of the man who came as a visitor to my class. He had been writing prose, travel journals, essays, I can't recall, a commonplace book. There were more wrinkles on that face than on the average man's scrotum, and within that network of reticulations a thin smile was taking shape; his pale bluish eyes had a yellow cast. He looked pale and flaccid, was in a sweat, and the hair on his head had thinned to such an extent one could see the flaky skin of his crown through the bright overhead lighting.

Auden didn't seem to remember me, which was not surprising, but he was very gentle with my students. He told my class they should keep notebooks and avoid habit-forming barbiturates.

"Foster's only connect," he said, his hands trembling, "means trying to write even when you think you can't. So force yourselves. It will be good for all of you in the long run."

Over coffee later Auden confessed he was beset by thieves of all sorts. Perfectly charming young men would befriend him, visit him on St. Mark's Place, and make off with valuable manuscripts and letters from Auden's wide circle of admirers and friends "which they then sell to collectors for tidy sums."

"I don't like not trusting people," he said, and it was sometimes hard to follow his drift when he talked to my colleague about Rilke as he'd somehow managed to get drunk again.

We got up to leave.

Auden said, "This old Queen has had a long and tiring day."

We shook hands; his face was fissured and drawn, like a piece of arid soil after a quake.

"Thank you for coming," I said.

"Don't I remind you of somebody?" Auden said to all the assembled company.

"Maybe a little," I said, "a man I once knew."

"At least I don't resemble Flat Foot Floogie with a Floy Floy," Auden said, with a little shuffling shimmy, and he hailed a cab on upper Broadway and was gone.

Before the next New Year he had "disappeared in the dead of winter."

LITTLE RICHARD PENNIMAN

Of this great rock and roll performer I have the most vivid recall. When he played the Electric Circus on St. Mark's Place he was all over the room, on top of the piano, and even flat out, with his hair up in a high pompadour and gold tights and a gold and red satin cape.

When I went to interview him some mornings later at his invitation in his suite at the Times Square Motel at 10:00 A.M. about his former employee, the "soul" singer Otis Redding, who—like Penniman—was from around Macon, Georgia, and had even started out as Little Richard's band chauffeur, there was a naked couple fast asleep on the other twin bed in his chilly, air-conditioned room.

Penniman was also bare-ass naked when he came to the door. He said he didn't mind being interviewed, but why did I want to talk about Otis?

"I am the greatest," he insisted. "You should talk about me."

"This is a biography of Otis," I reminded him. "Maybe some other time . . ."

"Praise the Lord," he said.

We sat opposite each other on chairs, separated by a low coffee table on which was my tape recorder.

I asked Little Richard how he and Otis Redding had met, and he told me about the black Gospel churches around Macon and then began to masturbate, and after a while he came all over himself, a lava-like eruption that left him otherwise placid and unperturbed as he asked me to pass him some Kleenex from the box on the table between us and continued his narrative.

"Otis used to do me, sing just like me," he said as he dabbed at his chest and loins, "but we already had one falsetto rhythm and blues singer, so then he went baritone, and that was how the great Otis Redding came about."

I'd switched off the machine at the moment of his orgasm, and now I started it up again. "You were saying?"

Penniman started his monologue again, and within half an hour he was erect, masturbating another time, and again Wop bop! He came.

Afterward he asked if I'd like to interview his old friend James Brown.

"He's also from around Macon," Little Richard said, "and he likes to fuck . . ."

"That's nice," I said.

"You may not think so if it ever happens to you," Little Richard said.

He was naked except for a conk bandana on his handsome head.

"I hope you got what you wanted," he said at the door, as he let me out.

I shook my head.

That couple in the other bed were still out cold.

"Come again really," Little Richard announced.

When I told my friend Al Goldman, who'd arranged the interview for me with Little Richard, about what had transpired, he said, "He must have really dug you. He never did those kinda things with me."

GRACE PALEY

The first time I met Grace Paley was at a sit-in in City Hall Park protesting air-raid sirens and the need to have little school children take shelter. There were about ten people in the park, including Norman Mailer, as I recall, but Grace was the only person in good humor. She usually is, I've discovered, among strangers, but I was flattered that day when I identified myself as being "the reporter from WBAI" and she called me "darling."

A sunny face like that, I believe, had me blushing a little, but Grace wasn't even being flirtatious, I later learned; she was just being enthusiastic and friendly. She was another street kid like me, maybe even the big sister I'd never had. We were both second generation Russian Jews, though I towered above her in height.

I'd read some of the stories in *The Little Disturbances of Man* when they were first published in periodicals like *New World Writing* and was surprised to discover how successfully she'd captured her own voice in those stories. It was a New York voice but never rude or curt or lopped off from the side of the mouth.

Then the sirens went off, and all the people in the square refused "to take shelter" and Grace and some others were arrested and taken off with rough courtesy by the police to be booked. I had a press pass, so I was allowed to go back to WBAI and broadcast.

The second time Grace and I met was in Rockefeller Center in front of the Cambodian consulate the day the United States was forced to leave Saigon and Phnom Penh.

There were a number of exiled Cambodians among us, and they all seemed in an exultant mood.

"They'll all be going home now," a woman among us said. "It must be a wonderful feeling.

"Let's hope so" Grace said, who seemed happy for her companions but also slightly uneasy, as though concerned that our celebration might be just a trifle premature.

We were all busy congratulating the Cambodians, and they were shaking hands and being very enthusiastic about their plans to return home as soon as possible.

I've often thought of that day which was bright and sunny, but cold, as I recall, and those earnest smiling Cambodian faces. How many did actually go home as they said they would? And did any of them survive the depredations of the murderous Khmer Rouge? It was a moment of sunny optimism about an event I wish now I could bury forever and forget.

GIL SORRENTINO

Gil Sorrentino is now a distinguished Professor at Stanford, but when I knew him he was just barely getting by in New York and living in Westbeth. His wife was working for an auto parts distributor, and he rarely seemed to go out on the town anymore or make the scene, except to drop by certain late night jazz clubs infrequently.

Like the Prince of Aquitaine in his ruined tower, Gil surveyed the literary landscape with wounded contempt. He taught a little at the New School and had a hard time bringing out his novels with trade publishers. He once complained to me that his most recent publishers spent more on eating lunch than they did publishing him.

Gil was ambitious; he didn't wish to be another New York writer. He read voraciously against the poets of his day to pick out genuine voices, and these, like William Bronk, he would seek out and communicate with through correspondence. He seemed pretty cut off by quarrels and disagreements from his old crowd on the New York poetry scene and was no longer working for Grove Press where, he once told me, he'd been Samuel Beckett's editor. Gil said editing Beckett had been a strange assignment. The manuscripts would arrive letter perfect, single-spaced, and without margins. His main task was reading Beckett and then passing on his enthusiasm to Barney Rosset.

Gil was a powerful figure with good looks and a big voice, a defiant stare, a difficult manner. Because he was so convinced that so much he confronted was shamming, it was hard to relax in his company. He always seemed to be scrutinizing you for errors or illiteracies, or as though you would surely betray him. He'd once been best friends with Joel Oppenheim, but they no longer spoke, and Gil could be very harsh about his faltering colleague, calling him a "drunk" and a "scoundrel," among other things. He seemed to feel very wounded toward Amiri Baraka also, with whom he had once been close friends. Baraka had stopped seeing Gil when he more or less gave up on all his white friends, but Sorrentino seemed to regard his act as a special hurt. He would not say anything at all about Baraka.

His conversations with me in those days felt like a series of sly traps in which he tried to trip me up making misstatements of fact or misjudgments. He had very decided opinions about hipness and literature and claimed to despise cant of any sort, and he could seem very self-absorbed and felt overlooked. I never had the feeling he paid much attention to me except insofar as I could be of some assistance to his career. He had praise for no one else we both knew, and there seemed to be a degree of one-upmanship to some of his enthusiasms. He had great praise for a West Coast mathematician who wrote long, ruminative discourses and despised the faux naivetes of the Beats and their followers in the way that Orthodox Jewish *mithnagdim* are contemptuous of Hassidic enthusiasts.

Gil could be as severe with himself as with others. When I praised his early novels, he went beyond the standard ploy of the writer, which is to claim that such early efforts were naive; Gil made it plain he thought the vulnerabilities he exposed in such works feckless. He seemed all the more determined to be invulnerable from now on and to use every device of satire and burlesque to shift the focus away from himself.

Once I was asked to contribute to a special issue of a review about his work, which I was glad to do because I admired his poetry, as well as such novels as *The Sky Changes*, *Steelwork*, and *Aberration of Starlight*. These novels seemed to me painful about intimate experience, but brilliant the way they moved, and juxtaposed fantasy with reverie and scenes of observed life. But when I also pointed out in the piece that I did not find his ambitious Joycean satire *Mulligan Stew*—despite its displays of genius—either funny or moving, Gil stopped talking to me, too.

I gather this was a pattern with Sorrentino, who used to be very harsh on old friends in certain of his novels as well, such as *Imaginary Qualities of Actual Things*, which will be a great source book for future researchers into certain New York poets of that period, as it dramatizes all of their loutishness and cruelties toward each other, as Joyce did with Oliver St. John Gogarty through Buck Mulligan in *Ulysses*. The theme of betrayal is played out in his first novel, *The Sky Changes*, a wife with a trusted best friend and the authorial figure a sexual and emotional cripple, abiding in "silence, exile, and cunning" like Stephen Dedalus. Deliberate cruelties mark family interactions in *Aberration of Starlight*. In *Imaginary Qualities* friendship is two-faced, hypocritical, scheming. Perhaps that's one reason why Sorrentino's most recent fiction has grown increasingly abstract and seems almost exclusively to be about language and language games. When the plays of human personality are reduced to the nastinesses of individual acts, becoming entirely abstract removes the possibility of seeming simply misanthropic and provoking further enmities. Gil is a man of abundant instincts for comradeship which he is quick to repudiate; he was Hubert Selby's mentor and coach because they were friends. He took an interest in the early work of Mike Stephens and once admired Fielding Dawson, who wrote the preface to *The Darkness around Us* (1960). He once wrote a moving piece about the death of Paul Blackburn, but they were not close in the years before Paul's death. About the only writer I know with whom he has never really quarreled is Bill Bronk, but they live very far apart from each other and rarely communicate. Some writers are eager to insist they are not regular fellows. Such Jesuitical disdain is as much of a persona as pretending to be just another happy-go-lucky human being.

Gil's writing, at one time, was strongly influenced by the hard bop jazz of the fifties. It was the early cadenced riffs of his free syllabics I once found very appealing and wrote about with praise, the poems in The *Darkness around Us*, for example, and even the later more contemplative poetry in *Oranges*, and it turned out I was not the only person who thought highly of this poetry. Once when I was visiting with Sorrentino downtown, his son arrived home from school and announced he'd just been on the Eighth Street crosstown bus with saxophone player Sonny Rollins. The boy said Rollins had glanced at him for a few moments and then said, "You're Gil Sorrentino's son, aren't you? He's a really good poet."

That was the only time I ever saw Gil smile easily and happily.

C. P. Snow: The Name of the Game

When I was being published by Scribners I got to know the late Lord Snow just a little bit. We took lunch together once or twice and once had supper together with his wife, Lady Pamela Hansford Johnson, at the apartment of our editor, Burroughs Mitchell. C. P. Snow was always very affable in my presence; he claimed to be an admirer of my writing, told me he'd modeled his *Strangers and Brothers* series of novels after Proust, and once explained to me the secret of his success.

As I recall, it went something like this: "I'm a fairly able writer, but I'm surely not a Proust, nor Balzac, nor even Anthony Powell. I lack fire. Brainy enough, but just not a poet, don't you know. But I have a following here, and in England, and it has little to do with science and scientists. My fans are mostly middle-aged women who are interested in my Lewis Eliot. They're interested, don't you know, because he's middle-aged and a success in the world, but still unmarried. Still alone. Is he lonely? What about his old age? Who is taking care of him? Well, I take note of their worries and play to them, and so I have a following, the women who are concerned for Lewis Eliot, which doesn't interfere with anything serious I'm doing, really."

The Austrian Jewish writer Jacov Lind once confessed to me at Elizabeth Hardwick's flat that he had taken so much mescalin—or was it LSD?—after the war in Europe as a paid guinea pig for a "friendly" intelligence agency he was no longer certain all the time if he wrote fiction or fact.

I asked, "What do you think you favor?"

"Jacov Lind," he replied. "I write Jacov Lind."

Nelson Algren told me his confidential petname for Simone de Beauvoir was "EZ OFF" because she was always, in his words, "oven ready."

He said, "I figured her for an act. Hell, hookers often do the same thing."

I once owned Algren's copy of *Never Come Morning* which he gave to Ms. de Beauvoir. It was glossed by a copy editor of *Temps Moderne* for French equivalents of American words like *raincoat*, and it contained a very mawkish dedicatory poem in Algren's hand "to Simone." I wanted to sell it because I was, as usual, short of cash and showed it to a number of so-called dealers and Algren experts who said it couldn't be his composition because it was such a lousy poem. That's how little these people knew about love.

According to the biographer of de Beauvoir, Deirdre Bair, Algren came to Paris to be with his mistress, but she went off with Sartre somewhere and left him with the keys to the flat. In a rage he ransacked the place and took back some of the presentation copies he once gave her, including my book, which ended up in a tag sale in Selden, Long Island, after Nelson's death in Sag Harbor.

The book now rests in the special collections of a large midwestern library. They had no doubts about its authenticity, perhaps because they'd known of some other mawkish effusions by Algren to Simone.

I shall always be grateful to Joe Heller. We lived near each other for a spell on the Upper West Side, he in the Apthorp, and I around the corner on West Seventy-seventh Street, a hostage of the notorious Sullivanian cult. Joe had praised *An Education in Blood* when he read it in galleys. Once we met on Broadway, and I was in a funk. The Gang of Four in Sullivanian HQ had threatened to put a contract out on me because I wouldn't make a baby with one of their women. Joe was with his good friend Speed Vogel. He asked me why I looked so frightened, and I told him.

"Come on Speed," he said. "We'll walk him home."

And that's what they did, see me gently to my door, and then Joe said, "You see, Richard, there's nothing to be frightened about. Lock yourself in." And that's exactly what I did.

Donald Hall was poetry editor of the *Paris Review* when I was in college. I started to send him my poems for publication, and, at first, he sent me form rejection slips.

Once I wrote him an irate note demanding to know what he found lacking in my poems. Hall, to my surprise, wrote back, pointing out that if he had to criticize every poem he read for the *Review* he would never get any of his work done. But the next time I sent him some poems Hall wrote a brief note of criticism, and from then on for a couple of years whenever I submitted to the *Review* he always wrote me brief, informative, sometimes encouraging notes until, finally, some years later, when I'd graduated, the *Review* published my poem "Arbor Day." I learned a lot from what Hall had to say to me, including how generous he was being toward a young, unskilled novice, and I wish simply here and now to express my gratitude.

As I've already mentioned, Henry Miller once told me I should make up his life story, as he had done, and not bother him for information for a biography, as he was in his declining years and not very long for this world. The problem was I had read through all his correspondence at the UCLA library by then, and fiction and fact seemed intertwined.

Here are some of the unpublished results:

The finest lover he'd ever known was a young Parisian prostitute from the Dordogne named Solange. He attributed her success in the life to what he called "her milking hand."

"She'd been around cows all her life," Miller said, "and she knew how to bring on *crème fraiche.*"

He said many visitors to her establishment were married men, and they "felt guilty about cheating on their wives," but they did not reject the pleasures of "her milking hand." Miller also said she was the special favorite of many German customers and for that reason referred to the organ of generation as *le schmuck.*

He had a younger sister who was mentally retarded and he told the late Ned Calmer, who told me, he sometimes took advantage of her. All through his early threadbare Paris years he was sending money home to his father, a bankrupt bespoke tailor to the theatrical trade. He cajoled a Barnard professor visiting Big Sur to find June Corbett (Mona), his ex-wife, in New York and have her hospitalized and treated for alcoholism. She later became nanny to the professor's children.

His dentist's wife from President Street in Brooklyn wrote me once that in Brooklyn in his thirties Henry was always much more interested in cadging food than having sex. If they ever make a movie of my life, he told me, I ought to be played by Jean Gabin. They'll probably dub in George Raft's voice over the face of Rock Hudson. One of his fans once wrote Henry from a small midwestern town that all his life he had wanted to be a writer like Henry.

"There are many things to be said for a small-town life," Henry politely wrote back.

STANLEY EDGAR HYMAN

When I knew Stanley Hyman at Bennington he was a widower, living by himself in a large mansion of three floors, with a glassed-in tower room above, on the main street of North Bennington, Vermont, down the street from the old railway station. The tower had once been the domain of his wife, the writer Shirley Jackson, and her library of the occult. When Shirley died, Stanley seemed to retreat to the bottom floors of the old house and took most of his meals at a local French bistro.

He did not drive a car and employed Junior Percey, the proprietor of the local newsstand (and hearse), as his as-needed chauffeur. His four children from the marriage with Shirley were grown and living away from the house in neighboring communities or were at school. His face was bearded and largely hidden; he was overweight, a little sloppy-looking most of the time, and drank a lot, but I never saw him falling-down drunk. He was still a dedicated teacher and a generous colleague. Stanley once confessed to me that he was insomniac and couldn't fall asleep at night without downing half a bottle of whiskey.

He had a large collection of antique jazz recordings, and a good library (and was good about lending books) and had valuable collections of coins and ancient Roman artifacts, which he purchased at auction through catalogues, but his true vocation (and hobby) was reading. Since he had trouble sleeping, Stanley could go through a couple of novels in an evening, and he kept himself au courant about poetry, which he liked less well than fiction but considered a necessity for the *amour propre* of any civilized man, kept up with the magazines and quarterlies, and read books of literary scholarship, anthropology, and theory. He also played in a regular weekly poker game with a cellist, a garage owner, an abstract painter, and some other local Bennington types.

His office in the Barn at Bennington resembled the collections space at some small, provincial museum. There were amateur masks and fetishes on the walls and feathered assemblages, pieces of wooden sculpture, and brightly hued swatches of student paintings. He'd been teaching many years, and reading student prose had become a chore. He would, therefore, he informed me, allow some unlettered students to make artistic representations in place of term papers for his classes on language and literature. In some instances he was even known to allow the dancers to choreograph and perform for him their versions of short stories and poems in the privacy of that office.

He was, nevertheless, a professional man of letters of very high standards and taste and an enthusiastic reviewer of new fiction for the *New Leader* and writer of occasional pieces for the *New Yorker*, and, in person, he was genial and funny, even when he got a little snappy.

I can recall interminable meetings of the Bennington faculty to discuss and debate whether the college should go coeducational. Stanley had little patience with what he called "the bathroom people," those colleagues who were arguing that the present sanitary facilities in the dorms made coeducation "inadvisable." He told me some of his male colleagues were simply afraid of the competition they would have with "handsome young men available for the Bennington girls' affections."

He was truly very dedicated to Bennington and very reluctant to leave, even when he was offered fat academic plums at bigger universities with increasingly greater prestige. Aside from work as a "Talk of the Town" writer for the *New Yorker*, Bennington had been his only employment. He'd been hired and fired in the early forties, when, he said, he hadn't worked out well, and then was given a second chance and rehired again a few years later and never left, as though bewitched. Stanley said, "That first time I was very callow and a little ignorant. I learned a lot and grew up a little."

There came a time when Stanley had to stop drinking alcohol and lose a lot of weight, as his blood pressure had grown alarming; he would appear at college social functions a very frail and meager shadow of himself, with a glass of cold tea, his hand trembling, looking very morose. He had recently remarried, with an erudite and bookish former student, Phoebe Pettingell, perhaps three decades his junior, and, as she was carrying his child, he was trying to prolong his life. That really wasn't to be. Stanley had gout and did no physical exercise; his eyesight was weak. Instead of dieting, he sometimes fasted. He collapsed over a meal at the local bistro shortly after the birth of his new son.

Stanley was very good to younger colleagues and had a great esteem of talent. It was alledgedly because of Nick Delbanco's promise and talent (and praise for Delbanco from John Updike and Max East-man) that he got hired on to teach at Bennington when he was only a year or two out of Harvard. Nick's precocious early genius is only now beginning to realize his full novelistic potential, but he was to be a valu-able Bennington asset for many years as a fine writer and teacher and a friend to writers, and he eventually founded the Bennington writers workshops where I taught; he remains my very good friend. (Others Stanley admired fared less well. One young genius whom Stanley thought might just be the next Kenneth Burke served out his time at Bennington with few publications, aside from interoffice memos.)

Stanley was always very encouraging to me and friendly, though to this day I don't know if he ever read anything I'd ever written. He was from Brooklyn and a graduate of Syracuse, like me, and a former student of Leonard Brown, a man whose influence was larger than his reputation, and I sometimes thought that had something to do with his kindly regard toward me, except that he was not usually given to dis-plays of tribal loyalty. Stanley's demeanor, when he was still portly, reminded me a little of W. C. Fields and a little of the captain in the "Katzenjammer Kids," though usually he was affably crabby.

I've come to think Stanley just liked writers and that he had a sense of how difficult it was to make something out of nothing, and he judged their effort differently than that of other academics. He was truly proud of his long association with Bern Malamud and reviewed his writings enthusiastically and with special care. He also seemed proud that Ben-nington existed, in part, to foster the work of creative people, students and teachers. He told me once I'd get a lot of work done if I stayed on there, but "of course, you also have to be a little nuts."

He continued to be curious about new things and younger col-leagues. I can recall an evening at his house listening to the recordings of Aretha Franklin. Stanley liked the blues, and he wanted to decide for himself if she was in a class with Ma Rainey. In the end, Stanley stuck with Ma Rainey as more "authentic," for, compared to those early acoustic recordings, Aretha sounded to his ears overproduced.

He had great friendships with the trumpet player Rex Stewart, who lived not far away, near Troy, New York, and with the novelist Ralph Ellison, who would come to visit him in Bennington, but he seemed on equally good terms with many of the local people, who regarded him as no more eccentric than they were. Stanley seemed to have found sustenance and as much privacy as he needed in that small Vermont town, while yet remaining a member of the community. Local people used to point out he and Shirley's house on a rise overlooking town with some pride. If they regarded Shirley as "odd," Stanley was more or less a regular fellow, which he plainly wasn't.

Stanley's bookishness and his drinking problems seemed to make him more tolerant—not less—of others of aberrant behavior. It would not have occurred to him to insult a fellow for chasing skirts or boys, or for being such a depressive that he was unable to function. Stanley was very accepting of craziness. He was also very protective of the girls at Bennington, and they of him. He would get very upset when told of a young woman's personal problems and angry at any man who tried to exploit such. He seemed personally very fond of young women in an avuncular fashion, and to my knowledge fooled around very little. He wavered in his beliefs: sometimes he admired the imaginations of believers like Bashevis Singer; sometimes he was cynical and skeptical, a knowledgable but failed analysand.

Stanley once took great amusement in chairing a faculty meeting during which the main order of business was whether the college should offer a junior faculty position to a candidate named Heffelfinger or to another named Wexelblatt. After much discussion, Stanley thought both candidates were about equally qualified and suggested his colleagues vote according to which name seemed to them more euphonious.

Like Edmund Wilson, he taught a lot by his writing. He didn't enjoy writing negative reviews and seemed truly pleased whenever he could hold up a good new book he'd read before the reader and indicate with quotations how he or she could expect to be edified by the reading experience. Through Stanley's reviews I came to know the stories of Singer and the novels of Anthony Powell, William Gass, and Wallace Markfield. I also found his longer treatises on the New Critics or on Darwin, Marx, and Frazer learned and insightful.

His last writing was about Othello and the mysterious basis for Iago's malevolence toward the Moor. Stanley posited that Iago had a homosexual fix on Othello and was jealous of Desdemona and Othello.

This was not an entirely original thesis, but Stanley worked it out exhaustively, with extensive quotation, and was somewhat disappointed, I think, that his colleagues remained skeptical. It was the case even then that gay persons did not like to be characterized as homosexual villains.

"But that's just my point," Stanley argued in the lunchroom. "It's not openness that's the problem. It's repression, the classic Freudian jinx. You can't keep it in, so it comes out all screwy and mean."

"But," I interjected, "I thought you believed in the necessity for sublimation."

"Not so much that it hurts," he protested.

FAYE DUNAWAY

This beautiful woman once hired me on behalf of her boyfriend, to whom I had just lost three straight sets of tennis in Central Park, to write a treatment for a movie he would direct in which she would appear, in a cameo role, about the life and death of John Wesley Hardin, the Western gunman.

When we set out that day to meet my opponent's girlfriend over breakfast in her tower apartment in the Eldorado, I had no idea I would be talking to a beautiful movie actress. In those days I felt I was living on Pastemak's "aerial tramway" and in every moment there lurked the possibility of a significant encounter. My friend Harris simply told me he was taking me to his girlfriend's flat for breakfast.

As I recall, we went up to one of the towers in a special elevator, and when we came to a certain floor stepped out into a large, airy foyer with polished steel walls and portholes. I felt as though I'd entered the set of *Things to Come.*

Beyond us were vast blue areas of New York sky, a large airy sitting room furnished starkly, as I recall, with once again those tooled and polished steel walls and much larger portholes. Were we at sea? Or up above the stratosphere? A pair of French doors connected this to the private rooms of the flat. We entered, and then my friend called out a name, "Faye?" and a lilting and rather gay female stage voice responded, "Is that you, Harris?" as though it could have been anybody else.

The so-called stars of our universe are often shining brightly from the moment you encounter them. They come at you blazing with glamour, as though they never could look less than beautifully coiffed and made up. But whether that's really them or someone who is acting the part is often hard to figure out. Faye obviously had been forewarned of my coming and wanted to impress me with how she looked in her spontaneous dishabille, but she most certainly didn't wish to overwhelm me. Nevertheless, the woman who presently appeared was much more soft and willowy and beautiful than she photographed.

She was wearing some kind of gauzy, white negligee over another set of gauzy garments through which I saw the shadows of her long, slim legs.

And she was from the first extremely friendly and cordial about greeting a stranger. When I apologized for the intrusion, she said I was being silly to even mention it. Harris was always surprising her with guests at unusual hours. I thought she was being sincere and truthful up to a point, a perfectly beautiful and sincere imitation of graciousness performed by a good actress who really didn't enjoy being put upon. When Faye said she would rustle up some breakfast for us in the galley somewhere behind those French doors, I didn't protest.

I can't recall if there was a servant, but I do recall that Faye served us in the sitting room, from a tray, coffee and eggs and fresh rolls, and as we ate she informed me that Harris was a great admirer of my book *Fredi and Shirl and the Kids*, and did I think I would be interested in *working on* a project with them?

We talked a lot about violence that first time (it was a year or so after her hit *Bonnie and Clyde*), and they told me their interest in Hardin was stimulated mostly by the Dylan song "John Wesley Hardin was a friend of the poor . . ." which they hoped to use as theme music. The trouble was there were no women in Hardin's life that they knew of, and the only way such a film would be fundable with Stacy Keach committed to playing Hardin would be if I could figure out a way to invent a part for Faye.

When I left later in the day I had also more or less committed myself to the project. They gave me a reprint of a dime novel account of Hardin's life to look over and said we'd have to get together with Faye's lawyer, but as far as they were concerned we had a deal.

What deal? We hadn't even talked about money. I guess I thought I might alter the mood, or offend Faye with such a crass consideration. Percolating with movie dreams of Faye's allure, I called my agent to tell her of my good fortune, and she was furious with me. "I know what you want," she said, "and it isn't writing screenplays."

Nevertheless, I pressed her to make any deal agreeable to Faye and eventually settled for the Screen Writer's Guild minimum which, I believe, was about six thousand dollars. My agent thought I was a damn fool but agreed to read the contract and collect the money and take her commission. Faye gave me her private telephone number. Harris went out of town. I sat down to work. And I discovered almost immediately that Hardin was no friend of the poor, but a hardened psychopath who, according to one historian of the old West, had murdered close to fifty people before he was shot in the back in a saloon in

El Paso by the sheriff. Moreover, many of Hardin's antagonists were unarmed runaway slaves.

Sentimentalizing killers is an old Hollywood standby. Even moguls need a sense of recognition when they screen films, and the idea that a brute could be bashful, charming, enjoy pets, or have crushes on beautiful women, must have always been reassuring to such brutes. My own theory then was that people are what they do: some people murder, others do different things with their anger. When I reported this to Faye, she thought we ought to have lunch.

We met at a hangout for the theater crowd in the West forties. Faye came dressed in black with a dark fur piece clinging to her neck. It was now close to the Christmas season, and there was a decided chill in the air. Faye was cool and feline, nicely businesslike, and pretty to look at. I believe her hair had a new tint of auburn. She agreed with me that borrowing charm from Stacy Keach was no clue to a brutish lout such as Hardin. Had I discovered any part for her in his life story?

It so happened I had: Hardin had just arrived in El Paso after a long train trip. He could have met Faye, the sheriff's wife, on the train. Her name happened to be Rose La Rose. There would have been a flirtation, or more, and it was knowledge of this that prompted the El Paso sheriff to gun down Hardin as he leaned over a bar to have a drink.

Faye thought that would probably do for her, for the moment, if I could give the woman some character. She can't be just another broad, Faye reflected. She thought Rose La Rose had to see something in Hardin or bring out something, or vice versa. But I was still stuck about how to treat of Hardin, with or without a woman in his life. It was difficult to write sympathetically about a murderous loner. Faye paid the check and sent me back to my desk to work on my treatment.

I proposed to myself then that Hardin could be treated as a comic villain with a very bad temper easily provoked by slights and wrote an essayistic account of such a person for my own edification, and this time she invited me up to the apartment one evening to talk it over.

I think I was being seduced to stay with the project. She definitely wasn't interested in me as a man, for throughout our conference she was on the phone to Harris, and they were not talking business. Through the half-open French doors I saw Faye stretched out across a bed in another negligee and had coming at me a barrage of sighs and whimpers. We also spoke a few minutes more about Hardin that evening. Faye suggested I view some of Stacy's films. There was a wounded feeling to the man, a sense of deep hurt.

"You mean his hare lip?" I asked.

"That's really beside the point," she said. "He's internalized a lot . . ."

We met one more time for lunch, and by now I was *so* heated up by everything except my screenplay that I suggested to this lovely looking woman that we have an affair. I guess I was just a little bored with the project by now and didn't see how the proposed film's dramatic possibilities were enhanced by flirting. I thought, let's act this out in life. I'll be Hardin; you be Rose. Harris can play the sheriff. Also, by being blunt as I was, I hoped to pay Faye a compliment and to clear the air for serious business.

Faye couldn't have been nicer to me in saying no. She explained first that she could be a real bitch and wouldn't be right for me at all. She also told me I could never afford to treat her as she liked, which was also Harris's problem, in part, I gathered. Then she listed some of her previous lovers: a director named Jerry, as I recall, Marcello Mastroianni, Lenny Bruce. I had to admit I was in a different league. I'd miscast myself and probably everybody else in the scenario. I was a writer, not a casting director.

I did eventually turn in some sort of treatment to Faye's lawyer and never heard from either Faye or Harris again. They broke up shortly after all this, and Faye's corporation owned what I had produced, so that I don't even think I kept a copy. I got a Christmas present from Faye that year of a handsome volume of the paintings of Remington, and I got a final check from her lawyer to my agent, minus the commission.

I guess things like this happen a lot among Hollywood people, but it had never happened to me before. I can recall Harris and Faye saying to me that *psychopath* was just a name we put on certain people. My job would be to show how Hardin interacted with others.

The answer was he didn't at all, from what I could tell, and neither did I really in those days, nor she, nor he.

LOUISE VARÈSE

Louise Varèse always used to complain with some small fondness about her only son that he was "a stuffy old man." She was then in her late eighties, and he was chronologically her junior by about twenty years. They'd had little contact over the decades since Louise Norton and his father broke up and she went off to New York and Paris. Louise was a great charmer, and her son was perhaps a little dull, as I recall her also saying, but, if he ever felt put out by her seeming lack of tenderness or by what she said to his face, he most assuredly got his revenge on her. When she was older and beginning to fail, he closed down the townhouse on Sullivan Place in Greenwich Village which she had kept up as her memorial to her relationship with the composer Varèse and packed her off with him to Utah to die.

Poor Louise in Utah was hard to imagine. She had a hatred for the hinterlands from which she came, and going beyond her birthplace in Pittsburgh must have seemed true ignominy. She told me that when she toured the United States in the twenties with her great love, Edgar Varèse, who was then a distinguished visiting conductor from Europe, they were usually not able to share rooms in hotels because stuffy hotel managers and symphony patrons in the hinterlands regarded their not being married as immoral.

Varèse and Louise married toward the end of their long relationship. Here and abroad they shared an active and intimate life together, as her published memoirs attest. When I first met her at MacDowell, she was a widow, an elegant old woman in her early eighties, and she wore very chic Schiaparelli suits and still knew how to flirt. I loved to visit with her after a day's work, and we'd take cocktails together, and she'd regale me with stories of New York at the time of the armory show and of Paris during the twenties and thirties. She once told me she'd attended that great art event in New York with Marcel Duchamp himself, who had also taken her earlier in the day to the Brevoort for lunch, and that she'd also been a close friend of Francis Picabia from that time in New York. In fact, Louise seemed to have met just about everybody: Picasso and Colette, Sandy Calder, and "Madame Stein," as she called her, and Georges Simenon, for whom she translated for a number of years during and after World War II.

To illustrate Simenon's manic productivity she told me once that, during or shortly after the war, when she and Varèse and Simenon and his then wife were still living near each other in Connecticut "like exiled Jack Mormans," she'd called the Simenon household to invite the author and his wife to Sunday lunch. Mrs. Simenon answered. She expressed regrets that they wouldn't be able to come that Sunday "as Georges has just begun a new novel, but if you put it off until Sunday a week," she added, "he'll be finished by then."

I used to visit with her on Sullivan Street as often as I could, and she would read my poems and comment astutely and serve me Dubonnet sodas. She was growing somewhat hard of hearing but was as alert as ever, and her memory was extraordinary. She'd quote whole passages of Baudelaire and Rimbaud which she'd translated for New Directions (along with the Julian Gracq novel *The Castle of Orgel*, which she barely recalled doing.)

Since Varèse was a great innovator of electronic music and had a nineteenth-century background of studying with Busoni, he had many who wished to study with him, she pointed out. One such was Yardbird Charlie Parker, who arrived at their door one afternoon costumed as a butler and offered his services as chef and factotum to Varése in return for lessons in composition. Varèse was a great jazz fan and, according to Louise, told the Yardbird that the shoe should be on the other foot; he should be taking lessons from Parker's genius.

Once, in her last years, I dropped by in the late afternoon to keep an appointment, and, after ringing the front bell a number of times without hearing her voice, I started to walk away, discouraged, but a neighbor woman stopped me and said Louise was probably upstairs napping and had removed her hearing apparatus. Since I had an appointment and she possessed a key to the house, she would go upstairs and check on Louise.

I waited some minutes more, and then Louise herself came to the door, well coiffed and, smiling, chiding me gently. "I'm a very old woman, Richard," she said, "and I overslept. You mustn't be cross with me for keeping you waiting. At my age it's my privilege."

Once on a snowy evening in MacDowell, Louise slipped on an icy path and broke her leg. She lay exposed, in shock and pain, through the night until she was discovered the next day and taken to hospital and had her broken bone set. She was then an octogenarian, and such was her will to live an active life that she managed to recuperate and walk again through swimming and other exercises. I have never known anybody who had such a fierce desire to hang on a while longer. Louise was always asking me to suggest books she should read, especially poetry, and while she liked very little that was being written she was willing to pretend that she was the inadequate reader. She was a great fan of my autobiographical novel *Fredi and Shirl and the Kids*, however, and it so happened that her attorney was a member of the same synagogue as my family, and she had once asked him if my depiction in the book of my life growing up in Jewish Brooklyn, which was terra incognita to her, could possibly have been accurate.

When I came by for cocktails one afternoon Louise seemed most pleased and delighted to inform me that over dinner two nights previously "Irwin," her attorney, had indeed confirmed for her "that you really did not spring from the loins of the Olympian gods, Richard."

This was the sort of reassurance I needed then, as I was being rather harshly criticized in some circles for my "cruel" portraits of my middle-class family. Louise was the daughter of an upper-middle-class executive who had herself rebelled against respectable proprieties and restrictions in her own style, running off to New York and then Paris and marrying bohemians and never really going home to Pittsburgh again. Louise said the things in my defense I would never have dared to claim for myself. She even likened me to Varèse ("He was such a rebellious person, like you.") and to some of her Dada and surrealist friends. "Artists do exaggerate a little, and you're an artist," she would remind me when I was feeling low, "a poet. One can't have you kowtowing to too many false gods. There is such a thing as poetic license."

We knew each other over a decade, and those must have been somewhat lonelier times for Louise. She was writing her memoir of her life with Varèse and hoped to do a second volume, if her publisher, Norton, could be convinced to encourage her. She was very frightened they wouldn't. I sometimes think she used the memoir writing to extend her life span. Just so long as she had this project and kind or amusing people around her she could continue. But there came a time when she was told there would be no second volume, and that's when she began to decline, I think. The composer Ann MacMillan, who had been an assistant to Varèse, once told me Louise "isn't quite the way she used to be, you know."

"She must be close to ninety," I reminded Ann.

"Just the same," Ann said.

At such an advanced age Louise still seemed delighted to meet my girlfriends and occasionally seemed to get jealous if I devoted too much of my attention to them over cocktails. Then I moved out of town for a while, and I heard from friends that even then she was not without other male admirers. One in particular for many years was a doctor of medicine and a serious painter some twenty years her junior, who, allegedly, had proposed marriage to her once and with whom she continued to dine at least once a week at her favorite Village restaurant, Monte's.

Once a week at Monte's was probably no substitute for a life with people. She began to welcome visits from her son. She was too old to go back to MacDowell and lacked a project. For a while she was a part of a community of older gay women in a house in New Jersey. Louise missed Varèse and all her other contemporaries, nearly all of whom had already died. Though she was never as well known to Americans as she was in international literary and cultural circles, she still had stories to tell, memories to impart, a sensitivity to art and literature. She knew what was true to art and what was ersatz. She told me once metaphors should "taste in the mouth."

For most of her life, I gather, she'd been a lover of women as well as men, and some of her female companions were equally as celebrated as Duchamp and Varèse, though she seemed to find it indiscreet to gossip about them. She could at times, however, be very disapproving of her old acquaintance Anais Nin, whom she considered "a pretentious and truly silly writer," and she always had admiring words for the journalist Janet Flanner.

The last time I saw her was less than a year before her death. She had remained an elegant woman for as long as I knew her, slim and well turned out, with an eye for the fashions of when she was in her prime, her features finely modeled and enduring, ash gray hair silken against her long, elegant face.

In all the years I'd known her, therefore, I'd never once thought of her as failing, deteriorating, but as this terribly smart treasure I kept stashed for inspiring my life, so poised and exquisite and seemingly timeless and always prepared with a kind word of encouragement or a witty rejoinder to my lugubrious self-pity, whereas I—like her son—always seemed to be the one who was aging much too rapidly over the years.

It was spring in New York on that last visit, and she saw me into the hall leading to the front door. I was married and a father again, and she seemed very pleased about that. Louise had met my oldest daughter, Margaret, when Margaret was an adolescent. Now she asked about my little one. Was she pretty? Smart? Did she favor me or my wife?

I said I thought she looked a lot like my wife, but we also had some things in common.

"Do you want her to be an artist?" she asked.

I said, "just so long as she's happy."

"I don't suppose I'll ever meet her," she said, flatly, without energy. She was feeling very tired again from our hour together and thought she might go up to nap again.

"I'm so happy for you," she said, "and for seeing you again. Try to be happy too, Richard. Goodbye now."

I can't imagine words said by her with any more finality.

PETE MARTIN

Pete was a co-founder with Lawrence Ferlinghetti of the City Lights Bookstore and publishing house in San Francisco. He only wrote a few things in his lifetime that I know of, and they are mostly about movies and pop culture. If he ever thought of himself as a literary disappointment, he kept that to himself, except to make occasional self-deprecating jokes. Pete was usually careful never to use his disappointments to put down others who were trying to write and publish. He was a terrific talker when he was sober and sometimes even when he wasn't. He once told me he left the Bay Area "because I couldn't stand reading the *Chronicle* every morning." I choose to remember him mostly because he was my friend in New York when I was really in need of friends.

After being hospitalized for a while in a locked ward at Bellevue I lived alone, and I was unable to focus a lot of the time. So much thorazine was in my system I kept seeing other people from the same ward lying comatose on the streets of the Upper West Side as, later, in Central America, I saw actual corpses on the streets of some cities, usually with their faces skinned off. In my own private day and night horror show, I had simply too much time on my hands, with nothing much to do with any of it.

In New York Peter now operated New Yorker Books above the cinema of the same name owned by his landlord, the critic and producer Dan Talbot. That was all torn down some years ago to build another apartment house. The New Yorker bookshop had a small downstairs side entrance on Eighty-ninth Street next door to a sleazy corner frankfurter and orange juice stand. Downstairs you could buy newspapers, all sorts of periodicals, and the latest paperback releases. This was usually presided over by one of Pete's longhaired young male employees.

The upstairs shop itself was two large rooms and a storage space overlooking Eighty-ninth, which Pete had crammed with new hardcover books, all paperback titles, and, in the back, tables full of remaindered and secondhand books. To be in proximity with other human beings I used to go there often just to visit and browse. Here Pete himself was in charge in an old tweed jacket and khaki trousers, a shirt opened at the neck. He gabbed with all the customers, took special orders, and championed various Upper West Side causes, then imbibed a long and often liquid lunch at the saloon down the block on Broadway and stayed on until dinnertime, when he pocketed some of the receipts and put his trust for the rest in his various young assistants.

A crabby seeming man with a face red from drink, Pete reminded me with his beaklike nose and high cheekbones of a big, grouchy, and quite wise macaw. He was a neighborhood figure of some renown, knew everybody, and was hard not to notice. Mothers used to warn their children about getting him riled up. In fact, for such a red-faced man, Pete was usually gentle and funny, kindly and without pretensions, truly a supportive friend of all the writers in the neighborhood, who in those days included, among others, the crime writer Donald Westlake, Joe Heller, Jules Feiffer, Chandler Brossard, and myself.

Pete and his wife, Madeleine, were particularly kind and generous to me after I had that spell in Bellevue for mental problems. I had the feeling they'd hardly noticed me or my works before, though they always carried my titles, but when my piece "All the Thorazine You Can Drink in Bellevue" came out in *New York* magazine they were concerned for me, and they showed it. When my novel, *Fredi and Shirl and the Kids* was remaindered by Scribners, Pete at my request bought up the remaining 460 copies in stock for about a dollar a copy and sold them off to libraries and other interested customers a book at a time, which meant my book was not out of print for half a decade longer; this also made it possible for me to have copies for sale whenever I gave readings. They did the same for some other local authors I knew. Another title Peter carried and sold in abundance was the paperback *Conditions of Human Growth* by Jane Peirce and Saul Newton of the Sullivanian cult. All Sullivanians were required to own a copy of this tome and to discuss certain passages they knew by heart. Pete was amused by the Sullivanians and their Bible.

"I tried reading that," he once told me. "It didn't make a lot of sense. Just a lot of jargon. Don't those people ever have any fun?"

I assured Pete that there was a lot of sexual activity. "There'd have to be something," he said, shaking that thick paperback in my face. "It can't be this prose."

Once, after I'd gone through another bad time emotionally and was unable to write and just barely able to meet with my classes at

Columbia, I asked Pete if he could give me a job in the shop as a sales clerk as a way of passing time until I felt a little better. Pete had no real need for me, but he hired me on, and he and Madeleine took on the chore, as they'd done with others, of looking after me. They invited me out to their place on Fire Island with my daughter for day visits and for meals at the local saloon around the corner. I was paid minimum wage, and though I was okay at making change at the register and knew the stock pretty well, I was so physically weakened, after weeks of poor nutrition and going without sleep, I often couldn't really *shlep* all the big boxes of books by myself and was a bit of a drag to the other, much younger, sales clerks. Pete put up with me more or less as a point of honor and never really complained about my lethargy. He was just amiable in his way, a man who reached out to others and yet remained cranky and acute.

When Irving Howe was having problems with his teenaged daughter, Pete hired her on to help out in the shop because, he told me, "it can't be easy being Irving's kid." Sometime later Pete went out of business and moved back to California. He was having a hard time paying wholesalers and publishers on time (for he allowed customers to charge books and would special order any book in print a customer wanted). Eventually all those due bills caught up with him, even though he did a large volume of business and his store was becoming a literary landmark and a hangout. I blamed Pete's unfailing generosity and my sloth for some of his cashflow headaches. The subsidy he paid me may have been the ultimate drain on his available resources. "I'm not just another pretty face," he told me once, "but I sure as hell am a pushover."

Pete loved to drink and to gab and tell hard luck stories in his perpetually hoarse voice. He was the "natural son" of the Italian anarchist Carlo Tresca, and his mother was a sister of the Communist leader Elizabeth Gurley Flynn. (Tresca was apparently such a charmer that he managed affairs with both sisters.) Pete spent some of his childhood in Bisbee, Arizona, where his mother and stepfather, an anarchist trade unionist, moved when he was little as organizers for the Mine, Mill, and Smelter Workers. Pete still considered himself an anarchist, but he was also deeply disaffected from activist radical politics, the more so after marrying Madeleine, who was what we used to call a "bohemian," I suppose, but also a member of the Doubleday family.

He hated the poverty he'd known in childhood. "What's wrong with being middle class?" Pete used to hector me. "What's so terrible about living decently?"

When Pete and Ferlinghetti founded the City Lights Bookshop, he told me, they also started the quarterly *City Lights* and later a publishing house. Pete was both a contributor and an editor. One day, he told me, a skinny kid from the East with glasses came in with "this big long boring poem" and Ferlinghetti wanted me to read it. I thought it was lousy and "boring, you know," and I told that to Larry, but he thought it was just great, so we published it anyhow. That, according to Pete, was how Allen Ginsberg's *Howl* got into print. "And do you know what?" he always added then, with hoarse, unabashed candor that was unique to him and maybe Andy Devine, "I still think it's boring, lousy poetry, if you ask me."

Pete had little ear for Blakean music, but he loved movies, old, new, just so long as they made motion pictures before his eyes. Sometimes he would be missing from the shop for hours in the afternoon, and we knew he was next door in the dark at Dan Talbot's cinema, soaking up some classic thirties Hollywood comedy or Truffaut flick. The store had a first-rate collection of books on and about the cinema, and he was very pleased with me when I signed on to write the novelization of the film *Taxi Driver*. It was the end of my working at the store but by no means the end of my friendship with Pete and Madeleine. Pete thought *Taxi Driver* was my best book, "even better than the film," he told me, and he sold a lot of copies. He said, "There are guys like Travis all over the Upper West Side. Some are even my customers. They come in here to score dope. But the only dope we have around here is me, for hiring guys like you and running a shop like this which can never break even in a month of Sundays."

Pete was a man of strong opinions but easy acceptance of all the barflies in the neighborhood. He was especially fond of an old fellow named Sturman who'd been a writer in the early days of TV, until he got washed out to sea in a flood of alcohol. Pete used to buy hotdogs for Sturman from the stand downstairs and let *him* hang around the shop and browse the pornography. One day Pete tried to convince him he should become a vegetarian, as the hot dogs below us were so high in cholesterol. "I get all the grain I need and want in spirits," Sturman insisted. "If I feel like having a potato, I take a taste of vodka."

Pete was very proud that you could sometimes find movie people like Tuesday Weld and Faye Dunaway browsing not too far away from activists like Paul O'Dwyer or the black novelist John Williams. He especially liked journalists and crime writers and the authors of kids' books and was often hard on poets. "So many are just fakers," he insisted.

A truly gifted woman friend of mine was once briefly Pete's girlfriend in San Francisco, long before Pete knew Madeleine. It didn't really work out, she said, as Pete could be a lot of fun, but he just wasn't that interested in being a lover. He preferred bar scenes and gab. When they ended the affair, she said, Pete was very kind toward her, gentle, concerned. He didn't hold a grudge, and, in fact, they were still friends.

This was typical of what I knew about Pete's attitude toward women. He was courtly in a mildly besotted fashion. He was never much of a fan of Communists, but was always gallant when referring to his once beautiful "Aunt Elizabeth." Pete would tell interviewers she was a "marvelous woman" and should never have "done time, although I guess she was guilty of something, like having politics." He stayed close to Gurley Flynn until her death. And he always had humor about his radical pedigree. "They were pretty passionate, mixed-up people," he would say, "but sincere and honest. Not hacks. A hard act to follow . . . When I was a kid I felt like Jacky Coogan at the Haymarket Riots. It really wasn't what you would call a normal childhood, and it shows, doesn't it?"

Pete never really took himself too seriously. He had gout and swollen feet, headaches, a perpetual heavy cough. He drank too much and smoked too much, and sometime after moving back to the coast he was dead. That seemed to be the point of it all in Pete's case, to get on with living and with dying. A hard lesson for me to learn even now at sixty-three.

George William Booth

George William Booth is a tall, handsome, slow-talking, serious, and wonderfully deranged *New Yorker* cartoon artist from Missouri who, for the past twenty-five years, has inhabited a small pre–Civil War saltbox in Stony Brook where I live. Loping down shady Christian Avenue in his sky blue denim work clothes toward his studio or the post office, where we sometimes meet, rangy George bestrides the sedate main drag of this colonial village like a colossus strung out on white-out. His smile is genuine, which means he hasn't got one for just everybody, and his husky voice is like Walter Brennan's poured through maple sugar by a sober Andy Devine. "How are you?" from George is never faked.

It's an open question whether all cartoonists are artists; Booth's nervous, deep-bitten lines and feverish comic distortions distinguish him as one of our great popular graphic artists. A sculptor friend of some distinction once confessed to me, "I wish I could draw like George Booth." From neurasthenic cats and dogs and cranky dogfaced people in their drafty, ill-kempt houses, Booth has moved on to "early people" communicating in an "iptalk" akin to the language of "Finnegan's Wake." Lately, his increasingly absurdist metaphors for our world show him walking a tightrope strung above a trampoline between Charles Addams and Daumier. A recent Booth *New Yorker* cover, for example, was a bluefaced troglodyte trying to swallow a huge suppository-shaped bullet against a wash of soft greens and purples, the edge of which discreetly reproduced the thin, green margin of a Federal Reserve note. One would be hard put to confuse this message with the slogan Happy Days Are Here Again.

Booth is sly about the increasing bite of his popular art. He points out calmly enough he's just a little nuts, and he considers that a positive; he's an admirer of Lautrec, Laurel and Hardy, and the Marx Brothers, but also of Miro, Van Gogh, and Picasso, who, he says, was "also a cartoonist." "When I see a fine painting," he says, "I want to ask, What's the caption?"

Increasingly, Booth is teasing our postmodern nerve endings with expressionist renderings of the anxious plights of the Clinton era middle classes. In a cartoon on managed health care, the bewildered patients stand in their flimsy hospital-issue nightgowns on the front lawn, while, from a second-story window, a gargoyle nurse explains to an irate sufferer of hospital policy: "You don't get a room, Mr. Reinschreiber, because you didn't pay for a room. That's the whole point of walk-in surgery."

Color came late to Booth's art. When he was in art school in Chicago his watercolor teacher took one look at his raw reds and yellows and told him, "You should work in black and white." But for the past twenty years Booth has been doing occasional *New Yorker* covers. In these the brushstrokes are freely applied with a wonderful fluency. A few years back Booth did a charming syndicated cartoon strip for big city and small town papers who could afford his subtle, closely hued panels and quiet humor. Booth says it was "a dream come true, working on a strip." He grew up on Krazy Kat and Al Capp in color and since then his humor and his color have turned much more brazen. For his *Bite the Bullet New Yorker* cover he used a wide brush and vivid background swathes, tinting the face of his trog a lugubrious blue, with a swatch of pink tongue and gums showing. When his *New Yorker* editor asked why blue, Booth told him, "Because that's the way he feels."

"What I want to do," he told me, "is to look for the in-between happenings that happen to everybody and we're not aware of them until we see them on paper and they touch us and then we say, hey, that happened to me."

Booth grew up in small Missouri towns during the Depression. His father and mother taught in poor rural schools and farmed a little, and once they even had to live in a schoolhouse in lieu of rent money and for backpay ate the produce of some cherry trees. He's always been drawing something or other; his mother was an amateur cartoonist and poet in the local paper. Booth learned early from such experiences to detest cant, the slick and comfortable, easily glib. Now in his late sixties, he never uses profanity, is a careful abstemious man, except when he's making jokes or drawing his visions of the way we live today. When his demons overtake him, roofs leak, teenage babysitters join AA, and demented husbands and wives confess peculiar sexual yearnings amid the detritus of their porch steps before running off to blab on "Oprah."

Some years back I conned Booth in return for a free Vermont weekend to give a slide show of his cartoons to the hip, literate audi-

ence of the Bennington College summer writing workshops, an
evening that still gets talked about by old Bennington hands. Viewing
Booth's panorama of suburban dysfunction, paraded huggermugger,
was hilarious for the pithiness of his caption readings, his delight in
the faces he drew, the words they said. Booth loves words. He finds
them in the letters of friends, in the press, talking with neighbors. His
cartoon people gush, rhapsodize, soliloquize: "She wants high
romance and a baby while her husband wants to be, and is, a very successful broker who takes graduate courses at night and wants no baby
and at the same time she has more or less recovered from being in love
with the welldigger."

I knew even back then George was not a drinking man, but I had
never heard a sober man giggle quite so much with pleasure from his
own visionary company and realized I was in the presence of one of
those divine fools. As George stopped being broken up, his audience
was only just beginning to lose their minds, so in that close firefly
darkness we were all purged of pity and terror, a certain overly literate New York sangfroid.

Though Booth's sense of life is gently comic, he has a dark side
and even believes the tragic "can be funny too, humor, if you look at it
a certain way." His old blue Jaguar was in and out of the shop so often
he found comic pathos in the shoulder shruggings of garage mechan-
ics in their vast bays, one of whom happened to be his next door neighbor.

An honest man laughs at his own stuff because who would, if he
didn't? And how, pray tell, does that sound? Like a giggling Ozark
spring in a mudslide of India ink. Or when he's cross? Then the words
of Booth's "stone age" followers of the great Maloop bear a striking
resemblance to certain aggressive late-twentieth-century arbitragers:
"Yee yee hee hee haw haw yip yip! . . . Hom Tont Ho. Dass Krok-Tron
Gul! Huppy Dod Klop Klop GUL! WHU IP DOON HUPPY DOD?
OSSA IPS!"

Lyndon Johnson

I was opposed to the war in Vietnam. I marched against it, wrote against it, signed petitions, tore up my draft card, and sent the pieces with a note to the Selective Service. To this day I think those of us in opposition did the right thing and that our opposition mattered and helped put an end to our killing of the Vietnamese and to the U.S. military disaster there.

My father was a regular Democrat and a supporter of Lyndon Johnson. He thought I was misguided, ungrateful, and unpatriotic, and probably going to get into a lot of trouble. As the casualties mounted and the conflict spread, my disagreements with my father also increased. I stopped seeing him, in part, because he supported the war.

I met Lyndon Johnson once when he was president, and that was before the worst warfare in Vietnam had gotten under way. It was maybe six or seven months after the assassination of Kennedy. I was hired on to write narration for a film about the American presidency. The filmmaker had a grant from the USIA when Kennedy was still alive, and he was given great access to Kennedy at cabinet meetings and in the privacy of the White House. All that footage was scrapped when Johnson was sworn in. Johnson's people decided they only wanted a film made about his presidency, and they were much less willing to give the filmmaker access to the president. As a consequence there was a great deal of footage of Johnson stepping in or out of Air Force One, or at ceremonial events, but no intimacy and no anecdotal material. Johnson felt uncomfortable about giving the cameras that sort of access. The film threatened to be a dud, a bore, so the filmmaker arranged with Johnson's press secretary to allow me to hang about in the White House pressroom for a few days and gather material for the voice over.

It was a very hectic time, as I recall. The U.S. presence in Vietnam was growing, but Johnson was still fairly popular for pushing civil rights and all his other Great Society programs. He was also in the midst of a fight with Bobby Kennedy, until recently attorney general, about who would be the next leader of which Democratic party.

In those days the White House press hung out and waited on releases and leaks like Pavlov's dogs. They'd suddenly be animated anticipating an event but most of the time seemed indolent and gossipy. One day Press Secretary George Reedy invited me in with them from the pressroom to attend a bill signing in the Oval Office. It had something to do with preserving natural resources, and many from both houses of Congress were on hand.

After signing the bill with a lot of ink dip pens, Johnson passed along a file of us assembled by Reedy's people and greeted each one of us and shook our hands. Critic though I was of the burgeoning Vietnam War, I ended up with my own souvenir pen. It was as though I were being bribed or rewarded for not being disruptive of Johnson's performance in public. A setup, I thought.

There were, apparently, no limits to Johnson's hands-on approach to the press. A reporter nearby later told us he had a collection of such pens. I thought of how movie theaters used to hand out Depression glass and china.

Johnson also had been briefed about my name and occupation. When he came in front of me to hand me the pen and I accepted his gift without rebuff, he said, "Well, Mr. Elman, how's the New York novel writing business?"

I was much too startled to do anything but grin and nod back.

He seemed very tall and very tanned and well groomed, better looking than I'd supposed from all the cartoons and caricatures. His shoulders were narrow, and his drape suit hung off his large body a little, with handstitched lapels.

He took my hand in both of his big, warm mitts and smiled and grinned and exuded a wave of aftershave and showed off his teeth, and then he moved on to the next person in line, doing the exact same thing.

I was a little flattered, and I asked Reedy's assistant how the president had managed to remember everybody on the line like that. The man said, of course, he was a real pro. But I could have sworn Johnson was wearing a wire that resembled a hearing aid next to his ear. Maybe he had a prompter?

Johnson's head was big and sort of oblong; his hair was thinning and slicked back. He seemed to have me all figured out: even rebels liked souvenirs. When he shook my hand he grinned as though I'd just been caught swiping some of his silverware. Said to me, "This is something to save for your children." Said to my neighbor on the line,

"How's the rug business these days?" and waited for no reply before moving on.

I don't recall him making a speech. He came and went, and the room emptied out again. In the pressroom there was a briefing about future events.

Reedy was a big, clumsy, grumpy, but sweet-natured, man, and, later that morning, in private, he stood among us as a reporter and told a few colorful off-the-record stories about his boss, which were all about Johnson's playfulness toward the truth. One I remember was about inviting the president of Pakistan, a devout Muslim, to the ranch in Texas for a barbecue and serving him pork ribs. Then somebody on the staff panicked, remembering how Muslims didn't eat pork. A major diplomatic incident might have occurred if Johnson had not quickly informed the staffer to tell the Pakistani's people when they inquired that they were feasting on "wild turkey barbecue."

That afternoon the president took a walk in the Rose Garden and the press were invited to come along and ask off-the-record questions. Johnson was walking his hounds, as I recall, and the questions were mostly about who he thought might be his running mate were he to stand for a full electoral term. Johnson came on as cat-and-mouse obscene. He seemed fully aware that some of us thought of him as devious, perhaps even an assassin, and with every word spoken, though reminding us he now had the upper hand, he seemed compelled to be abusive.

"I don't suppose you fellas really want to know my thinking on the Great Society," I can remember him beginning. In fact, his questioners had far more mundane and petty inquiries to make. He had few rivals back then, but had a dismissive way of talking about every one of them. He referred to Robert Kennedy with contempt as "Bobby." Humphrey was "Hube." About Sargent Shriver, then still head of the Peace Corps, he said, "Sarge is just awful nice, a nice enough guy, and he's doing a good job, but he's no genius politically. In fact, if you blindfolded him and bent him over backwards, he probably wouldn't be able to find his own asshole."

Johnson couldn't seem to extricate himself from the knots of his own rage. Senator Ribicoff was, with a hint of sarcasm, "Honest Abe." Working the crowd for derisive laughter, validating his contempt, he reminded me of a comic bombing to a full house in the Catskill Mountains. He really was not a handsome prospect. In those days he took great delight in consensus, building people up to tear them down with a word, a glance. When questions were pointed he seemed to rub raw and did not look as sedate and well appointed as he did on the recep-

tion line, but meanspirited and feisty, slightly sedated. Whenever anybody asked about Indo-China he passed out valiums about "credibil-
ity" and "honoring commitments."

On the reception line I'd had a brief moment of recognition of
Johnson as a self-made man like my own father, but in the Rose Garden I saw the President as full of hubris and self-doubt. He kept anticipating hostility and came on strongly, hoping to distract people from
who he was and what he was about. It seemed pretty clear to me he
was afraid of all of us.

When I left the White House that day I stopped by Reedy's office
to thank him for his assistance.

"Did you get what you wanted?" he inquired, glumly.

"Probably not," I said.

My remark caught him short. He hesitated before nodding at me
and turning away. Sometime later he resigned. Bobby Kennedy was
assassinated, and the war in Vietnam worsened. I was one of those in
the streets chanting

> Hey, hey, L.B.J.,
> How many kids did you kill today?

BILL KENNEDY

In the sixties I used to visit Bill Kennedy at Burden Lake when we were both poor writers scratching our way up. He had a tough life in those days, had quit newspaper reporting to write and couldn't get himself arrested, as we used to say, as a free lance. He had a wife and kids, and it wasn't very easy getting by, but he always was gracious to me, and friendly.

Nowadays Bill is much more successful, and some people say he seems gruff. Such seeming gruffness, I suspect, is the impression a harried man gives off in seeking to keep in focus and connected to his writings. Bill and I have sometimes argued, but I never felt he kept grudges, accountings of old grievances.

He was really struggling a lot in those days, and his closest friendships, I'm sure, date from loyalties formed then, when he found it hard to get work at any of the local colleges, even teaching freshman English. One who was connected to Bill then as now was the critic and novelist Doris Grumbach, who was married to an Albany physician and sometimes taught at the College of St. Rose, a small private Catholic girls school in Albany. Bill is also old and good friends with the fine novelist Edward Howar, a former Albany resident, who used to work in a juvenile home not very far out of town.

Nowadays Bill is friends with former Governor Mario Cuomo, and also with a startling literary gent who seemed to live most of his spoken life between parentheses, the late Tom Smith, with whom he had been active in founding and finding support for the New York State Writers Institute. It's one of those happy pieces of bureaucratic haphazardness that such an institute exists, to provide readings to neglected writers, make awards to the accomplished, and provide a stimulus to the literary community outside New York City. Writers come to the institute, get treated to good wine and food and honorariums, and they have good company, a good audience, whenever Bill and Tom, while he was alive (or Toni Morrison when she was in residence), could be in town and in attendance.

I think Bill felt it as a happy obligation to make certain others of talent were not as entirely neglected as he was for so long in his career. He now seems to touch gold with nearly everything he does: seventy-five-thousand-copy first printings of a children's book he collaborated on with his son, while his masterpiece *Ironweed* initially sold only about seventeen thousand copies in hardcover. He's been translated widely, and when people like Francis Coppola fly to Albany for a meeting about a film project, they usually bring along their checkbooks.

Kennedy is now in the pretty fortunate position of being able to call his own shots. He followed *Ironweed* with a popular oral-style history of the Irish in Albany and a novel about Irish rivermen in the nineteenth century.

Last time we were together at his newly expanded quarters in the same old, large white house across from Burden Lake, a large party of friends was in progress. There must have been thirty little kids of all ages in the outdoor pool that late August night, and the pool was kept at the temperature recommended by doctors for the treatment of lumbago. Steam rose from the guests, the drinks, the barbecue pit. Kids bobbed about on floats like *zeppoli* at the Feast of St. Gennaro. Bill and his wife, Dana, and their grown kids circulated; his Puerto Rican in-laws helped with the drinks, joined in the fun. When my head emerged from the pool, I felt as though I'd just broken a long fever.

Night was heavy with chatter around Burden Lake. Bill and I talked a bit about Nicaragua. His Caribbean Basin reporting and family ties make him no great fan of the American empire. He'd just come back from seeing then President Daniel Ortega and his wife, Rosario Murillo, at a private meeting in a liberal Brooklyn church.

I was no great fan of Ortega or his wife. Bill was a more tolerant man. He thought Ortega was a bit of a bonehead, but his right to defend himself against the U.S.–Contra onslaught was undeniably just, and Bill was willing to help out if he could. He thought he might even be going to Cuba for a visit. Nevertheless, though we argued, he listened to what I had to say, and I did not feel afterward that we were enemies.

I tried to tell Bill that I thought Rosario Murillo could run for the Great Neck schoolboard and eventually, having captured the old Margiotta machine, wind up a Nassau County supervisor. He listened, and we drank. A few days later I sent him some materials about the regime, not because I cared to change his mind, but because I did not wish him injured through his associations. When he wrote back to thank me, he made it clear there were no hard feelings.

At the party I'd found myself thinking of Rip Van Winkle. There are certain resemblances between that prototypical old New York State recreant Dutchman and Bill's Francis Phelan, both returning home after long sleeps, and Bill finally gaining his due after twenty hard years in his self-imposed cocoon upstate, after disastrous fires and poverty and soul-bleeding neglect, and somehow coming away from it without malice, with compassion and care for others.

He's been kind to me in recent years, too, and he always was a fine host and kind to all his guests. I asked him about the filming of *Ironweed*. Was it to be done in Albany? I wished somehow to compliment Bill, so I pointed out my true feeling that no director could get from film what he'd been able to imbue in his prose, an inward outwardly directed hallucinatory and dramatic language of Francis Phelan which can imagine infant corpses growing beards and conversations beyond the grave.

Bill seemed to take offense at my compliment. He claimed as scriptwriter to be more interested in the "visuals." He strayed from me then to glance at the pool, where Doris Grumbach steamed on a float, like a pirogi, with a plastic glass of booze floating beside her.

Bill was driving a big, black Chrysler, and on one visit, he took me around Albany on foot, and all the local pols and wisealecks seemed to know him and were proud. Bill probably has different financial problems than he once had. Nevertheless, as our friend Nick Delbanco has pointed out, having more money has not changed Bill's life that much: the same friends, though perhaps a better brand of booze.

He remains a courtly man, with a glass in his hand, dedicated to proving that *Ironweed* was no accident. It's true, the same places which once refused him employment are now offering him large honorariums, probably even honorary degrees. He does not seem to find the need to be bitter about the bad times. If you ever get invited to Bill's institute, I'm sure you won't go away thirsty.

A Postscript

I've always gotten along well with Irish people like Bill. One of my nicest girlfriends was Irish, a Gallic speaker. My friend, Tom Flanagan, the novelist, and I have a regular date, whenever he's in town, to drink at a local boit. But I really can't keep up with Tom and alcohol anymore than I can with Bill Kennedy. It seems to me long custom has made them invulnerable to the tipsyness that easily overwhelms me after one or two.

I started drinking because I didn't like the notion of Jewish sobriety. It seemed chauvinistic and basically untrue to my nature. Like Jews don't collect welfare . . . I much preferred drinking to flirty conversations with Cynthia Ozick. Though I had a hard time swallowing whiskey at first, there were other things I was asked to swallow about the person I was supposed to be and how I was supposed to behave that I found even more difficult.

My favorite drinking pal was my old friend Hannah Green. We'd sip Old Heaven Hill bourbon neat in her studio on Barrow Street for a whole evening and just chat about everything. I loved Hannah and her husband Jack Wesley, the painter. Hannah had been a student at Stanford when I was there. She had the world's richest laughter, the greatest smile. Her long sickness and death was a real loss to me. She was such a good writer, and she loved to sip Heaven Hill and smoke Gitane cigarettes and giggle and sigh and just talk.

Roberto Sosa

I've visited La Ceiba, Honduras, more than once. It's a pleasant enough little port city, once you get used to the heat and poverty.

Honduras is the poorest country in all of Central America, and in the summertime the visitor to La Ceiba is spared from the putrid heat and the scorched faces of the drunken moneychangers on the streets by an occasional refreshing breeze off the sea. There are places along the wide beachfront where for a few lempira you can sit for hours with a bottle of cold Salve Vida beer staring at endless white, sandy beaches and the slow surging, dirty-looking Caribbean, and sometimes the haze lifts and you see off in the distance the even, green, throbbing mass of Roatan Island, one of Honduras' few tourist attractions, embedded in emerald bays.

On the mainland Hondurans are a poor frightened people. Though nominally ruled by constitutionalist civilians, the populace is under the thumb of the army, and its G-2 is surprisingly effective at torture and at making dissidents disappear.

At my beachfront hotel in Roatan the rooms were named after famous Central American adventurers: Columbus, Captain Morgan, William Walker.

Once in La Ceiba I went into a small local bookshop to buy some poems by Roberto Sosa, who is as close to a national poet as they have in Honduras. The lady in the shop seemed surprised that a gringo wanted to read Sosa. Was it some sort of trap? She told me he would be of no interest to me as he wrote only about the poor, and, when I agreed that he did, she announced loudly in Spanish she had no such books in her store anyway, but she could sell me the poems of any number of deceased leftwing Spaniards such as Alberti and Lorca, even Pablo Neruda.

Honduras has always been a military dictatorship run principally for the benefit of the United Fruit Company, which still cultivates bananas along the east coast above La Ceiba. It's a country of muddy villages and men with guns, where the spindly legged children wear

T-shirts with Harvard and Princeton and Hard Rock Cafe logos. Running from the law in Texas, William Sidney Porter (O'Henry) passed through there en route to San Salvadór. He found the locals unreliable and the North Americans bossy. An English lady traveler of the nineteenth century was somewhat kinder, though she suffered from cramps and dysentery and the heat. The men are always courteous, she pointed out. On the Bay Islands the shrimpers speak English and their wives attend chapel. They say, "we are not really Hondurans. We're Garufinos and Scots and St. Vincent Maroons and Creoles."

During the Contra civil war against the Nicaraguan state there were a number of CIA installations around Roatan and La Ceiba, and the wreckage of Nicaraguan fishing boats would beach among the coves. The population was fearful of the Sandinistas, but they also feared the Americans and their surrogates, the Contras. The incidence of AIDS and gonorrhea increased exponentially.

A nineteenth-century poet once said of his country, "You could write the history of Honduras inside a tear." Sosa's vision is even more stark: "The history of Honduras can be inscribed inside a bullet, or a gunshot wound, or, better, in a drop of blood."

Once in the tiny Guaymuras Bookshop in Tegucigalpa, while I was browsing through a rack of books by Sosa, I literally bumped into the poet as I was going toward the cashier.

He was a thin man of medium height, with a light cocoa complexion and a small moustache. His manner was agreeable, even friendly. He wore a straw fedora. After complimenting me on my good taste in poetry, he signed my copy of his *Secreto Militar*.

We talked for some minutes, and I told him of my experience trying to buy one of his books in La Ceiba. "I don't know why I'm so ill-liked there," he teased. "Could it be that I have made certain people unhappy with my poems? Or is it because I come from Yoro?"

Yoro is in the mountainous interior. There are famous lakes for sportfishing of bass in the interior and the magnificent Mayan ruins at Santa Rosa de Copan and hunger and poverty. Sosa has depicted the children of the Honduran poor as having the faces of "indignant gods." He has a collection of history poems on the depredations of the United States throughout Latin America, a history of treachery and blood.

In the Guaymuras bookshop he told me, "All Hondurans are afraid of the G-2. Possibly I am too, and I don't even know it."

He was planning to be an honored guest of a Latin American bookfair at N.Y.U., but shortly after arriving in New York he returned home again. His hosts told me he seemed "uncomfortable" being so close to the Beast.

Like the wings of furious birds
the poor obliterate the air.

Poems from poor lands, like certain fabled wines, do not always travel well because they do not flatter our palettes. Sosa writes for Hondurans about the enormous human costs to being poor. He was good humored when I met him but with a pained and bitter expression that he hid behind some delicate courtesies.

Some of Sosa's words about the Honduran poor remain with me because, once having read them, it is also impossible to forget cities like "accumulated ruins" and doctors in "illuminated cages" eavesdropping on the sadness of the poor.

Of the fearfulness of such lives Sosa depicts seeking justice, "the hope of something that doesn't exist . . . in the temples of enchanted snakes," and being incarcerated on rainy days to dream of "swift sailing on windy lakes"; his Indian poor "walk and die slowly."

All of his signifiers are in Honduran reality. In translation his poems seem tastelessly harsh. "The poor are numerous," he writes, "and for that reason/it is impossible to forget them."

SUSAN MEISELAS

Ernesto Cardenal once looked down from a small elevation at Managua's neon lights at dusk, under Somoza's rule, and noted in a poem:

> If I had to give testimony
> about my era
> it is it was barbarous
> and primitive but poetic.

When Susan Meiselas first went to Nicaragua in June 1978 to photograph the burgeoning Sandinista insurrection as it became a popular uprising, Somoza's barbarism still ruled. This was then some weeks in advance of the major world press, which was still not convinced that what was going on there was really important enough to cover regularly.

Meiselas was drawn by the terse and accurate reporting of Alan Riding of *The New York Times*. Covering a beat from the Rio Bravo River at Mexico to Panama, Riding seemed to be spending more and more time in Nicaragua reporting on what he, at first, called "the National Mutiny" of Nicaraguans against the Somozas. They had owned Nicaragua forty-four years, more or less, as their private plantation, brothel, and slaughterhouse; and when the sons and daughters of their middle-class collaborators became restless, inspired by a crusading newspaper editor—Pedro Joacquin Chamorro—to believe they did not have to walk about on their knees forever, the last Somoza assassinated Chamorro. That brought more than twenty thousand Nicaraguans into the streets. It also brought some members of the press to Nicaragua for a little while, but they didn't stay long. When Meiselas arrived there were no big stories, just demonstrations, street incidents, seemingly random assassinations, and guerrilla provocations.

She came as a free-lancer to a small country that had produced few datelines since 1973 when an earthquake destroyed most of the capital, Managua, and killed thousands, making many more homeless. The U.S. Marines had once laid down a fairly good road system in the western populated portions of Nicaragua, and this meant that one could use a rental car to visit every one of the principal cities in a day's tour. Meiselas lived in lodging houses or the homes of friends. She rose early in the morning to visit the offices of the opposition newspaper, *La Prensa*, which had stringers in every town and village. Its professionals often could guess knowledgeably about what would be going on throughout the countryside on a given day.

Because of Meiselas and Riding I also became interested in Nicaragua, then involved, and eventually I was able to get there, too, for a short while. The sequence was this: some photos Meiselas made of manifestations surrounding the assassination of four students in the marketplace of Jinotepe attracted the German-American photo magazine, *GEO*. These were gaudy, fantastic shots of masked rebels ("upstarts," the Somoza press used to call them), banditos with pistols and kerchiefs over their faces at Matagalpa, school kids in baseball caps making contact bombs, and so on. The slant was obviously toward the people making the rebellion, but the photos were of more than just professional quality: to the jaded New York–Hamburg crowd they were most assuredly the stuff of pretty great images of photojournalism.

GEO had the photos but no text. They were of the opinion that a great take-out on a Central American revolution should be colorful stuff, and they'd already scheduled Nicaragua for late fall without having a single line of copy on hand. I got the assignment because I was known as a fast writer who could fill in around pictures and because I knew something about Central America. It was also true, of course, that I had to agree to another assignment: writing about a shopkeeper in Brooklyn. This was not exactly a transcendent number for one who had spent far too much of his miserable childhood bounded by the Shore Road and the Gowanus Parkway.

I'd read a few good Nicaraguan writers (Dario, and Cardenal, and Arguello Harss), and I was interested, in a desultory fashion, in Latin America. My Spanish was a clotted, rudimentary Spanglais which contrasted hugely with that of Susan Meiselas, a Sarah Lawrence graduate, who spoke something more resembling Franglais, with Spanish verbs and French verb endings. But having seen photos and read in the dispatches of bloody moments of hope and pain in Central America, I went on assignment, trusting to good luck and the abilities of my professional peers.

It was just about the most frightening, confusing, fulfilling experience of a lifetime of forty-seven years, stalled at the brink of being with people. When I got off the plane I was detained briefly for bringing in a military poncho. I took a jarring cab ride to meet Meiselas at the Hotel Inter-Continental. She already seemed like a veteran: cool, careful, just a little spacy from hard labor.

The Sandinistas had only just captured the National Palace and successfully extracted a ransom from the Boss, Somoza. But his army was still intact and equipped with U.S. and Israeli weapons. I arrived with a new long lens to deliver to Meiselas from Magnum, her photo syndicate. Unlike some other reporters, we didn't sit around the hotel pool drinking coffee; within an hour we were out on the road together.

We did that every day and night for three and one-half weeks, traveling about the countryside, racing from city to city and *barrio to barrio*, up early and to bed late. We sometimes took breaks for supper with some of the world press who were also beginning to arrive (for, by then, a full-scale armed revolt had broken out in seven major cities and towns, throughout the verdant savannah lands of the countryside); and mostly what we did was see and talk to people, watch, listen, and record, and bear witness.

That first uprising was eventually crushed by the Somozas, but it came to be a major turning point in the revolution because people did not just stop living and surrender to their oppressors. They became even more involved. Those who were not murdered and brutalized gained an even greater revolutionary resolve and coherence, through experience and better organization; and they eventually went on to take baths in Somoza's marble tub in the basement of his command post bunker, next door to the Inter-Continental.

The photographs reproduced in Meiselas's book, *Nicaragua*, are representative of the course of a revolution from small demonstrations to armed revolt to the seizure of power by the Sandinistas on behalf of the Nicaraguan people. It's as much of recent Nicaraguan history as Susan Meiselas witnessed, though not the whole story. That could begin with the building of the Panama Canal, or the revolt of Augustus Sandino against the U.S. Marines who occupied Nicaragua during much of the first three decades of this century; or with his assassination by the first Somoza; or with the first Somoza's assassination by the poet Rigoberto Lopez Perez; or the endless atrocities, student revolts, manifestations, strikes, and resentments in which a dynasty and a people were engaged that finally led large segments of the population to take up arms. The part Meiselas witnessed was a period of heightened activity and intense conflict. Wandering among the city streets and farms of Nicaragua, she took many more risks than others who came and went there and just made transparencies for the news magazines; and the result was that she made for herself many, many more opportunities.

Although Susan did not bother to hide her sympathies for students, peasants, and women and children in Nicaragua, she also managed to establish overtly correct relationships with that killer government and its national guards, and she was rarely harassed by them.

Enshrined in her book, for example, are some of her firsts: photos of Somoza's son's Tigre Battalion in training—Tachito's Tigres trained, GI-style in U.S. camouflage fatigues, by chanting that they drank the people's blood. Susan also took photos of the boss himself and his cronies at official and unofficial functions, and she talked to members of the student underground MPU, and to the middle-class members of the "twelve," which was set up as an underground bridge between vanguard Sandinistas and the disaffected Nicaraguan establishment.

Some Nicaraguan friends called her "Susanah" and the Hebraism "Shoshana," for she could seem, at once, very girlish, and yet well-set-up physically, womanly, a person of stamina and cool reserve, invariably friendly to women and children, and efficient about bestowing her feelings. Susan was slim and long-legged, with a full figure and fine features, an abundance of warm light brown hair, a Grecian profile, not surprisingly, since at least some of her Sephardi ancestors hailed from Macedonia. Such a face one might imagine decorating certain antique coins, though Susan rarely seemed aware of her appearance and didn't primp or pose. She was much too preoccupied with documenting others.

She was not well-disposed toward the middle classes as a matter of political conviction, though she was born into the upper reaches of that class herself, her father being a bureaucrat of academic medicine; and though we traveled together, ate together, and sometimes were lodged together in hotels and private houses, she was never sexually provocative or flirtatious, except that she would sometimes flirt with Somoza's military if she thought this might expedite her achieving a particular "foto" in a particular location. I have to say Susan was one of the most determined and disciplined professionals I've ever known and easily deserving of the Robert Capa Award which she later received for her Central American photography.

Alma Guillemo Prieto, a Mexican national who was a former dancer, also joined us toward the end of that first tour and was a useful addition, as she was fluent in both English and Spanish and more knowledgeable than either of us about Central America. A tall, handsome, dark-haired woman, Alma became Susan's close friend and mentor, and they worked side by side on some stories while I was writing other things. Alma's English prose was a little uncertain, and once I went over her copy before she faxed it to the *Washington Post.*

That was the evening of a massacre of civilians by Somoza's army in the same seven cities they'd recently recaptured from rebel hands. When Alma and I had finished, I was so outraged by the events she described from her visit that day to the city of Esteli that I went down into the lobby of the hotel and called the Pacifica station in Berkeley, California, and delivered extempore a five-minute report on the day's events, without clearing my copy with the military censors. I would do this every morning and evening for the next week or so until things quieted down, and inexplicably, though the phones were bugged, never once was I called on the carpet by Somocista authorities.

But while all this was going on I did sometimes worry for Susan's safety. She was taking great risks to get her photos, and it was clear to me that she, like Alma and I, was openly siding with the revolution and putting herself in situations where she was increasingly vulnerable to assassination.

In a postcard I received from Alma some time after I returned to the States, she wrote from Guatemala of assassinations and car bombings and the hardships of being a woman on the road. The patron at her hotel would not permit a woman friend to take a shower in Alma's room out of prudery, but, if she was staying in the hotel, he would permit her to visit.

Susan's photography of Nicaragua at that time is clear, colorful, composed largely in the middle distance. Her images are truly startling, exact, so obviously there that they do not need carping words of comment or explanation. We see (as Conrad believed one could show by words), scenes out of time enacted on a page in close-to-living color.

On a bluff above a mountain valley, for, example, we stare down from above at the bleached and desicated remains of a peasant, headless, with only his vertebrae showing, dumped there by paramilitary torturers for the vultures to feed upon. The look is so obviously shocking to our eyes that, at first, we are not sure what we are seeing, and we stare all the harder. That photo always reminded me of the smell of burning corpses which, a friend pointed out, startled us so by making our mouths water because even we were reminded of pork, or roast beef, cooking in an oven.

Susan Meiselas taught me all I really know to this day about covering a war, or a revolution, and she did it because she was learning how to do it herself. We learned a few things together. Get up earlier than the other guys and go to bed later. Try to talk to ordinary people about politics. Don't condescend. Listen. Ask questions. Be with people. Be fearful, of course, for fear is human, but don't let fear rule your life. Be curious at almost all costs and then get behind the barricades whenever you can; it's probably a lot safer there than in the middle. But, if I can believe my eyes in one of these photos, Meiselas is actually standing in the line of fire of a Sherman tank and less than ten feet away, while a Sandinista slings a bottle of gasoline, grenade-fashion, toward the same vehicle.

We could never really agree on just what sort of story we were writing about Nicaragua. Meiselas seemed surprised and even disappointed when I refused to outline the text in advance. I thought my job was to provide actuality, verisimilitude, images of a people in revolt and a social system falling apart, and she thought that was what she was doing and that I should probably just supply certain dry facts, dates, and other such information.

Out of all this a certain conflict developed between us. But when the fighting of "little summer" got under way in early September and the Nicaraguan people had to endure point-blank bombings, and the daily massacre of innocents and insurgents alike, our differences came to seem less important than was our task of showing there really was a popular uprising to an ignorant, superstitious, and largely uncaring audience of German and American middle-class editors and consumers.

The triumph of the revolution, which came after I had left Nicaragua, was, as Susan's photos envisage it, a national accomplishment, a gift of love and sacrifice to the people from the young, an act of self-renewal and much else, too. Until the last vestiges of such a tyranny and colonialism are expunged from Central America it will never be complete. A different elected government now rules in Managua, and they are politically conservatives, as we continue to support the business classes on behalf of the status quo. Meiselas has continued to photograph the ongoing struggle at times, bearing witness always, and recording as photo-journalists must and do.

The toll of working so close to the action was often cruel, and even grim, heavy-handed. Susan went many days without decent rest or good nutrition. She got dysentery and hepatitis. In El Salvador she was almost killed and suffered injuries in her neck and skull and bruises all over her body when her jeep accidentally touched off a mine implanted by insurgent forces to ambush government units. (A colleague did perish in the incident.) She was going down a remote country road, I presumed, to be there first where an action was anticipated.

"Death most quickly singles out him who is afraid of death," General Augustino Sandino once reportedly told his troops. But it was also true, from my own experience, that getting over the fear of death comes and goes, especially if you are older and have acquired more hostages to fortune. So we often quarreled, Susan and I, about what risks we should be taking, and once in Masays, in the middle of a gun battle, actually had an argument and were separated for nearly twenty-four hours.

She had accepted an invitation to jump inside a Toyota jeep with armed insurgents and travel through a crossfire to a point behind the insurgent barricades. Timorous and concerned, up against a wall with some other members of the press, as I watched her zigzagging into the fire, I decided to make it my own way by hugging the walls with a friend until we had reached the same point. But I was also feeling extremely angry with her for deserting my company.

Ciudad Masaya was being encircled by elite troops of Somoza's national guards, and they were just about moving in for a massacre. Susan knew the story was with the people, and she was truly risking her life to be among them as the whole interior of the city was bombed and strafed preparatory to a door-to-door search for rebels. During the bombing and strafing she found some sanctuary in a Red Cross building in the center that was crowded with Nicaraguans.

I had also stayed around for as long as I could bear, huddling with a grocer and his family and another photographer friend on the outskirts of that small city, and afterwards, during the eerie calm and lull in the battle, had wandered the streets in the center, enthralled with myself for suddenly, briefly, acquiring something resembling quiet courage and equilibrium. But as soon as I could leave, I did, whereas Meiselas was compelled to remain overnight.

The next morning, as I was worrying for Susan, I received a scribbled note from her passed to me by a Red Cross worker at my hotel. She wished me to know she was OK, although exhausted, and would be coming back soon. It was a note full of weary bewilderment, pain, and loss. She described how Somoza's soldiers went from person to person among the huddled refugees to seek out insurgents and take them from their sanctuary, presumably to be interrogated and perhaps even executed.

Susan's crumpled message to me was cryptic and full of pain, as if she had just been witness to her own endurance of a very great and horrible ordeal. Returning to our hotel later she rested a little while, ate, took a swim, and then we both went out and back to work again without any further reproaches, to take photos, talk to people, and take more risks as they came along.

Susan Meiselas's outstanding contribution to the art of photo-journalism proves once again a major and enduring difference between photo-journalists and those of us who merely write day-by-day for a living: good photo-journalists just can't hide and get their work done. It's a matter of always being willing to stick your neck out. To take the photo that gets the work done is often a life or death matter.

ERNESTO CARDENAL

San José, Costa Rica, is a hilly city high in the sun. It's a grid city, avenues all running one way and numbered streets crisscrossing. There are no huge slums on the order of Managua's or San Salvador's, but class divisions are fairly rigidly zoned. Wealth now has the high ground where the air is cooler and less miasmal.

In one of the more prosperous suburbs of this pleasant tile-roofed city, in a large, white, three-story house built against a hillside of bright flowering shrubs, I first met the poet Ernesto Cardenal on a warm day in September in the late seventies. I had trudged uphill at noon from the Soda Palace Cafe in the city's busy center to keep an appointment with this Maryknoll priest, and though tired and sweaty, I was keen with expectations, like a pilgrim—not a journalist—an admirer of his courageous and funny epigrams about the tyrant Somoza and his elegy for Marilyn Monroe, his modernist vocabulary, and his great patriotic ode, "Zero Hour," depicting the assassination of Sandino.

I had read Cardenal in New York more than once, but in San José had recently stumbled on some anonymous political poems in a clandestine publication that were clearly from Cardenal's pen, as well as a naive early ballad celebrating the pleasures of exile in San José. Cardenal had found sanctuary in that city in the fifties in the aftermath of a failed plot against Somoza, and he evoked a San José where pretty girls danced on balconies and the president of the Costa Rican Republic went about the city "on foot."

When I arrived at the front door of the mansion where he was hiding out, feeling "barbarous but poetic," Cardenal was eating his lunch, I was told after being guided to a louvered porch at the front of the house by a young, armed bodyguard. For the next half hour I sat alone, listening to the scrape of plates, rush of faucets, pouring of drinks. I must have been sitting directly over the kitchen and the rich odor of pot-roasted meat kept my mouth watering. There were no ashtrays, and I thought I probably shouldn't smoke.

When he appeared Cardenal was pale, white-haired and white-bearded, a little pot-bellied, wearing a black Basque beret and a gauzy white guayabera shirt and khaki trousers. His feet were shod in thick, leather-thonged sandals. This was his preferred costume at the time, and he looked so much like the photos on the jackets of his books that I thought for a moment I'd been sent an imposter dressed as Cardenal by his Sandinista handlers to distract me while the real Ernesto conferred with his *companeros* about revolutionary strategy, but the eyes of the man who encountered me on that bright, warm, sunny porch were large and taking very full of notice of me.

Cardenal didn't bother to ask my name; he'd been briefed by one of the young Sandinistas. He was neither friendly nor unfriendly at first, but studious of my demeanor. He did not attempt to set me at ease and did not offer me any refreshment. He also preferred not to speak English, so our conversation was carried on in my rudimentary Spanish, and once we began, though he seldom returned my glance, he was patient about my setting up a tape to record him.

In the FSLN propaganda films he was shown serving mass in the field in the same mufti, tearing pieces off a loaf of bread to serve to his insurgent communicants with rum or Spanish wine. He had some time back renounced violence and spent a period in contemplative silence at a Trappist monastery, but, after the destruction of his arts community on Solentiname Island in the middle of Lake Nicaragua, he was now in San José in exile from the Somoza regime in Nicaragua, under the protection of the Costa Rican government, but also serving as an emissary of the Sandinistas, whom he called *la gente*.

"So many of your people," he said to me, "are only now learning there is even such a country as Nicaragua."

Some Sandinistas like Cardenal liked to call their revolution a "revolution of love," but it was not an optimistic moment in the history of that movement. As I had recently witnessed, a rebel offensive in seven Nicaraguan cities had just been halted and turned back, with heavy civilian casualties, and the remaining lightly armed rebels had fallen back into the hills of Segovia. Some of Cardenal's housemates in that mansion were only recently arrived: a dentist named Casimiro from Managua who was for some time in the Sandinista Directorate, a pretty young woman insurgent. They were briefly introduced by Ernesto's bodyguard but did not join us on the porch as we spoke about poetry and Cardenal told me of his great admiration for North American poets: Pound, Whitman, and Kenneth Fearing, "who should be better known than he is among North Americans."

He recited some lines from the Cantos I did not recognize, with a hoarse Spanish accent, and then softly inquired if I thought the United States would intervene in Nicaragua.

I told him I didn't know, but thought he probably did.

"We admire the United States so much," he said, "but they do not admire us. That's the history of Central America. So Nicaragua will have to make other friends."

He'd been to New York many times, had been a student at Columbia, and said he had many good friends in the city. He mentioned radical Catholics Thomas Merton and Dorothy Day. He mentioned the St. Mark's Poetry Center. He said he hoped to return when there's no more fighting, but wondered if he would truly be welcome. He said he remained a Christian but also a Marxist. They were not contradictory ideologies. He said he'd learned to hate capitalism through reading Pound and once had been attracted to Fascist ideas like Pound's, to which he had been introduced by the Nicaraguan poet Coronel Urtecho, whom he called "our one great modern poet."

It was clear to me that he was speaking to me as somebody who had not yet earned his trust and expected appropriate reverence. He was also not revealing much about himself that wasn't already public. When I asked about violence, he spoke of Somoza's national guard. He seemed uncomfortable with my informality, my stumbling Spanish. He asked me if I knew the North American poet Muriel Rukeyser's work. When I said I did and had once corresponded with her, he seemed very pleased with me, as though I'd just passed a test.

He glanced at his watch. He was to give a reading at the university that evening. He would need to rest a while. When I thanked him for his time, he told me I was not to despair. He believed a Sandinista victory inevitable. I recalled the end of "Zero Hour":

> The hero is born where he dies,
> And the green grass grows from his ashes.

"Patria libre," I found myself saying, and he grinned a moment and said, "We will surely meet again," and he left the room, allowing the female housekeeper to show me to the door.

Less than a year later he flew back to Leon on a private plane with members of the new Provisional Junta and wrote of peering down into a countryside illuminated by battles signifying new hopes for his countrymen born of that not-yet-concluded struggle.

The next time we saw each other was in the States some weeks after the Sandinista triumph, when he came to Stony Brook and gave a reading to a large university audience. I was seated near an aisle in the center of the hall when Cardenal entered, and I stood with others to welcome him. He saw me and beckoned me to come forward, spread out his arms when I was close, and embraced me with a tender ferocity.

As I recall, he was dressed in the same costume as in San Jose, and I was a little puzzled and embarrassed by the theatricality of his greeting. What had I done to deserve such attention? Had he perhaps read something I'd written?

I realized later that Ernesto Cardenal was grandstanding a little, not for my benefit, but to impress his audience. He wanted their approval, and he was aware that some public opinion was already hostile to his new government. So it was I became a part of his public performances here and, again, at St. Mark's Church when he read there some days later. The U.S. sponsored counterrevolution was already commencing, I was to discover. On a trip to Managua in September 1979, I had found the bar of the Inter-Continental Hotel teeming with spooks from the US buying drinks for the journalists and asking *faux naive* questions about the Sandinista leadership. What were they really like? Were their numbers still capable of putting up a good fight? One businessman who claimed he was from Compton, California, was prepared to outfit a whole Sandinistan division with any type equipment or uniform they desired.

Some weeks later, at a Ministry of Defense briefing, a major with a pointer showed us places along the Honduran border where bands of national guardsmen were reforming. It seemed as though I was also watching the Sandinistas tighten security and bear down harder on their newly liberated constituents. There were closed sessions of party self-criticism, and at social gatherings people were reluctant to talk openly to each other.

In Mexico City some months after that, at a conference of intellectuals in solidarity with the revolution, Cardenal and Rosario Murillo, the wife of Danilo Ortega, led the Nicaraguan delegation. There had been death threats made against the Sandinistas, and every evening in the dining room of the hotel, Cardenal took dinner by himself, dressed in his usual costume, which now included an olive fatigue jacket similar to Fidel's. He was guarded by a young Indian bodyguard in combat fatigues, armed with an Uzi machine pistol, and once when I tried to approach him his bodyguard's stare encouraged me to retreat.

Was he being contemplative in public? Gabo Marquez was in the room and Juan Bosch and Mario Benedetti from Uraguay. Cardenal addressed the delegates and left to fly home again. He seemed very alone, cut off, and, though I observed him at every meal, I never once saw him talk to his young bodyguard.

He was a revered public figure, a figurehead of the new regime, one of only two leftist governments then in power in Latin America. But he was obliged to eat alone in full view of everybody, guarded by a man with an Uzi.

One of his assistants in Mexico City was a pretty young woman from a well-to-do background. She had a lame leg, as I recall, as though from polio, and she told me at some point during the conference that Ernesto would like to invite me back to Nicaragua, but there was just no money. I said I would pay my own way.

Some weeks later in Managua, I tried to visit Cardenal in his offices at Somoza's former hideaway, El Retiro, which were now the executive offices of Cardenal's Ministry of Culture. The patio of the house was now a music class for guitarists and marimbists. It was a place to which Nicaraguan mothers brought their children to have their talents validated and to point out the sybaritic lifestyle of the former dictator and his mistress, Dinora.

A lot of young women of good family comprised the office staff, and they were all very busy planning events. I was told that Cardenal was organizing street theater and poetry workshops in the poor barrios, and I was hoping to find one I could attend, but the decision would have to be made by the minister himself, I was informed, and I was kept waiting.

I was not the only literary "gringo" waiting around to see the poet. A man from the West Coast who had translated all of Cardenal's "Zero Hour" and was hoping to get his approval for more translations was also on hand and running out of funds. For more than two weeks he'd been kept waiting, and he was losing his patience. He seemed very hurt by Ernesto's seeming neglect. "But if you ever tell anybody I said such a thing," he told me, "I'll have you killed."

At last Cardenal called us both into his office and, muttering about all the demands that were being made of his time, pointed to a desk covered with papers. "I no longer have the concentration," he said, with a wave of his hand. "I'm distracted. Forgive me." After welcoming us back to Nicaragua, he then dismissed us.

We never spoke again, though I often saw his black beret bobbing up and down at literary receptions and began to hear a lot of complaints about him from some literary Nicaraguans. They said he was now very vain and only wrote propaganda for the revolution. They said he was unreceptive to criticism and kept certain poets from seeing their poems in print. "He publishes so much," went an often repeated witticism about his own poetry, "it's a pity he doesn't have the time to write."

To be a satirist against a regime surely requires courage; it's probably less chancy being an apologist for the behavior of politicians. As the U.S.-sponsored counterrevolution intensified and his government defended itself with more and more arbitrary power, arresting large numbers of dissidents and Indians, instituting an unpopular draft, berating the middle classes as sellouts, expropriating farms and residences, intimidating and censoring the press, Cardenal found himself in the unenviable position of justifying these acts on behalf of the people while appearing at somewhat glitzy official receptions for Salmon Rushdie and other literary celebrities.

He complained in the press that he had no privacy to write. He visited Iran and wrote a lengthy panegyric in the party newspaper *Barricada*, as a religious, celebrating the pietist rule of the Ayatollah Khoumeini with his firing squads for prostitutes.

Sometimes the poetic results were equally bathetic, as when, in a poem celebrating the achievments of the revolution, he contrasted the shutting down of Nicaragua's only brassiere factory, which presumably uplifted only middle-class women, with the installation of new sanitary facilities in the villages beyond Boaco.

I came to appreciate my own powerless status as a resident of the New Grub Street. Not being a national poet, I was not required to defend bureaucrats or firing squads. Scurrilous rumors were now making the rounds that Cardenal was choosing to bestow publication only on his various homosexual partners. Defenders of the old regime were pleased to point out that he had a Jewish ancestor "from the William Walker expedition" and was a Cuban agent. "All things love each other" was a running joke at a party I went to among some centrists at a ranch near Masaya. He was reproached by the visiting Polish pope on TV and required to kneel. He was threatened with ex-ordination. How far it all seemed from the community of love Cardenal had once espoused as the future Nicaraguan polis. It seemed to me that ordinary people were once again being asked to abide an ordeal and that the Nicaraguan public was fickle in its love of Cardenal's international prestige. When he was the darling of certain cosmopolitain intellectuals, he was revered as a national treasure. When the economic situation worsened, the priorities of the empty stomach meant that people blamed him, along with his comrades, for lending his prestige to the regime,

When Nicaragua's ties to Arab insurgencies summoned forth accusations that the Sandinistans were anti-Semitic, Cardenal and some others of Jewish descent in the party publically acknowledged their Jewish ancestry to disprove such canards, but that only encouraged some rightwing anti-Semites to berate him as a "Bolshevik sissy."

The more conspicuous he became, the less he was loved. If he seemed to demur at some of the regime's tactics of self-defense he was seen as silly and softhearted. A hardline leftist told me, "Ernesto just has his head in the clouds all the time."

The electoral defeat of the Sandinistas was a surprise to many in the movement. Despite the population's war weariness, it could not have been predicted, or else there probably would not have been such elections. For a poet like Cardenal it meant a return to the contemplative life, and, hopefully, the writing of more poems.

TOMAS BORGE: "FALTA NADA!"

Two different legends existed about Commandante Tomas Borge: that he'd been castrated by Tacho Somoza during his long confinement in El Chipote prison, and that he was a great lover of women.

It sometimes seemed to me Borge was responsible for creating both. He was a small, Napoleanic figure, and he liked to dress the part in various costumes and uniforms, looking especially fetching with the red and black Sandinista *panuello* tied about his neck above well-cut khakis or olive green fatigues, a sort of aging cutthroat boyscout.

He had a soft, wide, womanish face and was known to be highly intellectual and literary, as well as a man of action. Once, for about nine months, Somoza's jailors had tortured Borge by making him sit in his cell with a hood covering his face so that he could not see his inquisitors, living in total darkness. A man who had been through all that and remained sane, I thought, would be attractive to many, many people.

Women from abroad were often seen in his company, celebrities like Bianca Jagger and Italian female journalists, pretty young "Sandalistas" from the States, older women with mature bodies and advanced views. In their company Borge always comported himself without apparent bitterness; he seemed subdued and moody. Over a drink, or coffee, at a cafe he sometimes held women's hands, like a high school swain. He looked attentive, if not even a bit fawning. Yet he was known to be a man of steely determination, a founding Sandinista, a ruthless adversary. As minister of the interior, he ran a small empire: some elite military units, the quasi-governmental paper *Nuevo Diario*, all funds collected from traffic tickets and fines, a restaurant at Tiscapa volcano much favored by government people and tourists.

I was lonely a lot of the time in Nicaragua and without female company. Whenever I saw Borge at the hotel or the cafe with a different attractive woman I would become resentful of his seemingly masculine prowess and power. Some Nicaraguan friends would then point out that such socializing was about all he could manage. *"Falta huevos,"* they would say, "He lacks balls."

My friend Marco, a hidalgo of the center right, once exhorted me at length about the enigmas of Borge's "manhood." "If he lacks," Marco said, "what he also had in abundance is that from which he has been deprived. A man who reads Flaubert is no *maricon*. The instinct was undiminished by the cruelty of the Tyrant's act. He lacks nothing really, since we are all afraid of him, also. Then why do I trust him more than the other Sandinistas as a man of honor? He knows what it means to be injured and to suffer."

"What does he lack after all?" Marco went on. "What woman would not want to be with him? He has no friends but the people. They know he is no priest, and he doesn't pretend to be one. I don't even think he pretends to be a man. He lacks nothing I tell you."

I thought about what Marco said. If Borge had indeed been castrated, he would act differently, I decided. He would surely be indifferent to women; then I berated myself for my crude and reductionist views. Sex was only one way men and women befriended each other.

Once in the hotel I saw Borge emerge from a room on one of the top floors accompanied by two uncouth but well-armed body guards, and he was buttoning himself up. I'd seen a very handsome woman of undetermined Europearn origins occupy those premises only the day before. "*Falta huevos*," I told myself as I let myself into my own room for a cold shower. "*Falta huevos*?"

We met only once or twice and rarely talked, though sometimes it seemed he was addressing himself to me at press conferences or other public gatherings called to discuss the security situation. I could actually feel his eyes on me, and it was not a pleasant feeling, more like I'd been found out and was to be exposed. This may have been because I was conspicuous, taller than most of the other press, and older, a contemporary of Borge who must have been then in his early fifties. His eyes seemed always to be seeking me out to broach an understanding of sorts. I was fearful and glanced away. How I should have liked to put the question to him directly: "*Es verdad faltas huevos Commandante?*" Intimidated by his reputation as interior minister, I never asked him any questions, even when they seemed pertinent.

Once I went with Borge and some others in caravan to the Zona Franca prison to inspect some Miskito Indian prisoners. Borge had all the Indians summoned to a courtyard, and under bright lights with television recording the scene offered the prisoners liberty if they would only join the revolution.

His address was long and eloquent. He said they would be given land they could farm away from the combat zone and could sing their own songs and dance their own dances and worship as they chose in the Miskito language.

When he was finished nobody moved, or cheered, or made a sound. His speech was in Spanish, and somebody among the prisoners eventually explained to the comandante after his raised arm was recognized, "These men are Indians. They do not choose to understand Spanish."

Borge had the speech read aloud again by a translator into Miskito and stood silently and accepted the prisoners' subdued applause afterwards.

Later that evening, at the restaurant in Tiscapa, he came to sit among the journalists. He said all Nicaraguans were "loco" which was why so many wrote poetry. He said he no longer wrote poems because the singing of Managua's birds bothered him in the mornings when he sometimes thought he wished to write. Someday, he said, he would enact a statute to rid Managua of all its birds.

Borge said he would like to visit the States but was afraid the Yankees might assassinate him with a little pill he would not notice, and "three months later in Managua I'll be dead."

I allowed to my neighbor as that might really happen.

"He's much too smart for pills," she said. "*Falta nada!*"

Borge was smiling when we all got up to leave the restaurant. The minister of interior was paying for our meals, and there was no way he would allow any other arrangement, his aides explained. We were asked to file past and shake his hand. Borge's touch was womanish and soft, and I thought again of the castration legend. Borge's skin was light tan, his eyes shadowed, his lashes fulsome, big ears.

He held me in his gaze a moment and would not release my hand. His smile was mocking; he seemed to know I was an adversary.

"I wish you a safe trip home," he murmured, peering up at me.

"I'm not leaving yet," I replied.

"*Sin embargo*," he said, wryly, and glanced away to set his face for the next person in line.

The following afternoon he was taking coffee with a beautiful Costa Rican poet and her husband at a table by the swimming pool at the hotel. His body guards sat some yards away on some steps with their weapons on their laps.

I was crossing from the patio to the hotel lobby, but I saw the way was barred. It would be extremely provocative of me to pass near where Borge was. I might even be detained. I started back again toward where I'd been on the other side of the pool, when I heard Borge's voice. "Let him pass," he announced, and then *sotto voce* as I made my way around his table,"Is this not Nicaragua Libre?"

I walked on past his table, and Borge glanced away from his charming companion for a moment to nod at me dismissively. "Cowards," Borge was telling his listeners, "are enemies of the state, but not all enemies of the state are cowards."

When I was some steps beyond them I heard rude laughter. As though for my benefit alone, he added, "Sandino was short, like me. Do I look like I have blood on my hands? Did Tacho Somoza?"

Now that his party is out of power, I ask about him when I meet people who are visiting Nicaragua, and they tell me he's writing. He has published his memoirs and mentions tortures and factions, but not castration. I ask if he's still seen with many women. "He's getting older now," people say. "It's wrong to gossip. But if he is lonely he never writes about it in the newspapers."

TEARS

Tears, a psychiatrist once told me, are the greatest leveler.

They came easily enough to me when I was young. In middle age I discovered that when I thought I wished to cry I sometimes ended up laughing. That happened to me the first time in Nicaragua. A Somocista informer had been assassinated in the front window of a barber shop. When I was brought by one of the street kids to look, he still had hot towels covering his lower face and his corpulent form was sprawled back in the barber chair as though he'd just asked for a once-over-lightly with the razor.

There was no show of blood except for a small hole in the center of the man's forehead, which lined up well with another hole in the spider webbing of glass in the shop's front window.

The boy next to me said, "He was known to enjoy a facial massage and a hot towel."

Indeed, was my comment.

In the tropical heat the man's absurd posture was beginning to bloat.

The first time I'd experienced sudden violent death I'd cried. When I was a young journalist I was sent to cover a train wreck in Newark Bay. A commuter train one Rosh Hashanah had fallen across an open drawbridge into the water with more than forty persons decapitated, including Yankee baseball star Snuffy Sternweiss.

At the temporary morgue, attendants were trying to match up heads with bodies. As I broadcast this horrifying scene to my radio audience while clinging to a stanchion on the bridge, I was crying— humiliation, embarrassment, a pained chagrin. I cried intermittently all the way home from work as I drove along the Pulaski Highway; and that evening at dinner when I was served sliced tongue, an old favorite, cried again, until my boiled potatoes were salty from tears.

When other people I do not know well have broken down in front of me, I find that much easier to deal with than if the weeper is somebody I know well. Often, then, I am unable to respond as I think I should and start telling jokes and brewing tea.

For that matter, the older I get, the more I feel I no longer need to be afraid of acting like a cad. Intimate matters between myself and a certain well-known screen actress and high fashion model, for example, I tell now, aware that the price paid for caring has forbidden me from speaking out before this time and that my experience was as much of an embarrassment to me as it should have been to her.

("What's all this talk of gray hair and wisdom?" the Prague poet Seiffert asks. "When the bush of life burns down, experience is worthless.")

The first and only time she and I ever met was at a restaurant party along Cahuenga Boulevard in Los Angeles. It was the year I published *The Twenty-eighth Day of Elul*, a fine but difficult novel, tearful though angry, to many praising reviews. She claimed to recognize me from a photo printed alongside a notice of my book in *Newsweek*. She never once spoke to me by name.

She was with her current boyfriend, a jock. They weren't really getting along. A man was telling me how to prepare elk liver, and I felt her warm, caressing stare, an invasion of my body space.

"I don't really have any time no more," I heard her tell a photographer with easy vulgarity. She seemed poised on the other side of her image, peering out at me and the world about her.

I stood admiring her voluptuous figure, and then I went up to her and said, "Let's get out of here."

As I turned away and walked out of the restaurant, to my surprise she was following me. We went hand in hand to my car and by car to a place along Sunset where they seasoned the food with sensamilla, and then, stoned, drove to her place in the foothills. In bed she was passionate, gentle, and physically intimate. I had no trouble being generous with pleasure.

In the morning she seemed like a different person. She kept her head turned away like an advertisement for a certain mouthwash, and she went on and on about the New York literary scene, calling me by an unusual pet name, Phil.

"Why do you call me that?" I asked.

"Oh come on," she said. "I'd recognize you anywhere, Phil Roth. I loved every minute of *Portnoy*."

Richard Ellmann I could understand. The tears came again to my eyes, masking my spurious joy, beneath which I felt the eerie calm of the impostor. My previous feelings of well being after making love were being dragged down by a loopy mistake in identity; and I was afraid to destroy an illusion she had so carefully nurtured and sustained throughout our night of lovemaking.

"You'll be surprised," she said, "how photogenic you really are. I bet I'm not the first."

"Feeling's mutual," I pointed out. "Happens all the time."

So I allowed her to ring for coffee and rolls, and we took breakfast together in bed, and when that was over we kissed and I showered and dressed and said goodbye.

"Come and see me in New York," I said and left, and never saw this beautiful woman again. I hope and trust Mr. Roth did. If not him, maybe Lennie Michaels?

AFTERWORD:
HOMAGE TO ISAAC BABEL

I read and reread the stories of Isaac Babel and the stories about Babel in Konstantin Paustovsky's *Years of Hope*—of his care with language, of making draft after draft. "A comparison must be as accurate as a slide rule and as natural as the smell of fennel." Not only because we are both from Jewish families do I find affinities with this long dead Soviet writer. He inspires me to try to be less slothful and feckless. He has even begun to inhabit fantasies from my own childhood.

In one such the year before his arrest and death Babel journeyed to New York. He knew nobody in America but was befriended by my Aunt Esther when he went into her Cotton Shop in Orange, New Jersey, to buy a dress for his wife in Brussels. Esther invited my family to her house that Sunday to meet the great Babel.

The man we saw was bald and goggle-eyed, and he laughed a lot, but nervously. Though he was a bit tubby, he ate very little of Esther's flanken for lunch. Afterward, my Uncle Max took him along to meet their neighbor, the prize fighter (Two Ton)Tony Galento.

"What Joe Louis did to me," Galento said, "shouldn't happen to Mussolini."

"Mussolini," Babel replied, "is D'Annunzio with the syph."

We all sat under the grape arbor in my Aunt Esther's garden. Babel asked if any of us knew Buster Keaton or Joe Penna, and Esther said she personally didn't move in such circles. It was a gay time, I tell myself, for all except my father who seemed a little sour, and grumpy.

Babel and my Aunt Esther were clearly an item, he having done for her what no mere man until that moment ever could. My mother, Esther's younger sister, was also anxious to flirt with this fellow Esther affectionately called "Izzy."

"Izzy," she said, "you sure you wouldn't like a glass of cream soda?"

"Troublemakers, the lot of you," said my father.

Babel chatted with Uncle Max about how to pickle Baltic herrings. "The important thing," Max pointed out, "is there should be no vinegar. Just salt and dill, and maybe a little mustard seed."

"Maybe so, maybe not," Babel said. "But mustard seed doesn't always do the trick. It's like depending on Jesus Christ. One has to be audacious with spices but careful and select only olive wood for the barrels."

Then Babel took an interest in me. He missed his daughter in Brussels, he said, and though I was hardly a substitute, I'd have to do.

He said, "I really don't know how to talk with little boys anymore since the Cossacks."

"Did you really fight and kill people?" I asked.

"Mostly I just looked and made notes to myself. I also had saddle sores. It's hard being in the saddle night and day," he said, "but worth it, if you don't get a hernia. That's no way to make the gentile women happy."

"Is that so hard?" I asked.

"It's a man's work," Babel said. "Slave labor but also our pleasure. Be a *mensch*. Don't ever be a shirker, and you'll get rewards."

He said I looked like I could chase women someday.

"How do you know?" I asked.

"In Odessa," he said, "a little boy like you is a rarity nowadays. We Soviets can't afford pampered brats. Too bad . . . I was such a lad myself, but I grew up fast with the pogroms, and then came the revolution. You remind me of myself when I was little. I had my first girlfriend only after I got married. I advise you not to follow that route. Be a good stout lad and serve womankind," he said, "and always come last."

My mother and aunt were blushing and my father very angry to have this said in front of the children. Just then Aunt Esther served tea and fruit, and shortly thereafter Babel made his excuses. He would have to catch the tube train back to New York.

He stood up and shook my hand, a little balding tub and short of breath from asthma. "Just what my little copycat kid needs," my father asked, "a bum like this?"

"He'll be dead within a year anyway," Uncle Max said. "A mouth like that in the Soviet Union puts you up against a wall with a blindfold on your eyes."

Babel disregarded such kibitzers and spoke only to me: "Don't be too self-centered. You can't grow groats in a desert. Love life. A good Communist always waits his turn," he said. "Only Stalin is the exception, and if that doesn't prove the rule what will?"

When I woke up, Babel was dead in the Gulag and my parents

long dead and Aunt Esther and Uncle Max and "Two Ton" Tony
Galento. And Odessa of the former Soviet Union is now in an independent state they call "Ukraine"—a world that is no more except in
Babel's words of advice in a book, still more vivid than my own: "A
man should think twenty times before he decides to be a writer."